MURDER AND SOCIETY

MURDER AND SOCIETY

Peter Morrall

University of Leeds, UK

WILEY

Other Wiley Editorial Offices

John Wiley & Sons Inc., 111 River Street, Hoboken, NJ 07030, USA

Jossey-Bass, 989 Market Street, San Francisco, CA 94103-1741, USA

Wiley-VCH Verlag GmbH, Boschstr. 12, D-69469 Weinheim, Germany

John Wiley & Sons Australia Ltd, 42 McDougall Street, Milton, Queensland 4064, Australia

John Wiley & Sons (Asia) Pte Ltd, 2 Clementi Loop #02-01, Jin Xing Distripark, Singapore
129809

John Wiley & Sons Canada Ltd, 22 Worcester Road, Etobicoke, Ontario, Canada M9W 1L1

Wiley also publishes its books in a variety of electronic formats. Some content that appears in
print may not be available in electronic books.

Library of Congress Cataloging-in-Publication Data
Morrall, Peter.
    Murder and society / Peter Morrall.
      p.   cm.
    Includes bibliographical references and index.
    ISBN-13: 978-1-86156-455-9   (pbk.   :   alk.   paper)
    ISBN-10: 1-86156-455-4   (pbk.   :   alk.   paper)
    1. Murder.   I. Title.
    HV6515.M64   2006
    364.152'3 – dc22
                                                2006017995

British Library Cataloguing in Publication Data
A catalogue record for this book is available from the British Library

ISBN-13 978-1-86156-455-9
ISBN-10 1-86156-455-4

Typeset in 10/12pt Palatino by SNP Best-set Typesetter, Ltd., Hong Kong
Printed and bound in Great Britain by TJ International Ltd, Padstow, Cornwall
This book is printed on acid-free paper responsibly manufactured from sustainable forestry
in which at least two trees are planted for each one used for paper production.

CONTENTS

ACKNOWLEDGEMENTS

To family, friends, and colleagues whose support keeps me (nearly) sane, thank you.

To the students whose interest in murder has been encouraging (and worrying), thank you.

To all those nice people at Wiley, whose editing (and patience) I have valued tremendously, thank you.

INTRODUCTION

I didn't know Tim Parry, but I wept over his murder. Tim was a 12-year-old child when he was blown-up by Irish Republican Army (IRA) bombs in Warrington, England, on Saturday 20 March 1993. His parents, Colin and Wendy, compiled a book about their loss and how it subsequently changed their lives (Parry & Parry, 1994). The title of book, *Tim: an ordinary boy*, is a description of the Parry family's sheer normal existence until that unanticipated and momentous event. I had bought this book, written in the first-person of Colin Parry but endorsed by his wife, whilst searching for a way of understanding what happens to those left behind after a murder (a key part of *Murder and society*). The press cuttings printed on the outside cover and first page of the Parry's book made it obvious that this would be an emotionally-charged read. Therefore, as I try to do with any research into the awfulness of life that I tackle (as part of my job), I employed the knack of 'academic detachment'. This means trying to suspend one's feelings about the content of the material under examination and deal with the hellish images that are conjured up from accounts of disease, poverty, abuse or war 'objectively'. Avoiding sentimental engagement I review the 'facts', which then I utilise in my job as social science lecturer and writer in the same way as a medical practitioner uses professional disconnection as protection from the otherwise unbearable pain, worries and whinging of their patients.

But I failed spectacularly – and publicly. My tears were uncontrollable, my sadness and sympathy overpowering, all of which disconcerted my fellow passengers as my reading was taking place on a long train journey. Moreover, this was England, where crying openly on public transport is not as unacceptable as talking to the stranger sitting next to you but is still a faux pas.

My son, David, was 6 years old when Tim was killed, and 16 as I read the book. I couldn't prevent, in Freudian terms, the transference of me for Colin and David for Tim. Reading this book was certainly achieving the comprehension I sought of what it is like to be a victim of murder, the hurt, anger, depression and physical exhaustion. Although the people who shared my carriage were not to know what had caused my culturally impertinent emotionalism, the book would be read by thousands of others who presumably have undergone similar sensations. *Tim: an ordinary boy* was, hence, a catharsis for Colin and Wendy's personal suffering, and a catalyst for social suffering.

Humanity in general is defamed by its predilection to violence. The global murder rate per annum is rising towards one million. The global arms bill is US$1 trillion each year (Stockholm International Peace Research Institute, 2004). All of the health planning in which Western societies indulge, the healthier lifestyles that the governments of developed nations demand 'good citizens' follow, all of the financial and social investment made by inhabitants of rich countries to ensure a secure, happy, and healthy old age, means not a fig when death occurs early through a wilfully fatal attack by a lover, fanatic, mugger or crazy person. All of the international effort made to prevent or cure such fatal maladies as AIDS, malaria, dysentery, cholera and Ebola, and increase the woefully short life expectancy of people in developing countries, is not worth a bowl of rice when they are caught in a genocide made efficient by weapons designed by the armaments industries of the West.

The ordinariness of Tim Parry contrasts with his extraordinary death. In most developed countries there is an expectation, particularly in such countries as England with a relatively low murder rate, that death will ensue at the end of a natural and extending old age. But, unusual as murder might be in the everyday experience of life in developed countries, its effect can be both dramatic and insidious. When a killing occurs it becomes a noticed event, unlike many other forms of crime (including those that involve violence) that are either not reported by the public to the police, or if reported then not recorded by the police. Certainly, within the vicinity of the killing people will deliberate over the particulars of the slaying, it is likely to become a headline story for the local TV and newspaper, and might reach the national press if there is anything associated with it that is salacious or panders to established prejudices.

Moreover, in most societies, but especially those whose economy and leisure are based on technological communications and widespread availability of written material, vicarious murder is endemic. Killing is experienced secondhand on a daily basis. Television, films, videos, DVDs, recorded music, the internet, newspapers, books and magazines are splattered with vivid details of factual and fictional killings. As both a consequence of, and stimulus to, the high level of killing in electronic and print forms, killing litters human conversation. In these 'advanced' countries people persistently watch, read and talk a discourse of human slaughter. It is a major element of the amusement business – *killing is thrilling*! 'Murder sells as entertainment irrespective of the fact that killings bring so much suffering to families, relatives, and friends of the victims' (Hickey, 2003, p. xxxii).

In developing areas of the world early death is much more common. For example, the inhabitants of parts of sub-Saharan Africa have a life expectancy below half of that of the West. Someone born in Zambia has less chance of living to the age of 30 years than a person born in England in 1840. Norwegians (top of the list for life expectancy out of 177 countries) on average will live until they are nearly 79 years of age (United Nations, 2005a). Life expectancy in the Russian Federation dropped noticeably following the collapse of the State socialist system. Subregions (for example, the black townships of South Africa, and shanty towns of Brazil) and substrata (for example, the long-term unemployed in Europe, peasants in Indo-China, indigenous peoples in Australia and South America, and industrial workers in the 'Special Economic Zones' of the People's Republic of China) have early death as a common facet of their 'health' profiles.

Much of the (non-murder) early death in the developing world is the result of specific and interrelated factors: (1) disease (for example, as a consequence of HIV/AIDS, malaria and smoking); (2) poverty (associated with environmental catastrophe, trading arrangements and cultural values of the Western-orientated global economy, home-grown political corruption and financial incompetence); (3) accidents (related to unregulated working conditions and dangerous transport infrastructure). Within developed countries wide disparities in longevity mean that the executive, management and white-collar classes in such countries as the UK die older than those with menial jobs and those in the underclass. The reasons for the latter groups dying younger – perhaps up to 10 years – can be categorised in the same way as in the developing world: (1) disease (principally: cancers, cerebro-vascular trauma, cardio-vascular disorder); (2) poverty (associated with unemployment, long-term physical or mental illness and homelessness); and (3) accidents (for example, mishaps at work, on the roads or in the home).

Whilst the gauntlet of disease, poverty and accidents purges a small proportion of the population in developed countries compared with the populations of the developing world, those most vulnerable to these factors in any part of the world also have the greatest risk of being murder victims. The world's elites and middle-classes are not immune from murder, but those who are marginalised in global society (whether this is the developed or developing world) are far more likely to have their lives ended in this manner.

The possibility of being killed is higher if you are a *Cidade de Deus* (*City of God*) street-child scraping a living from the rubbish dumps of Rio de Janeiro drug-ridden *favelas* than if you are a wealthy petroleum executive living in a sumptuous penthouse along the coastline of Guanabara Bay. Death is more probable for a male youth living in rundown inner-city Moss Side, Manchester (colloquially referred to as 'Gunchester') than for a white British elderly female residing in the bungalow estates of the south coast of England. A female illegal immigrant working as a prostitute in a sleazy Hillbrow hotel, Johannesburg, has a far greater risk of being murdered than a white South African businessman ensconced in his gated and guarded suburb. Dying by the violent actions of another person is more of a hazard for a low-paid worker from south-central Los Angeles than for a well-paid employee who resides in hugely wealthier Santa Monica. Protesters from the slums of El Alto in Bolivia (who are against their government's collusion with multinationals exploiting local gas fields) are more likely to be killed by the State security forces than are the well-off demonstrators who disagree with the ban on hunting foxes in England (and invaded the House of Commons in 2004).

In circumstances where death through disease, poverty and trauma rather than old age is much higher, murders are an added component in the overall risk of early death. The pattern of many types of murder is: men kill other men; poor people kill other poor people; whites tend to kill whites and blacks kill blacks; men kill women; and killers and victims are more likely also to come from the same social pool (Hickey, 2003).

There is much controversy over whether cultural and economic globalisation is beneficial to humanity overall (Giddens, 2003; Legrain, 2003), advantageous only to the balance sheets of transnational corporations and the process of Western hegemony (Fox, 2001), or happening at all (Rugman, 2001). But what is happening is that globally the poor are getting poorer, hit by the environmental and financial self-interest of the Western world and westernising countries. Fundamentally, the 'war on hunger' is being lost (Food and Agricultural Organisation of the United Nations, 2003).

These social factors related to killing people highlight the quandary over defining murder. Are the Chief Executive of a transnational oil company, President of the United States of America and leaders of the World Bank guilty of murder perhaps more so than the jilted partner or even the serial killer?

Psychological, physical and social well-being is disrupted by a lethal pathogen. The lethal pathogen here is not a bacterium, fungus, spirochete or virus, but a whole human organism, and its infected host is not a cell, membrane, organ or bio-system, but another whole human organism. Moreover, the pathogen is pernicious with invasive collateral toxicity spreading through the global village.

Nelson Mandela, in the Foreword to the World Health Organisation's *World report on violence and health* (Krug, Dahlberg, Mercy, Zwi & Lozano, 2002, p. 12) writes with authority on the subject of violence given his personal experiences and political achievements:

> The twentieth century will be remembered as a century marked by violence. It burdens us with its legacy of mass destruction, of violence inflicted on a scale never seen and never possible before in human history . . . No country, no city, no community is immune. Violence is everywhere. It is everyone's problem.

But murder seems to serve a double-edged purpose. Murder is both dysfunctional and functional to society. The social sickness of murder is pervasive and perverse. Killing is imprinted on our lives and impacts on our health. Murder annihilates and undermines the health of individuals and society yet may enhance personal and social well-being. Whilst most of us abhor acts of murder, we are also absorbed and gratified by the gruesome details of the event and life stories of both assassin and victim. Murder is both malady and therapy.

To watch, much of it as it happened, the suicidal and murderous detonation of the Twin Towers of the World Trade Center in New York on 11 September, 2001 was an unparalleled media marvel. This was a killing event 'enjoyed' across the world. Wherever a television, radio, or internet news site could be found, people became spellbound by the unfolding disintegration of iconic property and human life. But this momentous drama occurred in a sphere of experience that is an amalgam of actuality (most of us were not physically in New York) and illusion (everything broadcast as news is inevitably mediated). This is not to agree with Jean Baudrillard that the media concocts a level of experience he describes as 'hyperreality' (which leads him to declare that such apparently factual and knowable events as the Gulf War do not take place (Baudrillard, 1995)). The Twin Towers did collapse. Thousands of people did die at the time and have died since because of 11 September, 2001, and it and its consequences continued to engage a huge audience with military action, human rights abuses, political manoeuvrings and beheading of hostages filling newspapers, websites, television broadcasts and films.

London, in 2005, was hit by bombs placed on its public transport system. On the Underground and in buses scores of people died. The media (as well as the police and the security services) broadcast pictures and videos of the aftermath of the attacks taken by those who were present using their mobile phones, camcorders and cameras. The travelling population became the purveyors of a media spectacle in which they had participated.

ORGANISATION OF THIS BOOK

The layout of the book covers the five questions implied in the above discussion, which correspond to the substantive chapters of the book:

What is Murder?

The concept of murder is analysed first using Michel Foucault's brilliant insight into how the presentation of 'facts' is affected significantly by the perceptual predisposition of the presenter, the culture and the historical epoch in which the murderous event happens. Foucault's recounting of the slaying of members of a family by another member of that family in eighteenth century France, using contemporaneous court documents, challenges the notion that either the killing or the incentive to kill are easily recognisable and knowable. With the backdrop of Foucault's 'deconstruction' of the process of murdering, definitions of murder enacted in criminal justice systems are reviewed. However, the main legal frameworks do little to detract from the problem of isolating murder as a specific and steadfast entity. But what seems knowable is the carnage from killing, although once again statistical accounts provide only a rough account of international murder rates.

Who Commits Murder?

Murderers and murders are usually collated within a typology that indicates different types of killers, victims or situations. However, any classification system is arbitrary. A murder could fit into other categories within that system, or other classification descriptors could be invented. No typology can be all-encompassing, and in time other major categories would need to be created given the potential for humans to discover novel methods for destroying fellow humans. Therefore, to answer the question 'who commits murder' I have merely presented case studies with differentiating characteristics. That is, in order to present 'types' of murderers and murder without falling into the trap of constructing a typology, comparisons are made between case studies that have apparent differences in, for example, the number of people killed, the social status of the killer and victim, and levels of personal responsibility that can be allocated to those involved in the murder event. This approach then extends to include the structural responsibility of corporations and governments.

Why Commit Murder?

Attempting to make sense of why people kill other people can in some circumstances appear all too obvious. That is, motivation for murder is explicit (for example, jealousy, loss-of-face or monetary gain). However, the obvious may actually be complex. Evolution, genetics, biochemicals, psychological characteristics and social factors could be underlying determinants.

Furthermore, if a reason cannot be discerned by the criminal justice experts and media, then default justifications ('badness' or 'madness') are applied. But these default explanations also have the same antecedent subtleties as those nominated 'obvious'. Asking why commit murder, however, presupposes that humans and their social environments are inherently fallible with regard to violence. That is, the implication is that the 'self' and 'society' have a faulty design that can precipitate murder, and that in some way this must be controlled if not eradicated. However, if this approach is turned on its head then other questions need to be answered. Specifically, why is murder committed so infrequently; why do most murderers only commit one act of murder (although there may be more than one victim); 'why are most people not murderers or even violent most of the time?'.

Why is Murder Devastating?

Murder directly affects the psychological and physical health of many people, the relatives, friends, neighbours, associates and communities of victims *and* perpetrators. Murder challenges the mores of society (contravening the elemental principles of every mainstream religion – except where there is fundamentalist bastardisation of these principles). Murder manufactures ontological and social disease. There is individual psychological and physical pain and illness. This is a distinctive form of bereavement, and has been included in the medical lexicon as a 'post-traumatic stress disorder'. There is also the radiated social sickness from murder, which contaminates communities and societies. The global epidemic of murder, hence, creates personal and social suffering. Moreover, there is a hierarchy of devastation: 'innocent' victims (for example, some, but not all, child deaths) elicit more sympathy than 'guilty' victims (for example, the killing of prostitutes). However, there appears to be a contrary effect after murder. Families may be devastated but they may recover, restoring their lives and completing remarkable personal and political goals.

Why is Murder Fascinating?

How is it that we seem to be living in a 'werewolf culture', the abhorrence about murder coinciding with a desire for the exhibition of murder? What purpose is served by extensive and prurient interest in murder? Is the curiosity about, and satisfaction gained from, exhaustive depictions of murder a remnant of an evolutionary drive for survival? Might it be an extravagant form of *schadenfreude*, a perverted sensuality gained from the desolation of others? Or could the fascination of murder be driven by the normal psychology of humans?

No matter whether the appeal of murder 'by proxy' is normal or deviant, it is a flourishing commodity, a billion dollar industry with producers (the killers), sellers (the media) and buyers (the murder buying public). However, not all murders evoke vast (if any) interest. Some (for example, ripper and cannibal killings) are highly marketable *because* they tap into the erotic senses.

Why have I written this book? I have taught students at the University of Leeds, UK, the subject of *Madness and murder* (Morrall, 2000) since the late 1990s. These students come from a variety of disciplines (for example: medicine, nursing, social science, education, physics, mathematics) and bring with them a mix of perspectives and expectations. A recurrent debating point for my students, no matter what their core subject, concerns the reasons for murder. Disputes amongst the students about causation virtually always centre on whether or not the killer's actions can be categorised as 'mad' or 'bad'. That is, at the level of the individual perpetrator, the incentives for people killing people are distilled into the two frameworks of mental disorder and evilness. But, this only goes so far as explanation for people-killing-people. What makes people mad and bad has to be examined. That is, what makes people mad or bad in the first place, is it evolution, biology or society?; what is the interplay between these factors?; and how much does individual volition come into play either to override these determinants of behaviour or to temper them?

Trying to gain insight into what leads to people being killed by other people reveals a further problem in comprehending the whole picture of murder as a social phenomenon. Murder enthrals my audience. Just as the evolutionary psychologist and academic David Buss (2005) was amazed to discover that the majority of his students had fantasised about murdering someone, I am both horrified and intrigued by the intensity of the effort made by the students to ascertain and discuss the most gruesome murder that can be found and to do this in immense detail both within the classroom and in their essays. Moreover, this is not confined to the male students, traditionally and stereotypically considered far more engrossed by and involved in violence, as the issue of murder attracts more females than males.

I still question my motive for being interested in murder. Certainly my students do whenever I question theirs! For sure, this is no 'objective' text on the subject, although my aim is to be scholarly. Primarily and unashamedly it is a polemic, my own moral fury, a cry to and for humanity to take control of and speed up its social evolution, reaching a stage at which violence along with other morally derelict primitive cultural practices (for example, female circumcision, slavery and rape) are cast into the evolutionary dustbin.

I have excuse enough, therefore for writing this book, a political, academic and impassioned concern about human unhappiness. But there is one further drive. All my life I have fought personal demons that can be traced to an upbringing within a culture of violence. At an early age I observed adults and children alike displaying a vicious streak, which I regarded as arising from the machismo values of the English lower classes. This vile layer of hostility is still around today exhibited by some sports supporters, binge drinkers and school bullies:

> Football clubs in West Yorkshire [England] have joined forces with police to combat hooliganism at games in the county. Launching the initiative on Tuesday, David Crompton, assistant chief constable of West Yorkshire Police, said: 'Football-related anti-social behaviour, including violence, disorder and racist behaviour, remain significant issues for the four clubs and the force'.
>
> (BBC News, 2005a)
>
> A specialist in liver disease at a Newcastle hospital [north-east England] has welcomed a decision to include information on Newcastle Brown Ale cans and bottles . . . It comes in the light of growing bad publicity about binge drinking culture.
>
> (BBC News, 2005b)
>
> A Northumberland [north-east England] teenager who killed himself had been bullied at school since the age of four, an inquest has heard.
>
> (BBC News, 2004a)

Reaction to frustration and apparent insult when I was growing up was to lash out with threats, fists, feet or head. To be in the playground, park or merely walking along the street, particularly after dark, might invite verbal hostility from an easily-angered passer-by ('Who are you looking at?'), the common verbal precursor to physical assault (a punch in the face or a kick in the gonads). How I wish I had acquired then the immobilising verbal put-downs used on hecklers I learned much later in the gladiator-like combat of after-dinner speaking.

Bullying was rife and even institutionalised within schools. Pupils competed within a hierarchy of 'hardness', those at the bottom persecuted mercilessly unless they could offer a distraction, such as humour, to their tormentors.

I know all too well, therefore, the human and social inclinations that appear to correlate with certain types of murder. With a culturally-charged limbic system, the 'fight' of the perpetrator and the 'fright' of the victim are familiar reactions. Red mist and terror are inculcated responses to supposed slights or threats. Perhaps that's why murder is also devastating but fascinating to me. It represents the ultimate slight (to my belated humanistic ethics) and threat (to the love of my child and my genetic potential).

My low-cultural heritage, along with a subsequent sociological training at a Marxist department of a London Polytechnic, means that I approach the murder of Tim Parry on the basis that social pathologies are predispositional to such tragedies (and therefore, change is necessary at a structural level). However, I have also been influenced by my long contact with the mental health industry (working within it, and writing about it), and in particular by Freud's spotlight on the murky depths of the human psyche. Such influences tend to promote despondency. However, hopefulness for humanity and society comes from the remarkable achievements of such people as the parents of Tim Parry.

Why did I use the word 'murder' rather than 'homicide' in the title of the book? I was asked this question by the renowned British homicide researcher, Mike Maguire, when I was delivering a seminar on the themes of this book (which was in preparation). My answer was rather lame referring to the more British use of the term compared with American usage. Moreover, I was aware that a killing only becomes a murder on conviction, unlike homicide which is applied on discovery of a body that the police assume has not met its demise naturally or accidentally. However, since then my ideas have sharpened and it is indeed 'murder' that I wish to explore.

Murder, like homicide, is a legal category, but, unlike homicide both in legal and lay definitions, it is associated with questions of intention, the inherent wrongfulness and appalling consequences. When told that 'there has been a murder', we conjure up images of badness, madness, sadness, and dissoluteness. Although I have used the term murder to refer to people killing people, I adopt the term homicide when it is used by the author to whose work I am referring.

Murder is not an emotionally sterile term. 'Homicide' is used legalistically and dispassionately. 'Homicide', therefore, is rarely employed or written about with any conviction stemming from ethical outrage at the loss of human life. *I am* outraged and intend this book to be both explanatory and an argument against complacency. It is the 'human' aspects of humans killing humans that are my interest. What is it about the human psyche and human society that leads to people killing others deliberately, when we know it is immoral (although viewed as morally justifiable, for example, in warfare or as legal sentence), and has awful consequences. Moreover, how is it that such either fictional or factual awfulness provides such interest and entertainment?

What I am not attempting here is simply an objective account of humans killing humans. Hopefully it is adequately erudite but it is not detached in the traditional 'objective' academic sense. I cannot remove my own feelings of disgust and horror at what I have uncovered in the researching of this book about human minds and deeds, but also the remarkable recovery and reconciliation that humans are capable of engendering as individuals (for example, Tim Parry's parents) or states (the post-apartheid South Africa). My reactions are not disguised. Killing people is wrong. Being entertained by killing is puzzling. Stopping the killing is the pinnacle of civilised society.

A word about the style adopted in this book: I have tried not to reference excessively. Information that is widely available and known in the public domain I have not necessarily referenced. This is so that the flow is not lost through the constant interjection of names and dates. Furthermore, in referencing internet sources I have been concise. That is, where an author, research project, report, or editorial is easily identifiable and traceable I have chosen just to refer to the generic web-site address. It is, in my experience, frequently easier to locate a reference by going to the generic address and entering key words than it is to type a long list of letters and numbers with the prospect of making mistakes in the process. What about jargon? I have tried to minimise legalistic, social scientific and medical terminology. But, jargon is needed sometimes. It allows sophisticated concepts to be described in short-hand, and for conviviality in everyday conversation. Otherwise our written and spoken communication would require us to have lifespans of thousands of years simply to get through the massively extended explanations in talk and print.

Recognising the complexity of murder, I conclude that there can be no 'grand theory' of murder. Altering personal behaviour and social patterns would lessen personal and social suffering from killing. But I question whether or not this is possible at this stage in human civilisation. The world you and I live in is in a mess. We have yet to progress to a point whereby everyone is fed, given health care, treated compassionately and lives the longest lifespan that is possible. Moreover, we continue to give sustenance to the barbarism that came from previous epochs. Such social atavism needs to be railed against passionately.

CHAPTER 1

WHAT IS MURDER?

I, Pierre Riviere, having slaughtered my mother, my sister, and my brother . . .

My brother Jule had come back from school. Taking advantage of this opportunity I seized the bill [a pruning implement], I went into my mother's house and I committed that fearful crime, beginning with my mother, then my sister and my little brother, after that I struck them again and again . . .

I regained my full senses, ah can it be so, I asked myself, monster that I am! Hapless victims! Can I possibly have done that, no it is but a dream! Ah but it is all too true!

(Extracts from Pierre Riviere's memoir written 10–21 July, 1835 in Vire gaol, France, whilst awaiting trial, in Foucault, 1975, pp. 53–121)

On 3 June, 1835, 20-year-old Pierre Riviere in the French village of la Faucterie in the commune of Aunay committed a triple murder, killing his pregnant mother, his brother and sister. They died in the family home, and according to the statements of the medical practitioners who examined the bodies, their heads had been 'cutlassed', leaving vertebrae severed, skulls crushed, and brains slashed.

Is this a straightforward murder with an obvious killer? The scene of the crime was seemingly, as described by neighbours and the officials who were summoned, awful but uncomplicated. There were bodies, blood and no indication that death had been caused other than violently, deliberately and without invite. There were witnesses to the crime and circumstantial evidence that would have convicted Mother Teresa or the Dalai Lama (bloodstained weapon in hand; leaving the scene of the crime). The accused not only admitted guilt to a bystander at the time of the crime but wrote a memoir detailing his motive (to save his father from 'mad dogs' and 'barbarians' – that is his mother and sister, whom he believed were giving his father a hard time), how he carried out the killings and his remorse.

Moreover, the debate during the trial was not about guilt or innocence. It was with regard to whether or not the expressed motive was an indication of madness or badness (with the accused, ironically, reneging on his preliminary claim to have had visions which led him to annihilate his kin, subsequently asserting that the killings were premeditated and evil). Medical opinion was divided, not only about whether he was sufficiently aware of the wrongness of his actions to be held responsible for them, but if not responsible whether his madness was worthy of such wonderfully inventive labels as 'homicidal monomania' and 'bilious melancholy', as well as 'imbecility'.

CONSTRUCTION

This was not a clear-cut murder at all according to the deconstructionist inclination of the influential French philosopher Michel Foucault (1926–1984), and his co-iconoclasts, who collected an intriguing collection of written reports relating to the event and trial. These were testimonies from inhabitants of Aunay, the village mayor, parish priest, the investigating and presiding assize court judges, the Minister of Justice, numerous medical practitioners including the eminent French physician Jean-Etienne Dominique Esquirol (1772–1840), the memoir of the murderer Pierre Riviere, and the appeal from the jury to King Louis Philippe against the sentence of hanging (Foucault, 1975).

Foucault and his collaborators viewed their intellectual work as 'knowledge-archaeology' (later referring to it as 'knowledge-genealogy'). Their task was to scrutinise historical texts on such subjects as madness, criminality, the medical profession and sexuality, excavating and exposing underlying meanings relating in particular to the connection between knowledge and power. Foucault's methodological brilliance (at least on this occasion) is to reveal, in the Riviere case, that the documents relating to the events of 3 June, 1835, rather than corroborating descriptions, represent what they describe as 'contesting discourses' and thereby not one event but a myriad of happenings each with its own meanings. These discourses are the linguistic styles, content and totems that hint at complex power relations within the local community but which also extend to influences coming from the very top of the French aristocratic oligarchy.

A superficial examination of the published account of the Riviere murders implies objective and complementary depictions leading to a comprehensive and truthful account. Knowledge-archaeology posits that what we actually have are rival and discordant narratives, which do not provide 'truth' but multiple self-defining, self-justifying and self-promoting constructions of reality (what Foucault refers to as 'epistemes'). For Foucault, the narratives in these documents point to a series of power struggles. The medical practitioners were fighting amongst each other for diagnostic dominance, eventually against the murderer (who inconveniently decided to reject all of the doctors' diagnoses having first supplied evidence to support the label of madness). They were also in a battle with those in whose territory they were attempting to gain a foothold (that is, the judges and lawyers) with psychiatric opinion on extenuating circumstances. The representatives of the criminal justice system (and ultimately, the King) had an agenda of controlling parricide because of it being linked to regicide as a threat to the social order. Killing one's own father, it was reasoned, undermines the King's position in a society in which the 'social compact' is legitimised through the institution of the family and paternalistic values. The local community, by attributing the murders to the faults of an individual, reaffirmed the inviolability of the family. Crime in the neighbourhood was also of great concern and the murders, tackled vigorously by the forces of law, would help to reassure the inhabitants.

Pierre Riviere's own power struggles are both superimposed onto these scenarios and emanating from them in a morass of cause and effect connections. He is at war with himself, his family, community and society. His behaviours, verbal and written accounts are not consistent, displaying the intricacies of his multi-fronted battleground. Riviere is not merely an individual, whether mad or bad, acting in a social vacuum, whose motives, actions and punishment can be located just at the level of him.

The French Revolution of 1789 and the subsequent atrocities of the Reign of Terror could be considered to set the scene for Riviere's actions and the resultant reactions to the murders. Indeed, David Andress (2005) argues that the Revolution and subsequent civil war in France has a long line of associations that have led to the 'War on Terror' initiated by the US government of George W. Bush in 2001.

There are, therefore, historical connections of French revolutionary violence and state power to the Riviere's murders. Punishments for acts that threatened the social order also alter. The exploitative French nobility set the stage for violent (and murderous and self-destructive) responses by the peasantry.

Not only was the episteme of madness available as well as that of criminality (offering alternative systems of control), but where a death sentence was given, hanging had replaced the guillotine. The guillotine in itself was regarded as the 'merciful widow' compared with what was meted out to Robert Damiens in 1757. Damiens, a man of low intelligence, had tried to stab the King (Louis XV). His effort at regicide gained him the unenviable experience of prolonged death: tortured with boiling oil and sulphur; ripped apart after being tied to horses; dismembered; and burnt at the stake (Andress, 2005).

For Foucault, the question of 'what is murder' is moot. Moreover, the questionability over murder illustrates well the construction of realities based on the wielding of power.

Murder it is that makes for the warrior's immortality (they kill, they order killings, they themselves accept the risk of death); murder it is that ensures the criminals their dark renown (by shedding blood, they have accepted the risk of the scaffold). Murder establishes the ambiguity of the lawful and the unlawful.

. . . Murder prowls the confines of the law, on one side or the other, above or below it; it frequents power, sometimes against and sometimes with it.

(Foucault, 1975, p. 206)

The killing of people by people is narrated (through, for example, government decisions with regard to warfare and criminal justice processes) as 'heroism' (the soldier) or 'infamy' (the criminal). Murder, therefore, is a social construct in that the very same act or even worse (in the sense of numbers, the vulnerability of the victims, and degrees of brutality) can be construed as legally justifiable and morally necessary if it is so deemed by powerful forces:

One man mentioned earlier, a very good soldier and later a non-commissioned officer (NCO), killed someone in civilian life some years after the war had ended. In prison he said: 'When I killed people I was told to kill when I didn't hate them at all, I was praised and given a medal. When I killed someone who had really wronged me, I was given a life sentence.'

(Hyatt-Williams, 1998, p. 123)

Alternatively, some murders, previously regarded as regretful but not unusual, become construed as so heinous that they command special approbation from the powerful because of the threat they pose to those with power. Magically, the very same killings and killers, if that threat has receded, can not only be returned to their former grading, but may be reclassified as non-murders and non-murderers.

Murder committed in Northern Ireland went through a noticeable process of construction and deconstruction. Political expediency dramatically readjusted the legally decreed life course of those found guilty of seemingly horrendous crimes. Under the terms of the Good Friday Agreement of 1998, hundreds of Northern Irish convicted killers from both sides of the Troubles were set free.

Michael Stone, a volunteer in the Ulster Defence Association, was seen on television throwing grenades and shooting about 60 people (young and old alike), killing three of them. They were attending the funeral of Irish Republican Army (IRA) members who were killed by undercover soldiers of British Special Air Service in Gibraltar, 1988, because they were believed to be on a bombing mission. Stone had also admitted to taking part in three other murders and further forms of serious violence. He was sentenced to nearly 700 years in prison, but was released in 2000. Stone, father of nine children, has written his autobiography and taken up painting. Sean Kelly, an IRA volunteer, was given a life sentence for killing nine Protestants (including a pregnant woman and a 9-year-old girl) in 1993. He was freed in 2000, later in that year rearrested, and re-released in 2005.

'Atrocious' acts are reconfigured as 'contextually understandable' when necessary to achieve aims other than those of the criminal justice system. The narrative adopted changes from one proclaiming 'justice' and 'retribution' to one espousing 'peace' and 'resolution'.

In South Africa a narrative of 'truth and reconciliation' has meant that killings spawned by apartheid are unpunished provided those culpable make public confessions (with or without the presence of remorse). During apartheid, which was finally completely dismantled in 1991 by President F. W. De Klerk, the white government through the security services 'neutralised' many of its opponents, virtually all of whom were black. However, the post-apartheid government of Nelson Mandela had to face up to its own history of violence, including torture and murder carried out by the African National Congress (ANC) during its 1960–1990 campaign against white dominance. The 'Truth and Reconciliation Commission' was set up to generate forgiveness from all sides and thwart vengeance in the 'Rainbow Nation'. Reconciliation in South Africa, however, became tempered with totems of victory proffered by the ascendant black majority. There has been a rewriting of (white) history to fit an account portraying the wickedness of the former rulers and the rightfulness of the present governors, and there is now a multitude of museums and artefacts symbolising black struggles throughout South Africa. Mandela's house in Soweto has become a shrine at which thousands of visitors pay homage to the lowly upbringing of a man who was pivotal to this struggle. Robben Island off Cape Town, where many of those fighting the apartheid regime were held (for example, Nelson Mandela for 27 years), has become a hallowed attraction for tourists with ex-prisoners acting as guides and selling autobiographies and poetry about their experiences. Apartheid as a social system is morally indefensible. But rewriting of the history of whose violence was and wasn't justified by inheritors of political power is no less inexcusable.

There are other social mores to be considered with respect to life and death. Peter Singer, renowned philosopher and adherent of a radical moral transition based on Darwin's theory of evolution, claims that animals have the same moral status and, therefore, rights as humans (Singer, 1975, 1979, 1995). Humans are animals in the evolutionary sense and all sentient beings should be regarded similarly with respect to suffering rather than through intelligence differentials or religious ideology that consider humans as superior.

For Singer, life and death should be re-evaluated. He regards 'persons' as those forms of life that can feel, reason, are self-aware and appreciate a future. Hence, humans that do not have these qualities are 'non-persons'. Humans with severe mental handicaps, or psychosis, and other somatic and psychological malfunctioning perceptions, are 'non-persons' and can be compared (morally) with animals having similar levels of perceptual acumen. Decisions to keep such beings alive must be taken on that basis: killing a healthy cow, pig, chicken, or sheep for human food may well, therefore, be more immoral than aborting a foetus with Down's syndrome, not resuscitating a hydrocephalic infant, switching off the life-support machine of a young man in a persistent vegetative state, or a doctor supplying a lethal injection to a woman with terminal cancer, or allowing a demented elderly relative to die 'naturally', presumably through starvation (a situation Singer was to face when his mother contracted Alzheimer's syndrome: Hari, 2004). Certainly, animal experimentation carried out to benefit humans cannot be defended. Pain should be prevented or minimised no matter what the species.

Such a view on what is worthy of living has major implications for what can be defined as murder. Moreover, Singer underscores the point that rich countries can be accused of multiple murder on a grand scale by not sharing their wealth with developing countries. Rich people should give poor people the excess of their wealth once basic needs are accommodated.

Hazel May (2001) recognises murder as a personal tragedy and an attack on the community. For May, 'community' has two possible denotations. First, it can be the imagined, fluctuating, transient sense of experience or belonging to a group of people. That is, we can 'feel' that we have a bond with others, and have values or behaviours in common, but we do not need physical proximity to feel united. Second, there is the geographically identifiable community, where people live and/or meet. May argues that changes to community through murder incidents include the redefining of personal lives, social relationships and localities. She also makes the point that although social disintegration is expected from killing incidents, particularly if there are multiple murders, the opposite could occur. That is, communities can become more integrated.

There is a 'symbolic assault' on the community in that the fragility of everyday life is exposed through the disruption of what turns out to be a social myth that, usually, routines and security are interminable. A murder flaunts insecurity and the fragility of normality. The resultant public indignation and grief is exacerbated where the moral and social order is threatened. There is, suggests May, a hierarchy of homicide with 'real murders' and 'less real murders'. Real murders are when there are totally innocent victims (for example, children, hostages, the elderly) and totally culpable perpetrators (for example, paedophiles, strangers, terrorists). Less real murders involve the victim's perceived culpability, such as: when there has been a drunken brawl and one of the contestants has died; during gang warfare when all sides are attacking each other; if drug dealing is implicated; in a domestic dispute and the deceased has been adulterous or abusive; if the victim was committing a crime.

In some less real murders, the role of victim and culprit can be reversed, as happened to some extent in the Tony Martin case. Tony Martin in 1999 shot in the back and killed Fred Barras with a pump-action shotgun. Barras, 16 years of age, and an accomplice (who was wounded), were burgling Martin's derelict farmhouse in rural England. Martin was convicted of murder in 2000. However, there was a high profile public-media debate about a householder's right in the UK to defend property. A 'Free Tony Martin' campaign was instigated, which projected this killer as the victim of an unjust legal system that punishes those who are protecting themselves or their property from the criminal actions of others. Martin, following an appeal, had his sentence reduced to manslaughter and was freed from prison in 2003.

Other considerations that influence the moral status of the murder are: victim–perpetrator relationship (intimate versus unknown); the perceived motive for the murder (was it spontaneous and emotional or planned and 'cold-blooded'); the nature of the violence (was it a 'brutal' murder, and/or did rape take place?); the power dynamic (was the victim defenceless, unwary and trusting, or first terrorised?); and the social prestige of the victim (a prostitute or homeless?) and the killer (a police officer or doctor?).

May comments, however, that even where a child is murdered this will not necessarily bring moral approbation from the media and public. Only where the murdered children become 'visible' (most child murders within the family go unreported) and the child's virtuousness is without question does it reach the top of the moral order of murder. If the young victim had ever been 'in care' or was regarded as precocious and 'streetwise', then the murder is unlikely to receive as much attention as one in which the child is considered 'hard-working' and 'popular'.

Miethe and Regoeczi (2004) regard historical interpretations of homicide, and therefore levels of killing, as unreliable. This is because what was considered to be homicide was both ambiguous and inconsistent at the time and also difficult to judge retrospectively. They refer to the definitions of infanticide, legal execution, abortion and self-defence as particularly problematic. Furthermore, newspaper, police and other methods of reporting today are swayed by both similar and idiosyncratic factors which mean that historical and contemporary comparisons are problematic.

Eric Hickey accepts explanations for murder overlap and are affected by cultural values. For example, Hickey (2003) cites the fact that a society that subjugates women may 'honour' the killing of women. That is, such violations may be either allowed legally, or because there is strong public acceptance (from men and women) of the practice, the law doesn't place great significance on these deaths. A society such as China may deem it socially unacceptable to have more than one child, thereby placing pressure on parents who conceive an 'extra' baby to drown it, especially if female. In Texas, Andrea Yates drowned her five children and the case had huge media coverage. Within the same period that this occurred, other similar cases (at least one involving the deaths of five children but carried out by a man) gained little attention in the press.

Fiona Brookman (2005) points out that legal categories are not clear cut. There are frequently fine distinctions, but sometimes huge differences of opinion, made about a killing in the eyes of the police, lawyers, judges, juries, media, the general public, and the families of victim and perpetrator. Moreover, social and historical comparisons reveal that what is considered a legal killing, as opposed to an illegal killing, changes.

For Fiona Brookman (2005, p. 3), illegal killing, as with all other types of crime, is undeniably socially constructed:

> Unlawful homicide is not an absolute. Rather, various categories have been constructed over the years that are said to comprise unlawful homicide. Crime cannot exist without the creation of laws by a given society to criminalise particular actions or behaviours. The fact that legal codes vary between different countries and across different historical periods is a clear indication of the socially constructed nature of crime and deviance. Hence the creation of crime categories is a product of societal interaction and reaction to particular behaviour.

Lawful killing, however, can also be critiqued from the social constructionist perspective. The Singapore authorities carried out the death penalty on 25-year-old Australian, Van Tuong Nguyen, at its Changi Prison in December 2005. Nguyen was convicted for trying to smuggle nearly 400 grams of heroin to Australia via Singapore in 2002. The death penalty is mandatory in Singapore for drug trafficking (found in possession of more than 15 grams of heroin, 30 grams of morphine or cocaine, or 500 grams of cannabis), as well as for serious firearm offences, treason and murder. Singapore has probably the highest rate of executions per country in the world. The death penalty in Singapore is of course legal. However, an editorial in *The Australian* (2005), a national newspaper from Nguyen's home country, viewed it differently:

> The Government of Singapore was due to *murder* a man this morning. Certainly, it is acting according to the laws of that country. Certainly, the means of

his death is known from long experience to be quick and painless. Certainly, no one in Singapore took any apparent pleasure in the decision that a man should die. But no qualification can disguise that they have planned an act of *murder*. And there is no explanation, no justification, that can excuse any nation from killing an individual who has broken the law. There never has been and there never will be. [emphasis added]

Brookman also raises the question about whether or not homicide should be regarded as a unique crime. Where a fight takes place and injury but not death is the goal behind, for example, a punch, then the law does take account of intentionality and punishments are differentiated on this basis. The English laws on homicide are at the time of writing (2006) under review, with the present homicide categories and punishments regarded as in need of reform to take account of certain unfair consequences of present legislation. Whatever the outcome, the fact that the laws are being discussed illustrates well the fluidity of what can be considered to be an illegal killing and just punishments. Euthanasia, death through dangerous driving, corporate killing, the right to defend one's house and family, and mandatory life sentences, may have their legal status reconstituted either at this juncture or in the future. The concept of murder, therefore, is both erectable and demolishable.

Measuring intentionality, however, can be a matter of considerable complexity. At what point in the assault, and to what level of conscious realisation and commitment by the perpetrator, does the act move from intent to injure to intent to kill? Of course there is little to debate over Mafia assassinations of rival family members, and lawyers, police officers and politicians who are attempting to curtail its protection, extortion, drug and prostitution operations. The video-recorded evidence of an embittered wife hiring a contract killer to murder her wayward husband leaves little doubt about culpability.

William Marcy's (1786–1857) maxim 'to the victor belong the spoils of the enemy' does not just imply material possessions. Virtue is also 'looted' by those who win politically and through warfare. When the governments of Soviet Russia and its satellite countries started to lose their grip on power and the communist ideology (as projected in the USSR and Eastern Europe) became unsustainable, then the actions of former State apparatchiks became vulnerable to reinterpretation. The victor was to claim the spoils of owning the moral high ground.

Following the building in 1961 of the Berlin Wall during the 'Cold War' between the West and the USSR and its allies, approximately 1000 people attempting to get away from East Germany were shot by border guards. The East German head of state and leader of the Communist Party, Egon Krenz, who opened up the Berlin Wall in 1989, was later convicted by a German court on unification of being responsible for the shoot-to-kill policy employed by the military patrolling the Wall. His defence was that he had not broken any East German laws. Arguing that he had acted legally under what was the East German legal framework, he appealed against his prison term for manslaughter to the European Court of Human Rights in 2001. He lost this appeal on the basis that he had broken international law, although he was released early from prison. Interestingly, the main victor of the Cold War, the USA, has refused to allow international jurisdiction over its actions during wartime.

Thomas Szasz's (1993) view is that law-makers are not managing but, rather, are inventing crimes. From this viewpoint, killing in itself may not be considered to be a crime, but only those forms of murder that are unsanctioned by the state and its regulatory bodies. For example, the mass extermination of civilians is, depending on its legal status, either 'genocide' or, when authorised by governments and therefore legitimised, a 'military necessity'. Moreover, in time of warfare, the conqueror has the power of veto over which events can be classified licit and which can be vilified. In the Second World War, the German 'blitzing' of London was compared unfavourably with the Royal Air Force and US Airforce blanket 'fire' bombing of Dresden in terms of its moral standing by the victorious allies. It was only years later that the morality of destroying Dresden and killing thousands of German civilians was questioned by the victors. By 2005, British and US ambassadors participated in a wreath-laying ceremony to mark the 60th anniversary of the bombing of Dresden, commemorating the loss of up to 35 000, mostly civilian, German lives in February 1945.

The narrative for the invasion of Iraq in 2003 has enveloped many justifications by the 'Coalition of the Willing' (President George W. Bush's phrase for a disparate collection of countries supporting the USA in its neo-conservative inspired military interventionist policies). This narrative referred to Iraqi links with those responsible for the 11 September, 2001 terrorist acts in New York, Iraq's alleged hoarding of weapons of mass destruction, and the need to remove the tyrant Saddam Hussein. An alternative narrative has been submitted in Michael Moore's 2004 film *Farenheit 9/11*. Moore suggests that the pre-emptive invasion of Iraq was conducted to protect the flow of oil to the West and the investments of US politicians in the Middle East. Numerous non-combatant deaths during this war were, as in most modern conflicts, constructed as 'collateral damage'. The tens-of-thousands killed by the Coalition forces after the USA declared a formal end of hostilities have been constructed as 'insurgents', or simply not acknowledged. Constructions by parts of the Iraqi population and Arab news stations such as al-Jazeera contend that these killings are akin to murder.

The meaning given to the deed of killing in times of war will alter depending on the motive, but how that motive is regarded (i.e. as either honourable or amoral) will be influenced by such variables as the status and power of the perpetrator. It will also rely on the manner in which accounts of the killing are disseminated to the home and world audience. All sides in modern warfare appreciate the need to utilise the services of media 'spin doctors'. These are used to present an interpretation of events that, as far as possible, ensures a sympathetic response from the public in whose name the killing is being conducted, and to reduce the possibility of the enemy gaining assistance (militarily or morally) from other countries by not appearing to be the aggressor. What, for example, is the difference between 'terrorists' killing Americans working in the Twin Towers in New York and American armed forces killing civilians in Serbia, Afghanistan or Iraq? Perceptions of these events will depend on who wins the propaganda campaigns propagated by the US government and by Islamic militants, and how free the press is to view and report on them.

So, the state can designate killing as legal, and under certain conditions actually promulgates the slaying of large numbers of people. During periods of warfare, a hero status is awarded to the most successful of socially sanctioned assassins. In some countries, a covert or overt policy of mass execution has been adopted by governments in order to address particular forms of criminal activity (drug dealers in China), racial impurity (the eugenic practices of Nazi Germany, intertribal massacres in Rwanda, and 'social reconstruction' in Stalinist Russia and Pol Pot's Cambodia) and civil unrest (colonial India under British rule, and Saddam Hussein's butchery of Kurds in Iraq).

Within postmodern critique lies the proposition that all knowledge is uncertain. For postmodernist thinkers, the world in the late twentieth century has been going through a series of tumultuous transformations. Established social systems have had to react to a reordering of previous economic arrangements between societies, the creation of globalised markets and communication systems, the death of the 'expert' as the purveyor of absolute truth, and a metamorphosis in cultural values. From this outlook, there is no a priori moral, political or legal authority available to judge individual and social behaviour. All conduct (including deviancy) thus becomes relative to the particular practices of the social group to which individuals belong. Definitions of crime change over time and between cultures, and no behaviour is inherently good or bad, true or false. Cannabis can be consumed legally in some countries, whereas in other countries a heavy fine or even imprisonment is imposed for its use. But even in parts of the world where using cannabis has been criminalised, it (along with derivatives of other prohibited drugs, such as heroin) may be approved for medical purposes.

What is the difference between a serial murderer killing his prey and the state killing murderers serially? The answer is: only the moral authority that governments can construct which allows killing with not only impunity but righteousness. There is, therefore, much enigma over what is a legitimate and what is an illegitimate killing; that is, what is prescibed or proscribed.

PROSCRIPTION

English, Roman, French and Islamic criminal justices have been the major influences on world legal systems. Murder has been, throughout the development of virtually all civilisations, considered to be one of the worst criminal acts, if not the worst. Punishments reflect this seriousness. However, punishments vary considerably between torture, long-term imprisonment and execution (or all three).

In Ancourteville-sur-Hericourt near Rouen, France, in 2004, a 14-year-old boy known only Pierre F (due to the restriction on identifying juveniles) murdered most of his family (Henley, 2005). In a two-hour killing spree, using his father's shotgun, his mother was shot and killed, his 11-year-old sister shot and seriously wounded, his baby brother shot and killed, and then his father shot and killed. After the killings, Pierre F fled on his bicycle but was later arrested. He confessed to police that he had murdered his loved ones because of being treated too strictly in particular by his mother. Whilst he waited for each member of his family to return home he apparently sat calmly watching a video. Pierre was not regarded as clinically or legally 'mad' by court psychiatrists. The maximum sentence a killer of his age can receive in French law is 20 years in prison. Pierre F was given an 18-year sentence.

But, Pierre Riviere, having been found guilty of parricide in 1835 in France, faced a very different fate. If his sentence had not been commuted to life imprisonment by the King's prerogative, he would have been taken to the place of execution barefoot, only wearing his shirt. On the scaffold his head would have been covered with a black veil, an officer of the court reading aloud his sentence. This would have been the cutting off of his right hand, and then being put to death.

As unpleasant as this sounds, when compared with the law of eighteenth century China, it was all but humane. During the Qing Manchu dynasty a parricide killer was scourged, sewed in a sack alongside an animal (from a choice of ape, dog, cock or viper), and thrown into the sea or river unless there was no water deep enough to drown the unfortunate in which case death was met by being given to 'wild beasts' (Bouvier, 1856).

However, in some Muslim countries (for example, Iran, Saudi Arabia and Pakistan) today payment direct to the victim's family ('blood money') can assuage punishment imposed by the state. A similar practice occurred in Saxon England with the imposition of a 'were':

> *WERE.* The name of a fine among the Saxons imposed upon a murderer. The life of every man, not excepting that of the king himself, was estimated at a certain price, which was called the *were*, or *vestimatio capitis*. The amount varied according to the dignity of the person murdered. The price of wounds was also varied according to the nature of the wound, or the member injured.
>
> (Bouvier, 1856)

There is not complete agreement on terms for human killing (that is, humans killing humans). Table 1.1, formulated from a variety of sources, shows those expressions that have general acceptance for various forms of human killing.

Table 1.1 Terms associated with human killing

Homicide	Killing a human
Murder	Killing a human (illegal and intended)
Manslaughter	Killing a human (illegal but unintended)
Filicide	Killing of offspring
Fratricide	Killing of brother (or possibly sister)
Mariticide	Killing of husband
Uxoricide	Killing of wife
Matricide	Killing of mother
Parenticide	Killing of parent(s)
Parricide	Killing of parent(s) or near relative (by extension, the Monarch)
Patricide	Killing of father
Sororicide	Killing of sister
Familicide	Killing of members of a family by other family member
Suicide	Killing oneself
Femicide	Killing a woman
Foeticide	Killing of foetus
Infanticide	Killing of an infant
Autocide	Killing with a motor vehicle
Genocide	Destruction of an entire group with a shared cultural identity (for example, ethnic, religious)
Populicide	Killing of all people
Mundicide	Destruction of entire world
Omnicide	Destruction of all living things
Ambicide	Killing of friend
Hosticide	Killing an enemy
Regicide	Killing a monarch (King/Queen)

Foucault et al. (1975) use the term 'parricide' (that is the killing either of one's parents or both), in the title of the book about Pierre Riviere's killings. Presumably this was to draw attention to the gravity of killing one's parent in nineteenth-century French society because of the connection made with regicide, and because the other killings were secondary to destroying his mother – matricide. Apart from matricide, however, what Riviere committed was fratricide; that is, killing one's brother. Confusingly, fratricide is sometimes used to describe killing one's sister (which he also did), although the term sororicide is more commonly adopted.

Moreover, in the twenty-first century, familicide is the expression applied when two or more family members are murdered by another family member (for example, a father killing all other members of his family). The popular description of the perpetrator of familicide is 'family annihilator'. Examples of family annihilators include: Welsh businessman Robert Mochrie in 2000, who murdered his wife and four children, and then swallowed slug pellets, weed killer and paracetamol painkilling tablets, before hanging himself from the loft hatch; English police officer Karl Bluestone, who in 2001 used a hammer to kill his wife and two of his children, as well as seriously injuring another of his children before hanging himself in the garage. Examining family killings in Australia, Jenny Mouzos and Catherine Rushforth (2003, p. 1) observe dryly: 'The family is viewed by most people as providing a nurturing and loving environment. But for some, the family environment can be deadly.'

The indistinctness of terms describing different forms of murder doesn't stop there. Parricide can mean not only killing a parent or parents (which can also be labelled parenticide), but the slaying of close relatives such as brothers or sisters. It is probable that this was how Foucault (1975) applied the expression as was more usual in the nineteenth century (Bouvier, 1856). But French law in the nineteenth century included the killing of non-blood parents (that is, adopted mothers and fathers) under the criminal act of parricide. This use of parricide to include parents and near relatives underscores the point made by Foucault (1975) that it was 'the family' that must be protected by law rather than merely individuals. The inclusion of non-blood relatives under parricide in nineteenth-century French law is emphasised further as reference is made to 'any legitimate ascendant' (Bouvier, 1856). The very highest 'ascendant' in feudal France was of course the king.

Whereas murderers in many parts of the USA may be executed, in Western Europe a gaol sentence will be handed out. If a country wishes to join the European Union (EU) it must relinquish the death penalty completely (that is, in times of peace, civil strife and war). Turkey placed a moratorium on the death penalty in 1984 in order to support its EU application.

Capital punishment was replaced by life imprisonment without parole in peacetime in 2002, and by 2004 it had removed it from criminal punishment possibilities.

In the People's Republic of China, the death penalty is given for a range of criminal activities other than murder (for example, drug dealing and political agitation). The Jordanian penal code allows a man to kill, without any penalty, his wife or a female relative if she is discovered committing adultery. Furthermore, political pragmatism and/or alterations in public opinion may dramatically affect punishment. For example, following the implementation of Section 2 of the 1997 Crime (Sentences) Act in England and Wales, there is a mandatory life sentence for a second violent or sexual offence. These second offences include attempted murder, manslaughter, soliciting murder, possession of a firearm with intent to injure, wounding or causing grievous bodily harm with intent, possession of a real or imitation firearm during a robbery, rape or attempted rape, and intercourse with a girl under 13 years of age. It is commonplace for punishments to be adjusted following the disclosure of an offender's previous criminal conviction(s). What is different here, however, is that, for a disparate assemblage of crimes, there is minimal opportunity for a judge to do anything but give a predetermined sentence.

Homicide (derived from the Latin *homicidium*, combining *homo* meaning man and *cidium* meaning the act of killing) is the catch-all category for the killing of humans by other humans. Homicide is not necessarily a crime, and hence implies no guilt but is legally 'neutral'. It is a necessary ingredient of the crimes of murder and manslaughter, but there are other cases in which homicide may be committed without criminal intent and without criminal consequences, as, where it is done in the lawful execution of a judicial sentence, in self-defence, or as the only possible means of arresting an escaping felon.

Although frequently used as synonyms, there is generally in the world's legal systems, and in particular Anglo-American law, a distinction made between 'murder' and 'homicide'. Murder is not legally neutral and does imply a moral judgement as it is the outcome of judicial processes. Homicide is usually the term adopted at the beginning of inquiries into a death where natural causes are not blatant. Murder is the illegal and intentional killing of a human being by one or more human beings. 'Malice aforethought' is the key criterion in the legal definition of murder (Blom-Cooper & Morris, 2004).

The term 'murder' derives from Saxon times (Blom-Cooper & Morris, 2004). After the conquest of Britain in 1066, disgruntled Saxons engaged in ambushes on the Normans. So outraged was William I about what probably would in the twenty-first century be described as 'terrorist outrages' that he decreed if the perpetrator of such a killing (a *murdrum*) were not found then a hundred people who lived where the death had taken place were required to pay a fine, also known as a *murdrum*. It wasn't until 1340 that this collective punishment for unsolved homicides was rescinded. In English Law, the legal category of homicide includes the offences of murder, infanticide and manslaughter, whereas in some parts of the USA homicides that are justifiable (killing in self-defence) are demarcated from those that are unjustifiable. In Scotland, criminal homicide is, as with the many states in the USA, distinguished from non-criminal homicide, where the notion of 'culpable homicide' is employed. Taking the classic definition of murder used in English law, reference is made to the unlawful killing with malice aforethought of 'any reasonable creature in *rerum natura*' (i.e. a living human being). 'Manslaughter' refers to unlawful killing when it is judged that there was an absence of the intention to kill, or substantial mitigating circumstances such as severe provocation or an 'abnormality of mind'. When the latter is applicable, a verdict of manslaughter due to 'diminished responsibility' may be given.

Actus rea (guilty act) is common in English law for murder, manslaughter and infanticide. Levels or the absence of intentionality (*mens rea* – guilty mind) influence what the police prosecution and court outcome will be (that is, either murder or manslaughter). Moreover, even with intention a conviction may be one of voluntary manslaughter rather than murder if there was provocation, a suicide pact (where one person survives), or diminished responsibility. A conviction of involuntary manslaughter may be given if there was no intention to kill and a death occurred through recklessness, gross negligence or a dangerous act (Brookman, 2005). There are patently enormous problems in assessing whether or not the indicted individual intended to kill (*mens rea*), whether he or she was induced to kill by the actions of the victim, and whether or not he or she can be held accountable for the killing. There are also fundamental issues concerning when the victim actually dies and what can reasonably be thought to be 'human life'. There was in English law an arbitrary limit of one year and one day on when the victim could be considered to have died from the (intentional) actions of the perpetrator. That is, prior to the Law Reform (Year and a Day Rule) Act of 1996, a killer was not found guilty of murder if the victim lived – or was kept alive artificially – beyond this period, even if the accused set out deliberately to take that person's life.

Deciding just who can and who cannot be considered to be a 'reasonable creature' produces a dilemma that demands a subjective assessment of the beginning and cessation of human life. That is, the perimeters of human existence are not steadfast, and hence verification of the extinguishing of a person's life may not be categorical. For example, at what point in the growth of a foetus does it change from a bundle of molecules into a person? At what point in dying does a body change from being a person to become a non-person?

With the advance of modern medical science, there is further blurring of 'life' and 'death'. Not only are there far more sophisticated technologies for detecting signs of cardiovascular and cerebral activity in an otherwise 'dead' person, and methods for bringing the dead back to life, but also the artificial elongation of life can be for perpetuity.

John Bouvier (1788–1851), a French immigrant to the USA and prestigious Philadelphia lawyer and authority on US law (whose legal dictionary remains in print), described three kinds of homicide: (a) justifiable, as when the killing is performed in the exercise of a right or performance of a duty; (b) excusable, as when done, although not as duty or right, yet without culpable or criminal intent; and (c) felonious, or involving what the law terms malice (Bouvier, 1856). The latter may be either manslaughter or murder. Suicide in English law was at one time included within the classification of 'felonious' homicide ('malicious self-murder'), and punishment, such as a 'barbarous' burial, meted out on the body and his or her possessions expropriated by the king (Bouvier, 1856). Moreover, in nineteenth-century America, although death from a fight would normally result in the assailant being charged with manslaughter, if the fight was a duel then the charge would be murder. But duels could produce complications for criminal justice officials of that time:

> If Peter, of *malice prepense*, should discharge a pistol at Paul, and miss him, and then cast away the pistol and fly and, being pursued by Paul, he turn round, and kill him with a dagger, the law considers the first as the impulsive cause, and Peter would be guilty of murder. But if Peter, with his dagger drawn, had fallen down, and Paul in his haste had fallen upon it and killed himself, the cause of Paul's death would have been too remote to charge Peter as the murderer.
>
> (Bouvier, 1856)

Laws dealing with the spread of deadly contagious diseases stretching back to the Middle Ages still have application in the twenty-first century's laws of murder.

> Lord Hale seems to doubt whether if a person infected with the plague, should go abroad with intent to infect another, and another should be infected and die, it would not be murder; and he thinks it clear that though there should be no such intent, yet if another should be infected, it would be a great misdemeanour.
>
> (Bouvier, 1856)

The connection between the plague in the Middle Ages and today relates to HIV/AIDS. People with HIV/AIDS may be charged with one or other form of homicide if they have sex with others knowing that they may be infecting someone who then dies. But there are major difficulties in proving homicide through HIV/AIDS transmission. It cannot be certain that an infected person has been infected by the alleged killer. Also, the victim may take years to die and in the meantime contract many life-threatening diseases which may cloud what has caused his or her death. Even in 1856 there were competing legal definitions of murder. The definition that remains the cornerstone of Anglo-American criminal justice is that of Coke. The pitfalls of Coke's description of murder, as outlined by Bouvier (1856), remain in the twenty-first century:

> And Sir Edward Coke defines or rather describes this offence to be, when a person of sound mind and discretion, unlawfully killeth any reasonable creature in being, and under the king's peace, with malice aforethought either express or implied.

> This definition . . . has been severely and perhaps justly criticised. What, it has been asked, are sound memory and understanding? What has soundness of memory to do with the act; be it ever so imperfect, how does it affect the guilt? If discretion is necessary, can the crime ever be committed, for, is it not the highest indiscretion in a man to take the life of another, and thereby expose his own? If the person killed be an idiot or a new born infant, is he a reasonable creature? Who is in the king's peace? What is malice aforethought? Can there be any malice afterthought?

In England, in 1624, infanticide was introduced into law under the Prevent the Destroying and Murdering of Bastard Children Act as a way of accepting the impoverishment and social stigma that would be the consequence of a woman having an illegitimate child. Three centuries later this was enshrined as a special sub-category of homicide. A woman will not be held fully responsible for her actions if, at the time of the crime, medical evidence suggests that the aftermath of giving birth to any of her children has induced mental instability:

> Section 1 of the Infanticide Act 1938 provides that where a woman by any wilful act of omission causes the death of her child, being a child under 12 months, in circumstances which prima facie amount to murder, but at the same time of such an act or omission the balance of her mind was disturbed by reason of her not having fully recovered from the effects of giving birth to the child, or by reason of the effect of lactation consequent upon the birth of the child, she is guilty of infanticide, an offence punishable in the same ways as manslaughter. By Section 1(2) of the Act, where a woman is tried for the murder of the child under the age of 12 months, it is open to the jury to return a verdict of not guilty of murder but guilty of infanticide.
> (Cross, Jones & Card, 1988, p. 261)

With the wide-spread defence of diminished responsibility, as well as not-guilty-through-insanity (although this is seldom used), it becomes unnecessary for a section of the homicide law that implies women are biologically prone to killing their babies to be implemented.

Unlike the defences of insanity and diminished responsibility, however, the evidence of a 'disturbed mind' presented by the defence has to be disproved by the Crown. Moreover, the infanticide legislation can be viewed as providing further advantage to the defendant as there needs to be a lower level of mental disorder established than for diminished responsibility. If found guilty of infanticide, women are generally given probation with a requirement to receive psychiatric treatment.

There has been, particularly in the USA, much debate about what could be considered a type of infanticide, 'partial-birth abortions'. These abortions take place late in pregnancy, perhaps, the sixth month. The live foetus is extracted from the womb into the vagina, and then removed but dies. The procedure was banned in 2003 by the government of President George W. Bush on the basis that it was medically unethical and tantamount to murder. However, since then various US courts have suggested that the ban is unconstitutional as it denies a woman's right to decide what she does with her own body.

There is much controversy about how the Koran (Qur'an) can be interpreted with regard to taking a person's life, as there has been about the Bible. Killing is forbidden in the sixth commandment of the Old Testament, but there is the thorny problem of 'an eye for an eye, tooth for a tooth, and hand for a hand' in Exodus for Christian ethicists. What should be done with infidels (that is, non-Muslims) has become a desperate moral battleground for moderate and fundamentalist Muslims, with the latter taking the view that executing them is sanctioned in the Koran. In both religious books it is a matter of how literally references to these issues can be taken and whether or not the context in which the reference is made overrides its apparent meaning. Islamic law allows the family of a murdered Muslim to have the choice of retribution: (1) to take the murderer's life; or (2) to take *wergild* (or 'blood money'), that is accept compensation from the killer or the killer's family.

Sharia law, an Islamic religious code for living based originally on the Koran and the Sunna, allows the death penalty for murder. The form of execution is not specified in Islam. Beheading used to be regarded as the quickest and most merciful way (as in Roman law, and, for example, the French guillotine). The penalty for adultery and other sexual offences, such as rape and sex before marriage, is open to debate. Where punishment is judged appropriate, it includes flogging and execution. Sharia courts in Iran and northern Nigeria have in the twenty-first century handed out death sentences by stoning for adultery and incest (although these have not necessarily been carried out). Honour killings have also been given legitimacy by some interpretations of Sharia law.

Roman law is the legal system of the Roman republic and Roman Empire, from its earliest days to the time of the Eastern Roman Empire and the Emperor Justinian I after the fall of Rome itself. *Black's Law Dictionary* (1999) traces the contribution of Roman law from the Roman Republic and Roman Empire (spanning nearly one thousand years, on either side of the birth of Christ), to the foundations of many present-day legal systems:

- Common law was originally based on Roman law, before it developed into a tradition of its own in England, from where it expanded to the United Kingdom, apart from Scotland, to the United States of America, apart from Louisiana, and to most former British colonies.

- By contrast, so-called civil law systems are more directly based on Roman law; the legal systems of most countries in continental Europe and South America fall into this category, frequently through the Napoleonic Code. These are sometimes called Latin systems (or operating *jure latino*).

By the thirteenth century, Roman law, with its emphasis on public rather than private justice, had influenced the French state. The sixteenth century saw a shift from an accusatory procedural system to an inquisitorial system. However, in France both private and locally inspired customs that defined criminality and decided punishments continued well into the eighteenth century. Religion also affected the working of French criminal law when infringements of Church property and heretical practices occurred, or particular types of immorality (e.g. adultery) were the issue. Pre-revolutionary criminal law was arbitrary, harsh and retributive (capital punishment by hanging, quartering or decapitation; flogging; amputation; branding; banishment; torture). A criminal code was produced in revolutionary France, moving the law from customary practices, excessive retribution, judgements made on the whim of the judge, and exemption through privilege or decrees by feudal lords and the King, to a more humanitarian, egalitarian and stable system.

It wasn't until the Napoleonic Code (*Code civil des Francais*), primarily dealing with civil issues, was implemented early in 1804 that a coherent and national rule of law became possible. Further aspects on criminal law were added in 1810. This combined aspects of Roman law with French law from pre-revolution and revolutionary periods. Due to Napoleon Bonaparte's (1769–1821) military expansionism, the Code was adopted by Italy, the Netherlands, Belgium, Spain and Portugal and their colonies. The Napoleonic Code has also had influence on the laws of Germany, Austria and Switzerland. The Napoleonic Code was only replaced in France in 1994 (Elliot, 2001; Hodgson, 2004).

Homicide in France is split into voluntary homicide (intentional killing: murder, assassination and infanticide) and involuntary homicide (non-intentional death, for example through a violent act without *mens rea*, and road accidents). In twenty-first-century France, the law remains inquisitorial (with the emphasis, certainly in the early stages of trial, on private hearing, written evidence, and the judge ascertaining 'facts'), as opposed to English law, which is adversarial (accusatory, with a public hearing, verbal and written reporting, and the defence and prosecution promoting their respective assessments of the case throughout).

Just what an accused can use as defence against a charge of homicide is very different cross-culturally. Aggravating factors, such as provocation or long-term abuse, diminished responsibility, or self-defence, may or may not be used as a defence or in mitigation; a hierarchy of 'good' and 'bad' motives exist; the method of killing may be counted in judgement and sentencing. Moreover, any particular country's laws on homicide might change. For example, the Law Commission declared the homicide legislation in England and Wales a mess and in need of review (Law Commission, 2005a).

Concurring with the Law Commission, Blom-Cooper and Terrence Morris (2004) argue that the current distinctions in English law between murder, manslaughter and infanticide should be abolished. Blom-Cooper and Morris focus on the idea of malice aforethought, necessary for a murder conviction, and view it as a completely misleading concept. They suggest that the concept of 'moral-guilt' implies that where there has been no direct intention to kill (that is, an absence of explicit malice), but a death(s) has occurred through the gross recklessness of another person (for example, corporate neglect of employees' working conditions, drunken driving) then this could be considered more heinous than if malice is explicit but either minimal or short lived although a death has been the outcome (for example, during a drunken fight, or a lover's quarrel). They propose that culpable homicide (a category already used in Scotland) should be the single crime for all present forms of homicide in English law so that the assessment of 'malice aforethought' is secondary to that of 'moral-guilt' for a human death. There is, they point out, confusion about the separation of grievous bodily harm from murder. Further, it is possible to be convicted of murder without actually wishing to cause the death of the victim. That is, the convicted murderer has no malice aforethought of murder, is intending to cause grievous bodily harm but a death ensues and they therefore will be convicted of murder.

The Law Commission (2005b) set out proposals for consultation on the structure of homicide offences. The main proposal was that there should be three tiers of culpability for homicide:

1. In the top tier would be cases where there is an intention to kill for which the mandatory life sentence would be retained.

2. In the second tier would be cases of killing through reckless indifference to causing death and intention to do serious harm but not to kill (including defences of provocation, diminished responsibility and duress).

3. In the third tier (manslaughter) would be cases of killing by gross negligence or intention to cause harm but not serious harm.

The USA, with its British legal heritage, still has principles that are similar to English law. But, as with other crimes, homicide in the USA is affected by the separation of federal and state laws. This leads to remarkably different outcomes in the courts (Hickey, 2003). Moreover, some killings (non-criminal homicides) are not illegal. These 'justifiable', 'excusable', or accidental killings include those that happen when defending oneself from assault, during conventional warfare, or in the 'war on terrorism', when perhaps a potential suicide bomber is shot to prevent them from endangering other lives, or causing a death without intention, negligence or recklessness.

Taking the example of two thieves in a grocery store: one of them standing by as his partner attacks, with a blunt instrument found nearby, the store detective who has spotted the pair stealing. The detective dies from his wound. The thief who took no part in the killing (and perhaps had even shouted at his partner to stop) could under certain legal jurisdictions be charged with murder and sentenced to death, whereas in others a murder charge would not apply.

It is, therefore, not possible to talk of one US law on killing, but Hickey (2003) provides the following outline of the homicide framework in which those charged with a killing are held responsible to a greater or lesser extent:

1. First-degree murder: the 'murder one' of TV and cinema police dramas is an intended and premeditated killing but one categorised as heinous due to the way in which the victim(s) died, because of the social status of the victims (for example, police officers or children), or if it occurred when a crime such as kidnapping or rape was being carried out (that is, a 'felony' murder).

2. Second-degree murder: the killing is intended but is not a premeditated, heinous, or felony murder, and is the result of an intention to do grievous bodily harm, or resist arrest.

3. Voluntary manslaughter: here the intention to kill usually only comes about close to the act, when it has been encouraged by the 'heat of passion' stemming from, for example, jealousy between lovers.

4. Involuntary manslaughter: there is no intention to kill or to commit grievous bodily harm but there is guilt through negligence or recklessness, or
where a death has occurred during an unlawful act.

In Western societies, there is ambivalence about how the business world
should be covered by the homicide laws, but in Sir Edward Coke's
seventeenth-century England, there was little doubt: 'They [Corporations]
cannot commit treason, nor be outlawed, nor excommunicate, for they have
no souls, neither can they appear in person' (Sir Edward Coke, 1612, quoted
in Blom-Cooper & Morris, 2004, p. 133).

Although many Western countries have laws that prosecute corporations if
they flout health and safety regulations, these laws are, in practice, used
infrequently and punishments are derisory, even if people have died as a
result. Certainly a charge of 'corporate homicide' or corporate manslaughter, that is death caused by decisions or omissions, is rare and as a verdict is
so uncommon as to be ignored in the homicide statistics, despite:

> . . . the slow and painful deaths of thousands of individuals exposed to pre-
> cious dusts, such as asbestos, despite ample evidence, known to employers, of
> the potentially fatal health risks, or the negligent and fraudulent safety testing
> of drugs by the pharmaceutical industry, or environmental crimes that cause
> death due to the dumping of hazardous wastes and illegal toxic emissions.
> (Brookman, 2005, p. 3)

Deaths caused in this way, if included in the homicide statistics, would be
the largest category of homicide. Essentially, however, it is very difficult to
identify who is responsible in the corporate decision-making process for a
particular act that leads to death. Corporations as inanimate entities could
be prosecuted, fined, their operations restricted or closed down altogether,
but this is unsatisfactory in terms of targeting culpability and prevention,
and is unrealistic in a globalised economy.

As Blom-Cooper and Morris (2004) comment, the absence of any soul or
attribute of being a human being as Coke proposed is no longer a bar to corporate liability where somebody has died. However, prosecutions for corporate killings are not often successful. The guilt of the company is
dependent on the guilt of an individual manager or senior director.
Company's generally delegate the responsibility for Health and Safety
further down the hierarchy and therefore can claim that they are not immediately responsible for any negligence.

What Blom-Cooper and Morris have set out is a new framework in the law
on homicide in England and Wales. Blameworthy behaviour leading to the
killing of a human being, which attracts the criminal tag of homicide
involves:

> A person, by any act or omission, intends to cause, or by behaviour manifesting recklessness, gross negligence, or by reason of serious failure of corporate management, causes serious physical harm to another resulting in that person's death, commits the offence of criminal homicide.
>
> (Blom-Cooper & Morris, 2004, p. 175)

Cannibalism has occurred throughout history, in many parts of the world, and for many reasons. During the Christian Crusades from Europe (circa 1096–1270 AD), about 20000 Muslims were massacred in 1098 at Ma'arra al-Numan in today's Syria. The Crusaders, who had an attitude of regarding Muslims as lower than animals, and because other food sources were in short supply, indulged in cannibalism. Adults and children were boiled or spit-roasted and then eaten (Maalouf, 2001).

In English law, however, it is murder for one human to kill another human for food. This is so even if starvation looms and whether or not you hold that person in low esteem. In 1884, the yacht *Mignonette* set sail for Sydney from Southampton, but it was ship-wrecked off the African coast. Its Captain, Tom Dudley, and some of the surviving crew took to a small dingy. After killing and eating the cabin boy (17-year-old Richard Parker) they were rescued. Subsequently, they were to be put on trial for cannibalism on the high seas (Blom-Cooper and Morris, 2004). The judge, Lord Coleridge, dismissing the defence of self-preservation, found the Captain and the Mate (Edwin Stephens) guilty of murder. They were sentenced to death but this was reduced to six months imprisonment.

Thailand, however, in 2005 could not find a law to prosecute a 50-year-old man who had been eating a partially cremated corpse. Sakorn Piengphon was arrested in a poor region about 500 miles north of Bangkok near the border with Laos, but, without a legal ban on cannibalism, he couldn't be charged. He had served a prison term of 15 years for killing his mother and claimed that, on release, his family had ostracised him and he was very hungry (AFP, 2005).

REALITY

In 2004, in a part of the city of Johannesburg that has one of the highest densities of murder not just in South Africa but the world, I decided to conduct rudimentary research. This entailed looking for possible socio-environmental causative factors that may be linked to killings in this area (for example, dilapidated housing). My method of recording any such evidence was photographic, and I did this by leaning out of the window of our taxi. The taxi driver had insisted that this was a safe and acceptable 'tourist' activity. I was accompanied by my increasingly nervous Australian colleague and friend, Mike Hazelton, whose academic interest in killing stretched only as far as perpetually exclaiming that he 'could murder a sirloin steak' and whose stereotypical Aussie bravado failed him on this occasion. We attracted attention due to the very obvious ethnic-clash between the inhabitants of this part of the city (black Africans) and the would-be criminal ethnographers (white Anglo-Australians). People around us were also captivated by the amusing sight of a taxi driving very slowly along busy streets with a worried-looking 'tourist' taking pictures of what must have seemed to be most unphotogenic scenes as he dangled half-way out of a moving vehicle, his reluctant collaborator trying to hide and the driver shouting encouragingly and repeatedly 'it's okay, it's okay.' This was a blundering and disrespectful venture.

A few days later, a prominent black jazz musician in South Africa, Gito Baloi, was talking with people in the same crowded part of Central Johannesburg as we had been photographing. He was shot in the neck, but managed to drive off, then got out of his car, walked a few metres, collapsed and died. He was then robbed (Peta, 2004). Two months after this killing, Darryl Kempster, a British dancer performing at the Nelson Mandela Theatre in Johannesburg, was shot and killed by a mugger whilst walking back to his hotel during the night. The downtown theatre is next to what Ted Leggett, senior researcher at the Institute for Security Studies in Pretoria, states is arguably one of the most dangerous areas in the country (quoted in Starmer-Smith, 2004). The part of Johannesburg referred to here is Hillbrow.

Hillbrow has a reputation for murder, rape, prostitution, firearm robbery, drug-dealing, shop-lifting, vehicular theft and illegal immigration. It is perhaps the most feared neighbourhood in a county which is infamous for its violence and crime. The above two murders were mentioned in the British press. However, most Hillbrow murders do not get reported internationally. In 2000, there were 205 murders recorded by the police (Leggett, 2003). That means approximately four deaths a week. But things change. South Africa's murder rate dropped in the early 2000s, and a concerted effort to sort out the social chaos that is Hillbrow is being made. Hence, listing statistics here is pointless as they will be out-of-date by the time they are read. Even trends, if dealing with short periods, have to be referred to carefully because, for instance, what might be a downturn in the number of murders in a city like Johannesburg over a couple of years might become an upturn in the following two years. I have, therefore, not in the main used specific figures on homicide. Instead, I comment on long-term patterns using the United Nations, the World Health Organisation, the British Home Office, the US

Federal Bureau of Investigation, and publications produced by various regional police departments, as principal sources.

Despite the dubiousness of criminal statistics in general, the official recording of homicides has been regarded as largely reliable (Smith & Zahn, 1999). For Gary LaFree (2003), it is a fairly safe assumption that cross-national comparisons are legitimate. The police are usually notified of unlawful killings, or bodies are found eventually which necessitate murder inquiries. Murder is usually not only reported to the police but is also recorded (which doesn't always happen for other types of crime). Criminal justice systems mostly take murder seriously, spending more time and resources compared with other crimes. Most murder crimes do not need a Sherlock Holmes or Inspector Maigret to catch the killer: 'The majority of murder investigations are solved relatively soon after the offence and with limited investigative effort' (Nicol, Innes, Gee & Fiest 2004, p. 42).

The police arrest and conviction rate for murder, compared with that of other crimes, is about 90% in many Western countries, which is very impressive. This is due primarily to the closeness of the victim to his or her killer; that is, the previous and current lovers to whom the police first turn in their investigations. It is also a consequence of murders carried out by lovers being, although possibly premeditated, conducted in a state of emotional turmoil and therefore not necessarily being well planned. In such circumstances, motives are far more likely to be ascertained (the victim perhaps having had a sexual affair with another person or having threatened to terminate the relationship), and clues are more likely to be left at the scene of the crime. Other common murders, such as those involving fights between men, by their very nature usually have witnesses. They happen in crowded bars or city streets.

Moreover, developments in forensic science allow for fragments of evidence to be used by the prosecution to establish connections between killers and crime scenes. DNA testing in particular allows culprits to be traced from tiny pieces of human discharge and skin debris left unknowingly at the time of the murder. This means that unsolved cases of murder that have been 'closed' for many years can be re-examined, using the evidence collected at the time to compare with the DNA of old or new suspects. The British National DNA Database, set up in 1995, holds millions of DNA profiles. In 10 years of operation it has provided the police with 600000 matches to suspects. The police can retain DNA samples taken from any arrested suspects, even if they went on to be acquitted in court. Each month about 15 DNA matches are made to help solve murder cases (Gosline, 2005).

This is also true for other countries. For example, Canada has a National Data Bank (Banque nationale de donnees genetiques). Winnipeg Police

(2005) used DNA profiling to track down and charge Robert Joseph Kociuk, aged 64 yrs, with first-degree murder 20 years after he is alleged to have committed a murder. He was suspected of sexually assaulting and killing 48-year-old Beverley Ann Dyke, who had been stabbed seven times in the chest and abdomen, twice in the back and six times to the arms.

The reliability of homicide statistics can be disputed. There is a disparity between what counts as the official crime rate, as recorded by the police, and that which is identified through research into victim incidents. The way in which police forces collate crime data, and what regions come under the province of a police force, alters over time, and therefore historical comparisons become problematic. Different surveys of victims (such as the British Crime Survey, and those conducted by the United Nations and the World Health Organisation) can reach widely different conclusions about the number of homicides committed, even in the same country and in the same year. Furthermore, how do these approaches that measure incidence provide an accurate reflection of prevalence? The numbers of missing persons in the world may run into hundreds of thousands, some of whom may have been killed.

Although homicide is universally a crime, there remains an absence of an internationally agreed definition of homicide. International crime statistics are faulty in that they are collated from different sources (official data and unofficial data). Biases inherent in methods of data collecting at a national level are transferred into global statistics. Internationally collated data may not separate intentional from unintentional homicide, and there are further anomalies such as legal executions being included by some countries (LaFree, 2003). The cause of death listed on a death certificate of a person executed in California is classified as homicide (Hickey, 2003). Brookman (2005) refers to the 'dark figure' of homicide, suggesting that we do not know how many bodies have been disposed of without trace, or if there is a body whether the person died illegally, by suicide, accidentally or through natural causes.

Moreover, there are three sets of data with respect to homicide. One set refers to the number of deaths considered at the time of discovery by the police to be the result of unlawful killing. Another set are those that are recorded as homicide within the active judicial process of prosecution. Finally, there is the actual sum of convictions. Hence, it is not possible to be certain about how many people have at any one point been murdered as some deaths perceived to be the result of homicide can be later reclassified as, for example, accidental.

Furthermore, none of the data reflects when the crime took place as some convictions may be related to murders committed years previously. The number of offences of homicide recorded by the police does not correspond to the number of people arrested. Not only are there situations in which no one is apprehended, but also more than one person can be charged with a particular murder, or one person may be charged with more than one murder. Nor do the statistics take account of miscarriages of justice that might be uncovered at a later date through, for example, the very DNA testing procedures that help to convict others.

Also, officially defined and recorded statistics omit certain deaths. In times of civil strife, such as the break-up and 'ethnic cleansing' of the former Yugoslavia, a calculation of the number of innocent civilians killed by soldiers representing the various warring factions, or by other civilians, can only be estimated vaguely. Moreover, it is debatable as to how to register intentional killings such as those occurring through terrorism: Northern Ireland; the Basque Region; New York's Twin Towers; Bali; the Philippines; and Iraq.

Interpol was created in 1923 and is the world's largest police organisation (182 member countries). Its General Secretariat is located in Lyon, France, and has a global police communications system and criminal databases. Interpol was, up until 2004, the most widely used source for homicide statistics. After 2004, it stopped supplying open access to its data bank for the public and journalists (only making it available to police agencies) because the collection of data was not regulated effectively (Interpol, 2004).

Also, there is the matter of the connection between aggression and violence. Although aggression is not synonymous with violence, there is a correlation between the two. Aggressive people tend to get more involved in violence compared with non-aggressive people. People who are aggressive in interpersonal relationships have a greater 'risk' of entering into violent situations, of being violent and of having violence done to them (Hickey, 2003). In 2002, the World Health Organisation published the first comprehensive report on global violence and health (Krug et al., 2002). Violence, according to the report, kills more than 1.6 million people every year. This figure includes self-directed violence (that is, suicide). This is just the tip of the iceberg as many if not most violent incidents do not get entered into official statistics, either because they are not reported or they are not viewed by the authorities of a particular culture or society as worth recording. Violence is among the leading causes of death for people aged 15–44 years of age, accounting for 14% of deaths among males and 7% of deaths among females. Almost every minute of the day, someone, somewhere is killed by homicide, and every two minutes another person is killed by armed conflict. During the twentieth century, nearly 200 million people lost their lives through armed conflict, and over half of those who died were civilians.

What can be said about homicide is that there has been a sizeable rise in homicide victimisation since the end of the Second World War, and it is expected to rise to one million per annum by 2020 (Krug et al., 2002). For most countries, the rate has grown inexorably since the 1950s. It has nearly trebled since the 1950s in England and Wales. A number of countries (for example, Chile, Japan and Singapore), however, have showed a decline in their rates (LaFree, 2003). Rates in the USA have been largely higher than other industrialised nations; they rose much more steeply than other industrialised nations during the 1960s and early 1970s but then fell more markedly during the 1990s. Homicide, however, in overall global crime figures, accounts for only a small proportion.

The regular publication of data by the United Nations and the World Health Organisation (using standardised rates of homicide, that is, rates per 100 000 of the population) does allow some international trends to be identified. For example, homicide accounts for only a small proportion of the overall global crime statistics. But there has been a sizeable rise in homicide victimisation since the end of the Second World War, and this is expected to rise to one million per annum by 2020 (Krug et al., 2002). Moreover, for most countries the rate has grown inexorably since the 1950s. It has nearly trebled since the 1950s in England and Wales. A number of countries (for example, Chile, Japan and Singapore), however, have showed a decline in their rates (LaFree, 2003).

The USA is commonly regarded as a country with a very high homicide rate, and homicide rates have been largely higher than other industrialised nations. They did rise much more steeply than other industrialised nations during the 1960s and early 1970s, but then fell more markedly during the 1990s. The EU, Australia and New Zealand do have much lower rates of homicide (England and Wales the lowest) than the USA. However, Russia has about 10 times more than the USA, Jamaica about 15 times more, South Africa about 25 times more and Colombia more than 50 times. Colombia is the country with the highest homicide rate in the world, and Malta has the lowest.

Moreover, you are far less likely to be murdered in the European cities of Brussels, Athens, Rome, Dublin and London than in the US cities of Washington DC, Philadelphia, Dallas, Los Angeles and New York, the South Africa city of Johannesburg, the Jamaican capital of Kingston, as well as the Russian Federation capital of Moscow.

Modes of killing are dependent on the availability of obvious weapons. In countries where gun ownership is high (such as the USA, Brazil and Finland), they are used frequently. The exception is Switzerland, in which although a high gun-owning society (due to its large reserve army), the murder rate is low.

The victim is frequently known to the killer. Nearly half of women victims are killed by a present or former intimate partner. Males are the primary perpetrators (usually 9 out of 10) of homicides, and they are also frequently the primary victims, although at a lesser extreme (over 6 out of 10 victims).

Murder is usually intra-racial, and is largely a matter of social class. The vast majority of murderers come from the lower section of the social strata. Drug or alcohol abuse is common amongst killing conducted by this group. The upper and middle classes rarely murder (Hickey, 2003).

In England and Wales, professional and skilled workers are considerably under-represented in homicide statistics. The victim's or perpetrator's home, bars and nightclubs, and streets near to bars and nightclubs late in the evening, are the 'hot spots' of killing (Brookman, 2005). The Crime and Society Foundation (Hillyard, Pantazis, Tombs, Gordon and Dorling, 2005) reported that in Britain poverty is the 'prime suspect' in murder. For Hillyard et al. (2005), people living in the poorest neighbourhoods are massively more likely to be murdered (nearly six times more) than those living in the richest. This inequality in murder (primary) victim-hood is, argue Hillyard et al., traceable to the social and economic policies of successive governments, which increased the gap in wealth distribution.

Dobash, Dobash, Cavanagh and Lewis (2002) reviewed 866 case files of men and women serving sentences for murder in England and Scotland. They also examined the annual homicide indexes for England/Wales and Scotland and interviewed 200 murderers (180 men; 20 women) in prisons (England and Scotland). They found that for male murderers:

- 61% had problems in schools

- 48% had at least one previous conviction as children (below 16)

- 39% were from 'broken homes'

- 24% had a violent father (towards mother)

- 26% had been in care

- 24% had multiple carers as children

- 25% had problems with alcohol as children

- 17% abused drugs as children

- most left school unqualified

- 10% have learning disabilities

- 67% were usually unemployed

- 50% had problems with alcohol as adults

- 25% abused drugs as adults

- 25% had mental health problems

- most had previous criminal convictions with 50% serving previous prison sentences

- the average age at the time of the murder was 28 years

- over 70% of the victims were known to the killers.

The characteristics of homicide in the USA, according to Miethe and Regoeczi (2004), are:

- Most homicides involve specific intra-racial and intra-age groups in urban settings – single male adult shooting an associate during an argument.

- Expressive homicides are more prevalent than instrumental ones (that is, killing because of heightened anger, jealousy, hate occurs more often than because financial or other rewards will be gained, during a robbery or mugging).

- Instrumental homicides are more likely to be carried out by strangers.

- Multiple-killers are more likely to conduct instrumental homicides.

- Expressive homicides are predominantly intra-racial, intra-age group, and carried out by single over 30-year-old offenders known to their victim, frequently over seemingly trivial disputes, with alcohol consumption being a factor as is victim provocation.

- Confrontational homicides (character contests 'saving face') often involve male as well as female offenders, both in public and private situations.

- Male killers mainly have victim acquaintances of the same age and race whom they shoot in public places during an argument. Female killers are more involved in killing members of their family and opposite-sex intimates in private places.

- Young juvenile killers (aged below 16 years) are more likely to shoot family members during an argument, whereas older juvenile killers are more prone to kill strangers for instrumental reasons.

- Male sexual jealousy and ownership are underpinning reasons for the killing of female intimates across ethnic groups, as is the threat to male honour (confrontational homicide).

- Stranger homicides are usually instrumental, involve guns, male against male within the same ethnic and age group within large urban areas.

Amongst the 15–44 year age group, murder is the third leading cause of death, but the riskiest age of being murdered is 0–1, and the likely murderer is the mother of the victim. Ania Wilczynski (1997), in her account of the killing of children of all ages by their parents or parental surrogates, suggests that there is an underestimation of these types of murder and that the figure may be as high as five times that recorded in official statistics.

Moreover, although extremely controversial, one research study in Britain conducted by a leading paediatrician has indicated that a small percentage of children diagnosed as having suffered from 'cot death' may in fact have been murdered – usually by their mothers (Meadow, 1999). According to Professor Sir Roy Meadow, coroners and pathologists are under too great a pressure to ascertain the cause of death in order to reduce psychological stress on the families of the dead child. In addition, he suggests that medical and nursing staff are not sensitive to signs of impending abuse (and potential homicide) when faced with harassed young mothers who attend paediatric units for no apparent genuine reason. Discordance about Meadow's stance on killer-mothers ruptured further in 2005 when he was struck off the medical register, and again in 2006 when he won his appeal against this decision (although the GNC may appeal against Meadow's successful appeal).

There is, of course, no chance of reoffending if a convicted murderer has received a death sentence (and it has been carried out). Whilst incarcerated, murderers have limited opportunity to kill again, and only rarely does a prisoner or prison guard get murdered (Hickey, 2003). However, only a very small number of convicted murderers reoffend following their release from prison. The circumstances of the initial killing, for example an extreme emotional outburst within a particular relationship or situation, would not be likely to be recreated. That is, killing does not become a 'career', although discharged murderers may go on to commit other crimes. The exceptions are, for example, serial, gang and Mafia-related killings. This may simply reflect judicious sentencing and discharge procedures in that potential repeat killers remain in custody.

SUMMARY

Murder is a perpetual social problem. But murder is, like many 'social facts', not necessarily easily defined or understood. What it is becomes dependent on whose perception has to be taken into account and in what context it is being judged. The intricacies of legal processes nationally and internationally compound the problem of deciding 'what is murder'. Although virtually always a major crime, some societies appear to condone rather than condemn some forms of murder. Most, if not all, societies appear to have a moral hierarchy of murder, both with reference to its victims and its perpetators. This means that even if all killing is proscribed, particular forms are given harsher punishments than others. Punishment itself varies enormously trans-nationally with non-custodial sentences applied in certain cases (for example, infanticide), whilst the death penalty is given for others (for example, fornication).

Furthermore, as with many types of statistical 'realities', it is a matter of interpretation as to what 'truth' is being expounded, particularly when politicians, journalists or other partisan groups are the interpreters. Take these three examples, all dealing with murder in Colombia. First, the BBC News used the following headline on 24 April 2003: '**Colombia murder rate soars**' (BBC News 2003a). This news item mentions data provided by the Permanent Committee for the Defence of Human Rights, a group based in Colombia. According to the article, 32000 killings had taken place in 2003. About 10000 of these murders were politically motivated, conducted either by terrorists fighting the government or by right-wing paramilitaries engaged in 'social cleansing' (that is, assassinating drug addicts, homosexuals and prostitutes). Per 100000 of the population, this murder rate is 78 (for the same year South Africa was 50, the USA was 6, Canada below 2, England and Wales approximately 1.5, and Switzerland about 1).

However, just over a year later (30 June, 2004), Reuters News Agency produced a contrary headline: '**Killings, abductions fall in Colombia – Police.**' Reuters used data from the Colombian police. This source stated that in the first half of 2004 the number of people murdered dropped from 11331 to 9790. The apparent dramatic fall was attributed to the new Colombian President's campaign to end police corruption and increase efficiency, along with the military tackling the violence carried out by paramilitaries and other armed groups.

Then along came Amnesty International's (2005a) report on Colombia covering 2004. What was stated in this report was that, notwithstanding a slump in civilian massacres, extrajudicial executions carried out directly by the Colombian military increased in 2004. Moreover, during the first half of 2004, at least 1400 civilians were killed or had gone missing.

So, what can be said about the reality of murder in Colombia? Whether or not the official account is accepted or versions offered by internal and external human rights organisations, the reality is either one of improvement, deterioration, or a complex mix of both including an obscuration of the distinction between legal and illegal killing (that is, government forces are allegedly killing people other than those who are an immediate military threat). Nevertheless, the reality is that Colombia is, compared to most other countries, a dangerous place.

One uncontested reality, however, is that Pierre Riviere hanged himself on October 20 1840 in the Central Prison at Beaulieu a few years into a life sentence, the King having commuted the punishment of death given at trial. Another is that Tim Parry, an innocent 12-year-old English boy, was killed in 1993 by the IRA.

CHAPTER 2

WHO COMMITS MURDER?

Glasgow: the scene is a crowded bar, night club, or street late in the early hours of the morning. Alcohol and a knife-carrying culture are factors, as is offending male pride and gang rivalry. There is an accidental nudge resulting in a split drink, an injudicious leer at a girlfriend, a heightened dislike of another man's accent, a gang intruding on another's drug operating territory, or a robbery is mishandled. Someone dies.

July, 2003, 17-year-old Thomas Loughery was stabbed and died in hospital from his wounds. James McCormick, also 17, was convicted of murder. He was later accidentally released from custody, and then he attacked and robbed two teenagers. April, 2004, Shaun O'Neill, 21 years of age stabbed and killed 28-year-old David McEwen in revenge for a road-rage incident. O'Neill had been cleared the previous year of shooting to death a fast-food retail manager, although three of his co-defendants, friends, were convicted of murder; February 2004, Ali Mohammid Karim stabbed and killed 21-year-old Anthony Farrell during a city centre fracas. Karim is an Iraqi Kurd asylum-seeker. Glasgow has had a long history of violence, a city with the reputation of having one of highest murder rates of all European cities.

Yetunde Price was shot in the back of the head and later died in Los Angeles's gang-ridden and poor southern suburb of Compton in 2003. She was sitting in a car late at night with her boyfriend when an argument with local residents began. Price was a mother of three children, a nurse and owner of a beauty salon. Price was also the elder sister of tennis stars Serena and Venus Williams. Aaron Michael Hammer, 23 years old, and Robert Edward Maxfield, also aged 23, were arrested on suspicion of the murder (in 2006 Maxfield pleaded no contest to voluntary manslaughter). Hammer and Maxfield are alleged to be members of the Crips gang.

Southern Los Angeles, like city-centre Glasgow and pockets of its suburbs around the commercial district, has a reputation for serious violence. Most killings in Glasgow are intra-ethnic (white-on-white), although there has been an increase in tension between the dominant Caucasian and ethnic minorities. Most killings in Los Angeles are also intra-ethnic (black-against-black and murders within the Latino community) and are much higher than those between whites (Leovy, 2003).

The black-against-black killings in Los Angeles and the Glasgow street killings have similarities but also major differences. For some instances in Glasgow ethnicity is an issue, as we have seen, where immigrants, refugees and asylum seekers may have something to do with the crime. In south central Los Angeles, skin colour most certainly has something to do with the crime because both killer and victim are black. However, the connotations of ethnicity in Britain compared with America are radically different. Secondly, the type of weapon that is used differs: knives in Glasgow, guns in Los Angeles. Thirdly, gangs may be part of the identity for Glaswegian youth, but not to the extent they are in Los Angeles. Fourthly, in Britain the homicide rates and also levels of violence are taken seriously across the board with some notable exceptions, particularly amongst refugee groups and prostitutes. In the USA, however, black-against-black crime, although politically debated as to whether or not it is a social problem or the cultural problem of the ethnic group concerned, doesn't seem to be tackled. Black-against-black crime in Britain has escalated in recent years in major cities. In response, the politicians and the police have specifically targeted black groups such as the Yardies (Britain's ruthless drug gangsters with the potential to equate to US, Italian and Russian Mafias, Chinese Triads and Japanese Yakuza) in order to reduce such crime.

Murderers who commit what appear to be crimes of a similar motivation or classification by style and process, numbers or status of the victims each have unique characteristics, and each are interpreted by themselves, the public, media, police, lawyers, juries, judges and social historians with added variations. No two murderers, or two murders even if committed by the same person, can be conflated accurately into one category. Terms such as 'mass', 'serial', 'genocidal' are meaningless, describing only the number of killings and attracting spurious theorising.

For example, Cedric Maake, given a 1340 year gaol sentence in 2000 for murdering 27 people, and Moses Sithole, sentenced to 2400 years in prison for the murder of 38 people, are both from South Africa. Both murderers were brutal, black and mainly preyed on women. But can they be neatly placed alongside each other on the basis of what? Their ethnic group? The number of victims? Presumed socio-economic causative factors? The labels adopted by journalists, local communities, lawyers, psychiatrists, criminologists? How can they be compared with, for example, a 'serial' killer, conducting his taking of human life thousands of kilometres away in India. Koose Muniswamy Veerappan, shot dead by police in 2004, after 17 years of banditry during which he may have killed 120 people and 3000 elephants, was considered to be either India's worst villain or a 'Robin Hood' folk hero with a reported tender side and a wife who became attracted to him because of his 'moustache and notoriety'! (Huggler, 2004). Could Veerappan be linked with other 'serial' killers out to make a profit through crime who are also regarded with ambivalence?

How can the following killings be categorised unambiguously?:

1. Cult leaders of 'The Movement for the Restoration of the Ten Commandments of God' kill 500 Doomsday Sect members by setting fire to their Church in 2000, as well as strangling others.

2. Tens of thousands of black Africans transported as slaves to the Americas, between the sixteenth and nineteenth centuries, left to die on route.

3. The Italian Mafia, during 2004, are thought to have killed 134 people in Naples as a consequence of an internecine organised-crime turf war; killings of gang members and innocent bystanders continuing into 2005.

4. Australian pie-salesman John Wayne Glover, attacked elderly women from 1989 to 1990 around the North Shore of Sydney, using a hammer and strangulation; six are known to have been murdered but more deaths are suspected, and Glover becomes known as the 'Granny Killer'; he dies in prison in 2005, seemingly having committed suicide.

5. Pakistan 1999, Samia Sarwar, 29 years of age and a mother of two young sons, was shot in the head and killed in her lawyer's office, Lahore; Samia's mother and uncle had been driven to the lawyer's office and it was the driver (Habibur Rehman) who shot her; she was seeking a divorce; her killer was shot by a plain clothes police officer who had been guarding the lawyer's office.

6. England 2003, Abdulla Jones slits the throat of his 16-year-old daughter, Heshu Jones, because she was having a relationship with an 18-year-old man of Lebanese birth; he then attempts suicide by first cutting his throat and then jumping from the third floor of his home.

7. Scotland 2005, Michael Hayes, who had a series of driving offences, is found guilty of 'careless driving' after colliding with and killing a motor-cyclist as well as his own son; he received a fine and a driving ban for the fifth time.

8. Switzerland 2005, Russian Vitaly Kaloyev is convicted of a pre-meditated killing after stabbing Peter Nielson; Nielson was the air traffic controller in Zurich when an airplane flying from Moscow to Barcelona collided with another airplane killing 71 people including Kaloyev's wife and two children.

What about *terrorism*? Is that a stable category of murder? That is, can those who kill for identifiable political reasons and use covert means be lumped together precisely because their motives and modus operandi are identifiable?

Timothy McVeigh and *Terry Nichols* on 19 April, 1995, park a truck full of fertilizer explosive and fuel in front of the Alfred P. Murrah Federal Building in Oklahoma City, USA. The explosion kills 149 men and women and 19 children, and 500 people are wounded. McVeigh and Nichols were American 'terrorists' but only in that they were antigovernment survivalists aggrieved by the State's handling of a siege at Waco, Texas in 1993 in which 84 people had died. Nichols was given a prison sentence for the rest of his natural life and Timothy McVeigh was sentenced to death by a Federal court. He died by lethal injection in 2001.

Reginald Dyer, a General in the British Army when India was part of the British Empire, ordered the shooting of hundreds of innocent Hindus, Sikhs, at Jallianwala Bagh on 13 April, 1919. He became known as 'The Butcher of Amritsar' (Collett, 2005). Dyer had grown-up in the army, gained a reputation for violence and of being head-strong, disobedient to his military superiors, arrogant and racist. When the First World War ended, 'terrorism' against British rule in northern India flourished. Dyer, who had taken command of Amritsar from the civil authorities, feared that another mutiny to match that of 1857 was possible. The introduction of censorship and internment without trial as an anti-terrorism measure had provoked public demonstrations. When telegraph wires were pulled down and a goods train was derailed, Dyer took the view that a repeat of the mutiny of 1857 might be looming in the Punjab. His Gurkha and Pathan soldiers were ordered to fire on an unarmed crowd that had gathered in the centre of the town. They began shooting without warning and continued for up to 15 minutes. The wounded could not be helped because a curfew had been installed (by Dyer).

Osama Bin Laden, a wealthy Saudi Arabian, had joined the jihadist war against Russian Soviet forces that had invaded Afghanistan in 1979. Bin Laden and his mojahedin were armed and trained by the American CIA and British MI6 security services (Milne & Bodi, 2001). Bin Laden then formed al-Qaeda, with loosely organised cells based throughout the world of Islamic extremists and whose members were willing to attack Western interests. Bin Laden has been implicated in the bombings of American embassies in Kenya and Tanzania in 1998, the 2000 bombing of the USS Cole refuelling in Yemen, an explosion in Seattle on New Year's Eve 2000, and the bombing of an Australian nuclear reactor during the Olympic Games also in 2000. Then came 11 September, 2001 ('9/11'). The National Commission on Terrorist

Attacks upon the United States in its final report (NCTAUS, 2004) detailed the events on that notorious day when passenger planes were hijacked over American airspace by members of Bin Laden's al-Qaeda. About 15 minutes before 9 am, American Airlines Flight 11 was forced to crash into the north tower of the World Trade Center in New York. Fifteen minutes later, United Airlines Flight 175 was forced to crash into the World Trade Center's south tower. Half-an-hour later, American Airlines Flight 77 crashed into the Pentagon in Washington, headquarters of the US Defense Department, followed by United Airlines Flight 93 smashing into the ground 128 km outside Pittsburgh.

In September 2004, Ken Bigley is kidnapped in Bagdad by the Tawhid and Jihad Islamic fundamentalist terrorist groups, both led by Abu Musab al-Zarqawi. al-Zarqawi was born in Zarqa, Jordan. A petty criminal in his teens, he later was gaoled for over six years in that country during the 1990s for storing guns. The groups, believed by the US government to be the link between Saddam Hussein and al-Qaeda, responsible for 1000 deaths through terrorist bombings, but with perhaps only 1000 members. The group's demands were for the release of women prisoners held by the coalition forces. Ken Bigley, from Liverpool, England, married to a Thai citizen, was in his 60s and had been working as an engineer in Iraq.

Ken Bigley did escape from his kidnappers, but only for 30 minutes. He was to be seen on videotape footage placed on the internet begging for his life on his knees with hooded and armed men standing behind him. A video-tape was released of Ken Bigley's beheading.

Abu Musab al-Zarqawi, an Islamic fundamentalist, is alleged to have masterminded many bombing campaigns, and his death toll is hundreds. His real name is Ahmad Fadeel Nazal Khalayleh, and he was born in 1966. The Jordanian courts, in his absence, gave him three death sentences (P. Harris, 2005). He was eventually killed in Iraq by American forces.

Prison, exposure to the degrading conditions in the Palestinian refugee camps within Jordan, working in Afghanistan after the Russians had ended their occupation, radicalised al-Zarqawi. On his return to Jordan, his criticism of the government and hoarding armaments, resulted in a 15-year prison sentence, but because of a royal amnesty he was released early. He then returned to Afghanistan (with his mother) where he set up Tawhid wal Jihad (Monotheism and Holy War), a terror group along the lines of Bin Laden's al-Qaeda. The end of the Taliban regime forced him to leave Afghanistan. Iraq was his chosen refuge where he continued his terror. Bin Laden and al-Zarqawi became key bogeymen for the USA, helping the neo-conservatives in George W. Bush's government to justify the invasion of Iraq in 2003.

Abu Musab al-Zarqawi was ruthless. He had been involved in the kidnap and beheading of several foreigners in Iraq (for example, other than Ken Bigley, US citizens Nick Berg, Jack Hensley and Eugene Armstrong), and allegedly shown on video-tape wielding the execution knife himself on at least one occasion. Al-Zarqawi is suspected of being responsible for the two suicide-bombs outside the Imam Ali Shrine in Najaf in Iraq, a sacred Shia shrine. The leader of the nation's Shia community, Grand Ayatollah Mohammed Baqr al-Hakim, along with over 120 other people, were killed. Al-Zarqawi is also linked to the suicide bombing of a hotel, used by Westerners, in the Jordanian capital Amman in 2005. One of the would-be bombers, a woman, Sajida Mubarak Atrous al-Rishawi, didn't manage to blow herself up. The woman's husband did die in the attack, with his bomb contributing to the death of 57 people. Most of the dead were not Westerners, the assumed targets, but were Jordanians attending a wedding. The woman, captured by the police, appeared on Jordanian television and re-enacted her failed mission, confessing:

> He [my husband] took one corner and I took another. There was a wedding in the hotel. There were women and children . . . My husband executed the attack. I tried to detonate and it failed.
>
> (BBC News, 2005c)

The woman is also believed to be the sister of a key aide to Abu Musab al-Zarqawi, Mubarak Atrous Rishawi (who was also killed in Iraq by US forces). In 2004, al-Zarqawi aligned himself with Bin Laden, becoming the Iraq commander of al-Qaeda.

Irving Horowitz (2002) explains, however, that when attempting to profile the terrorist there is first the problem of what definition can be used and who is applying that definition. Can, for example, the IRA (Irish Republican Army) operating in Northern Ireland really be compared to the PLO (Palestine Liberation Organisation)? Both have become political rather than military organisations, and both have had problems with splinter groups. Both have a history that is tied to foreign expansionism (the British in Ireland, and the Israelis in Palestine). But these similarities are outweighed by the dissimilarities. Their backgrounds, whilst seemingly analogous, are disparate. The British colonisation of Ireland was self-justified, and part of what was to become a large empire, and they had their own land to which to return. The Jews who took over Palestinian land with international agreement (the British Balfour Declaration in 1917, and the 1947 United Nations affirmation) as a consequence of, for example, Russian pogroms and the Nazi Holocaust. The IRA has always kept secret its leadership and disseminated violent activities to small groups, whereas the PLO flourished (and declined) under the known and charismatic leadership of Yassir Arafat. The contexts that led to the PLO and IRA terrorism have also been very different to that which gave impetus to Islamic terrorism. Seumas Milne and Faisal Bodi (2001, p. 40) commented about the destruction of the World Trade Center two days after it happened:

> Since George Bush's father inaugurated his new world order a decade ago, the US, supported by its British ally, bestrides the world like a colossus. Unconstrained by any superpower rival or system of global governance, the US giant has re-written the global financial and trading system in its own interest, ripped up a string of treaties it finds inconvenient, sent troops to every corner of the globe, bombed Afghanistan, Sudan, Yugoslavia and Iraq without troubling the United Nations, maintained a string of murderous embargos against recalcitrant regimes and recklessly thrown its weight behind Israel's 34-year illegal occupation of the West Bank and Gaza . . . the sense that the Americans are once again reaping the dragons' teeth harvest they themselves sowed will be overwhelming.

Apart from the historical discrepancies between terrorist groups, there are the blatant perceptual mismatches and reconfiguration of identities. That is, a terrorist in one culture is a hero in another; former terrorists become heads of state.

What about *euthanasia*? Is this kind of murder more classifiable than terrorism? Doctors and nurses deliberately covertly kill some of their patients, usually the most vulnerable: terminally ill people are given death-inducing doses of analgesia; malformed, diseased, or merely unwanted babies, and the elderly, are not given life-sustaining nutrition or medication; the instruction 'not-for-resuscitation', or a euphemism, is entered in the medical notes of those patients whose health status or quality and quantity of existence is assessed as not warranting further life.

This is euthanasia, and is practised in health care settings all over the world. But it remains an illegal practice in most countries for doctors, nurses (as well as loved ones of the victim) to kill for even the best of motives (that is, to relieve either immediate or impending suffering, or intractable infirmity). It is illegal so far in the UK. This didn't stop doctors, according to research conducted by Professor Clive Seale of Brunel University, carrying out euthanasia on 3000 terminally ill patients in the year 2005 (Seale, 2006).

There are of course those doctors and nurses who kill intentionally and clandestinely for reasons that are not meritorious. However, some medical practitioners and nurses calculatingly and blatantly collaborate to kill (either through their actions or lack of action), but do so legally. A senior court may sanction the ending of a life because of intractable suffering, or because there is no hope of consciousness being regained.

Christian Sandsdalen was convicted of murder in 2000. His crime was euthanasia, but this was Norway, although in the same year it had been made legal in the Netherlands. The retired medical practitioner murdered Bodil Bjerkmann. Bjerkmann, 45 years of age and suffering from multiple sclerosis, had requested the physician to end her life. She had been in terrible pain and was dying. The prosecution's case was that more should have been done to relieve her from pain without ending her life prematurely.

In New Zealand, a study by Kay Mitchell and Glynn Owens (2004) involving 700 medical practitioners revealed that physician-assisted death was commonplace. It occurred even when the patient was capable of making a rational choice about whether to live or die. But, in the same country, Lesley Martin, an intensive care nurse, was found guilty of attempted murder in 2004 because she had assisted in her mother's death in 1999. The police prosecution attested that Martin had revealed her actions in a pro-euthanasia book *To Die Like a Dog* (Martin, 2004). In the book she explained that administering morphine to end her mother's life, who had terminal cancer and was in considerable discomfort, was an act of kindness.

In 2000, the Netherlands became the first country to make euthanasia legal. However, there are stringent controls on who can be assisted to die. The decision must be a medical one; the patient must be facing an unbearable and interminable life of suffering; the patient must request the hastening of their death; both doctor and patient must agree that there is no alternative; a second medical opinion must be obtained; the patient's death must be conducted in a medically appropriate manner; a written agreement can be formulated prior to the patient's incapacitation if this is likely; and the patient must be of sound mind when making the decision.

Euthanasia is tolerated elsewhere with safeguards (for example, in Switzerland, Colombia, Belgium and the US state of Oregon). But the legal rules and implications, and long-term acceptance of the practice remain open to question. It is unclear as to whether or not foreigners can come to these countries to make use of euthanasia. In Australia, the Northern Territory did allow medically assisted suicide in 1996 but the Federal Government repealed the law within a year.

There is also the practice of 'living wills', a written statement by an individual who wishes their life to be terminated if physical or mental incapacity means they are unable to make that decision, which is becoming more acceptable as notification of that person's wishes, but not necessarily having legal standing.

Hence, killings that are ostensibly performed as acts of philanthropy will be treated very differently in different countries. They may be illegal but tolerated or simply not acknowledged. Moreover, where euthanasia is legal it is still easy to fall foul of the law, and laws change so that a legally acceptable killing this year may not be so considered the year after. Wherever euthanasia happens, the process whereby decisions are made to kill and how this is presented are likely to be complex. Personal resolve to kill will be influenced by cultural values and beliefs. Culturally-sensitised personal resolution over killing will then be mediated by professional, legal and media discourses. For example, a doctor or partner wishing to carry out euthanasia, once their own conscience has been consulted (a conscience that has been informed by their culture), may have to negotiate that decision with other relatives and health care staff, as well as reflect on the law and what the consequences would be if it became public knowledge. If made public it may either be construed as a 'mercy killing' or another 'murder' of a particularly immoral brand because the victim was defenceless and the killer gained from the death if only in the sense of a resource-consuming predicament being wrapped up.

Surely *child-killers* can be lumped together? To begin with, the term 'child-killer' is itself confusing as it could imply an adult killing a child, a child killing another child or an adult. Taking the first meaning, there have been many different kinds of child killings across many different cultures and historical epochs. Some are paedophilic (pathological love of children). Here sexual satisfaction is apparently gained through the abuse of children which then turns into murder for fear of the victim informing on the abuser. Some are paedophobic (pathological hatred of children). Here there may be an unadulterated loathing of one individual child; an inability to cope with an infant; a hatred of all children; or a politicised disapproval of children because they have become labelled a 'social nuisance'. Some are both paedophilic and paedophobic. Some are not connected to the child as such, the age of the victim being incidental to the perpetrator's motive.

The murder of a child, no matter how much it seems to be one of the, if not the, worst crime possible, has occurred throughout history and has been widespread across nations and cultures, and continues today. Children also kill adults. Some become child soldiers, thereby entering the adult world of killing that is either legitimised because it is on behalf of the state, or outlawed because it is part of a rebellion against the state.

Javed Iqbal was convicted in 2000 for murdering 100 children in Pakistan; Iqbal had kept a diary of his sexual abuse and the killing of his victims; vats of acid were discovered by the police in his house, which he admitted using to dissolve the bodies. The sentence given by a judge, who had assumed Sharia law could be applied, was decreed as strangulation using an iron chain 100 times and then he was to be chopped into 100 pieces to represent the number of children killed (the sentence was not implemented).

Marc Dutroux, in 2004, was found guilty of child-killings as part of paedophile activities that involved many others in Belgium. A 'social cleansing' policy in Honduras is alleged by 'Casa Alianza', a child-protection group based in Costa Rica, to have occurred in 2002. It was, according to Casa Alianza, conducted by police and security services. More than 300 streetchildren are believed to have been killed because they were linked by the police and security officials to a national problem of petty crime.

The killing of children may be linked to mental disorder, the unfortunate focus of a psychotic delusion or psychopathic gratification:

- Andrea Yates, was convicted of murder in 2002 in Texas because of deliberately drowning all five of her children (believing that by killing them she would save them from the Devil: Cleared of murder by reason of insanity at a retrial in 2006).

- Osaka, Japan, 2001, Mamoru Takuma, a schizophrenic, killed eight children, injuring 13 others and two teachers, in a knife attack at a school near Osaka.

- Ian Brady and Myra Hindley sexually abused and murdered three children in Manchester between 1963 and 1965, with Brady spending the rest of his life in a secure psychiatric hospital (where he was able to write a book analysing serial killing).

The killing of children has also been linked to the psychiatric condition described as 'Munchhausen's by Proxy'. Munchhausen's by Proxy was invented by British paediatrician Sir Roy Meadow who provided the rationale for the mysterious deaths of children. Mothers, it was argued, with this syndrome indulge in a grotesque form of attention seeking. They kill their children. However, this condition is not accepted as legitimate even within the psychiatric world, and further doubt about its medical authenticity was cast following the professional debacle of its inventor. Some mothers convicted of killing their children had been subsequently acquitted on appeal. In the 1999 trial of British solicitor Sally Clark, who was accused of killing her two babies, Meadow's expert testimony was given based on what became known as 'Meadow's Law': one cot death in a family is a tragedy, two are a cause for suspicion and three (unless there is evidence to the contrary) are murder. Meadow's position was that the chance of Sally Clark's children's deaths being natural was 73 million to one. She was found guilty of murder and sent to prison for two concurrent life sentences. But Clark was exonerated in 2003 by the Court of Appeal. Sir Roy Meadow was struck off the medical register in 2005 by the British General Medical Council (GMC) for his 'misleading evidence' in the Clark case. Then, however, in a government review of 30000 children, who were taken from their parents and put into care, just one case has been found to be based on flawed evidence (Frith, 2004). By 2006, the Attorney General concluded that the vast majority of reviewed convictions were safe, and Meadow had won *his* legal appeal against the GMC for striking him off the medical register.

Internationally, infanticide can come in various forms. During the 1990s, up to 300000 pregnant women crossed into China, some of whom were then repatriated back to North Korea (Hawk, 2003). The US-based Committee for Human Rights in North Korea (CHRNK) alleges that these repatriated pregnant women then had their babies killed at birth. The North Korean gulags (forced labour camps and prisons) contain thousands of political and criminal prisoners, as well as the North Koreans who had fled to China and were being repatriated. The CHRNK has used in evidence dozens of escaped prisoners' testimonials. Accusations about how the babies died included suffocation, being buried alive or just left on the ground face down. The perpetrators suggested that this was to prevent the survival of half-Chinese babies.

In Victorian Britain, infant killing in the 1800s appeared to be reaching epidemic proportions. Many of the babies killed were from women in the lower classes and many of the babies were illegitimate. The culprits might well be admitted to asylums rather than imprisoned. Today in Britain women who plead quilty to infanticide are likely to get a much lower sentence compared with many parts of the USA where infanticide may be regarded as 'ordinary' murder.

Whilst killing babies is a crime in most countries, some cultures allow (possibly encourage) its practice. In 1870, the British banned female infanticide in India (and also *sati*: the Hindu practice of burning widows). But infanticide, although illegal occurs in rural and impoverished regions. Both the abortion of female foetuses and female infanticide shortly after birth appear to be linked to the cost of bringing up girls in India (for example, the expense of a series of cultural rituals in the girl's upbringing, and also the handing over of dowries at marriage). Ultrasound has become big business for doctors in India. The expanding middle-classes, who are wanting to plan their family size and composition carefully, are paying for the gender of their babies to be determined at the prenatal stage. If the foetus is a girl and the woman already has one or more female children, or doesn't want a girl at all, then an abortion may be requested. One study calculated conservatively that 10 million female foetuses had been aborted over a 20-year period in India (Jha et al., 2006). It was not until 2006 that a doctor was given a gaol sentence for female foeticide.

Killings that take place in school usually receive wide media interest. They take place infrequently, but may occur anywhere in the world:

- In 1999, at Columbine High School, Colorado, USA, Eric Harris, aged 18, and Dylan Klebold, aged 17, shot 12 other pupils and a teacher before committing suicide; they had planted home-made bombs in the school cafeteria, but they failed to detonate.

- In 1996, Thomas Hamilton killed 16 children and a teacher at Dunblane Primary School, Scotland, before shooting himself.

- In 2004, a 15-year-old boy known as Fafael shot three class mates dead and wounded five others at The Isla de Malvines School in Karmen de Patagones, Argentina; he used a pistol that belonged to his father, a policeman.

- Yan Yanmin, 21 years old, was arrested in 2004 in connection with the killing of nine boys in a school dormitory in China in the town of Ruzhou; Yanmin was reported by his mother to the police as the likely killer; he was executed two months later.

Drawing parallels between one school killing and another, such as, for example, Columbine and Dunblane, is misleading as in the former case it was children who killed children, whereas in the latter it was an adult. Moreover, Harris and Klebold appeared to kill out of hatred but Hamilton had been investigated by police for being too fond of children. Harris and Klebold used guns of which they had no legal right to be in possession, whereas Hamilton had a legal gun licence (actually licences for six guns).

Comparing schools killings where there is the apparent link of children being the killers is also misleading. Bullying, revenge, availability of weapons, control in the classroom, a myriad of complex family dynamics, loss-of-face, dares, membership of subcultural groups (for example, satanic, supremacist or religious), and biological-psychological disposition may be factors, and it is unlikely that the same factors will be relevant to any two events. Furthermore, when a child kills, the family background and social environment are examined in detail more so than that of an adult killer. That is, there is a search for an externalised reason for the killing, but if this is not forthcoming then 'inherent evilness' becomes the default reasoning for a child to commit such an otherwise inexplicable crime.

Children kill other children not only in schools but in many other contexts. Mary Bell in Newcastle, England, was convicted of the manslaughter of two children in 1968. She was referred to in the press and in court as 'evil' and 'dangerous'. This description, however, was disputed after the publication of biographies of Mary Bell by Gita Sereny (1995, 1999). Sereny pointed out that Bell's abused family circumstances and poor environmental conditions should lead to a more sympathetic view of her. Another case, although recorded in the media as 'shocking', is that of Robert Thompson and Jon

Venables. These two 10-year-olds killed 2-year-old James Bulger, in 1993, Merseyside, England. On the whole, Thompson and Venables have not had a revisionist account of their crimes that equates to that given by Sereny on Bell. Publicly, the murder of James Bulger remains 'shocking', but the European Court of Human Rights did rule that Venables and Thompson had not received a fair trial. Their case had been heard in an adult court, and the Home Secretary, Michael Howard, had 'illegally' set their minimum sentence at 15 years (reduced by the Lord Chief Justice, to a minimum sentence of eight years).

However, contrast these English cases with a case in Norway. The English killers received custodial sentences, and were all given new identities on release. Two Norwegian six-year-olds (whose identities cannot legally be published in Norway) killed five-year-old Silje Raedergard in 1994; they were not prosecuted. Instead, they were offered understanding and support by their community in the town of Trondheim. The killers received counselling, and there was a degree of communal responsibility for the killing (BBC World Service, 2000).

PEOPLE

Exploring specific case studies of murderers illustrates the problem of categorisation. In this section, it is an *individual* who either carries out the killing or instructs someone else to murder. But, each of these individuals is very different to the others in many ways: nationality, self-justification for killing or lack of it and the degree to which the perpetrator and victim(s) attract approbation or sympathy.

Bertrand Cantat

Many murders are 'domestic' in the sense that they occur in private homes. Most of these murders, like domestic violence per se, are not reported by media, or are only mentioned briefly in the local newspaper, unless there is something unusual about the circumstances or the people. Both of these factors came together in Lithuania, 2003.

This time the killer, who attacked his lover, was famous; moreover, so was the victim. There was a typical lovers' argument about other people in their respective lives, emotional ties that threatened their own relationship. This resulted in Marie Trintignant, a film star, dying from a cerebral haemorrhage. Her killer was Bertrand Cantat, a rock singer from the band Noir Desir. Because they were famous and foreign, massive publicity ensued. Hundreds of (mainly French) reporters went to Vilnius for the trial. Intimate details of their lives were circulated over a long period of time in the media in both countries and for a while in other countries. Moreover, because they were French (and the killer was later sent to a French prison to serve his sentence; the victim was flown from Vilnius to Paris by private jet where she died), the crime was placed within the discourse of *crime passionel* (Bouchet & Vezard, 2004).

Trintignant had been in Vilnius making a television film for her director mother about the nineteenth-century French author Colette, and Cantat had joined her. Their relationship had lasted 18 months, and was characterised as bohemian. Jealousy surfaced between the two because mobile-phone messages sent by another man to Trintignant were discovered by Cantat. He questioned her about the other man, who turned out to be her former husband, the film director Samuel Benchetrit. She then told him to 'go back to your wife' (Webster, 2004). His anger became fury, fury turned into violence, and violence into murder. Lithuanian pathologists reported that the violence was severe, Cantat punching Trintignant 19 times, with four of the blows to the head. Cantat says he only slapped Trintignant a few times.

Cantat later admitted to attacking Trintignant on the night of 26 July, 2003 in the hotel room in Vilnius, causing her death on 1 August. In 2004, following conviction, Cantat was sent back to France to serve the eight-year gaol sentence in a Toulouse prison after asking in court to be able to 'purge the remainder of his sorrows' in his homeland (*Le Monde*, 2004).

The killing of Trintignant pushed the French into a state of national mourning. Although a contentious star, she was regarded as beautiful and talented. She was the daughter of the film star Jean-Louis Trintignant, who had starred with Brigitte Bardot in 'And God Created Woman'. Trintignant had a complicated private life, with four sons from three fathers and her boyfriend Cantat. In an example of art imitating life, the roles she played tended to be of vulnerable women, and in death Trintignant's fragility was paralleled with her cinematic persona. Moreover, her demise was made even more poignant because the film she was making in Lithuania was subsequently released. Audiences could therefore dwell on the last days of her life. Noir Desir was the most successful rock band in France during the 1990s, and Cantat was its charismatic and good-looking leader.

The hell-raising but ultimately self-destructive artistic persona of the rock star is also replicated in life by Cantat. The drama that is the *crime passionel* is complete with both the deceased and killer placed in the role of victims, their passion imploding: Cantat had been a hero to sections of French youth and those on the left of politics, having taken a stance against globalisation, racism, war and the environment. The dual victim construction of the crime of passion was also reinforced by the frequent shedding of tears by Cantat in court and reported by the media: 'I loved Marie with all my being. I loved her and I'll always love her. I think of her each second and I'll always think of her. I can't erase her from my memory' (Cantat, quoted on the day of his conviction, BBC Three News, 2004).

Sales of Noir Desir's album rocketed after the murder. Books have been written, with one by Nadine Trintignant, the victim's mother, being a vitriolic attack on Cantat, which became a best-seller. Her funeral in Paris was attended by a former French Prime Minister, Lionel Jospin. Comparisons were made in the French press with Romeo and Juliet, as well as with Sid Vicious and his girlfriend Nancy.

In court, different accounts were offered on the character of the killer: 'an honest, good and gentle man', states Cantat's former wife, Kistina Rady, whom he left for Trintignant; whereas Trintignant's former husband comments that Cantat is 'a madly jealous [man who had] cried more for himself than for Marie' (Henley, 2004). There is also a split amongst the French public, replicating that between the two families of the case, which was described as a 'clan war' (Henley, 2004). Jacques Chirac, the French President, calls Trintignant's death 'an injustice of a destiny so brutally broken'. These alternative perceptions illustrate well Foucault's deciphering of discourses in the Pierre Riviere case.

The crucible of the Trintignant–Cantat murder can be associated with other *crimes passionels*, but only superficially so. That is, apart from the places, people and trajectories being dissimilar, the bare bones of *crimes passionels*, the heightened emotions, do not necessarily come in the same form. Neither Cantat nor Trintignant had a known history of violence (that is, there were no prior incidents recorded by the police), and this is uncommon for those who become the players in fatal domestic dramas. Whereas the victim was the lover and the perceived rival that had ignited the murder was an ex-partner, in this example it is the person killed who was the partner of the lover and regarded as a rival. There was apparently no prolonged premeditation by Cantat, but in the case of Mariette Bosch, the planning was lengthy (if fallible).

Mariette Bosch

This 'domestic' killing occurred in Botswana. Mariette Bosch killed her best friend, Maria Wolmarans, so that she could then marry the dead woman's husband.

A few months after Bosch's husband was killed in a car crash, Bosch began a sexual liaison with Tienie Wolmarans, husband of Maria. Wolmaran's marriage had been in trouble. This passionate crime was carried out with malice aforethought long before the act. It was conducted with deliberate gain in mind and the removal of the obstacle to Bosch's avarice and desire.

The Cantat–Trintignant criminal event was contained within a relatively short space of time, with nothing but capture and punishment the likely outcome. But the Bosch–Wolmarans event was more complicated and therefore prolonged. It was a 'white murder' involving wealthy foreigners, South Africans living in a black city (Gaborone, Botswana), and a woman killing another woman.

Mariette Bosch, was a mother of three, middle-class, wealthy and had a maid and a gardener. Many well-off whites left South Africa for Australasia, Europe and the USA when apartheid ended in South Africa. Some moved to other southern African countries, such as Botswana, and this is what the Bosch family did. The life of a well-off wife in middle-class South Africa was replicated in Botswana – shopping, using casinos, playing bridge, attending with her husband game lodges and golf clubs at weekends, and membership of the Dutch Reformed Church.

Bosch began a sexual relationship with Tienie Wolmarans after her husband died in a car crash in 1995. Her lover, it would seem, was slow in making arrangements to divorce, so Bosch obtained a gun from a friend in South Africa. Driving to her neighbour's house (the Wolmarans lived two blocks away), she climbed over the security wall, entered the house and shot her rival twice. The police presumed that the fatality had been the result of a bungled burglary. Unfortunately for Mariette Bosch she had not taken care about the disposal of the weapon, handing it to her dead husband's brother, whose wife was Judith. Mariette and Judith hated each other. This was the killer's first mistake. Judith Bosch was eventually to surmise that Mariette Bosch had killed Maria Wolmarans and gave the weapon to the police.

The second mistake made by the killer was to tell her enemy (that is, Judith Bosch) that she was in love with Tienie Wolmarans and wished to marry him, prior to the murder. The gun had been borrowed from a mutual friend of Mariette and Judith. After the murder, Judith persuaded Mariette to return the gun to her and her husband on the pretext of giving it back to their mutual friend, but Judith Bosch then handed the gun to the police. Tienie and Mariette got married after she was arrested. At her trial, the defence expert witness, a psychiatrist, stated that Mariette Bosch was not guilty because she did not have a killer's profile and was incapable of lying. This was rejected by the judge. She was found guilty and sentenced to hang, but appealed against the sentence. The Appeals Court in Botswana comprises judges from England, Scotland, South Africa, Zimbabwe and Nigeria, a provision dating from Botswana's independence from Britain in 1966, but her appeal failed. Bosch's appeal for clemency to the President of Botswana also failed.

Although execution is mandatory in Botswana for murder, if the sentence was carried out she would become the first white woman to be executed post-independence. This would attract international attention, and, as Botswana is one of the few successful economies in sub-Saharan Africa, its government would not want 'bad press' about its human rights record. Publicity in South Africa and other English-speaking countries was much greater than occurred when a black African was murdered or a black African was convicted for murder. On the other hand, it was suggested prior to her appeal that she might be executed because the Botswana government would want to warn South Africans not to turn Garborone into Johannesburg, a neighbouring city (in African terms of distance) with a huge murder rate (McGreal, 2001). She was hanged on 31 March, 2001.

Amnesty International (2001), which is against the death penalty, expressed shock (1) over the rushed nature of the execution following the failed appeal and request for presidential clemency; (2) that her family were not allowed to see her before she was killed; and (3) the family only knew that she had been hanged after the event. Amnesty declared that it had been conducted in secret and quickly to avoid controversy.

This case was compared with the book by James Fox, *White Mischief* (1983), which was based on a true story about the time of the Second World War in Kenya, and was subsequently turned into a film (1987) starring Joss Ackland, Greta Scacchi, Charles Dance and John Hurt, and directed by Michael Radford. The plot encapsulates the lifestyle of British decadence in Empire. The rich older man moves from England to Kenya with his gold-digging young wife and becomes a wealthy rancher, although he eventually becomes bankrupt. She has a love affair with a British Army officer. The officer is killed and the husband is arrested and tried for the crime.

Cantat's premeditation (to cause injury or death) was much more immediate and far less potentially rewarding if indeed there was anything other than revenge to be gained. Cantat was enraged. Bosch was cool and calculating. Bosch did not have her lover to herself and was trying to take him from his wife. Cantat was trying to protect what he had. The lives of those in these two cases were European-bohemian versus African-White-middle-class. Public support for Cantat from the French population was split (roughly 50% for acquittal and 50% for conviction), whilst not much sympathy was offered to Bosch, except for a human rights organization being horrified at the sentence. Cantat will spend a few years in prison in his home country. Bosch was legally killed in a foreign country. Bosch denied she had killed her best friend, accused someone else of the murder, and showed no remorse to the end. Cantat, whilst denying murder, admitted the killing and publicly expressed deep regret.

China Keitetsi

Child soldiering has been made possible in modern times through the development of lighter and smaller weapons (Bell, 2003). Children can, with modern armaments, become nearly as effective in killing as adults.

The organization, Coalition to Stop the Use of Child Soldiers (CSUCS) (2004) argues that the European Union, the G-8 and the UN Security Council have failed to control the use of child soldiers. The CSUCS points out that children are fighting in almost every major armed civil conflict throughout the world, in both government and in opposition forces. Child soldiers have been used, for example, in Afghanistan, Sierra Leone, Sudan, Democratic Republic of Congo, Myanmar, Colombia and Zimbabwe.

The charity, Save the Children, reported in 2005 on what it described as a 'hidden army' or 'generation' of girls, some as young as eight, who are abducted against their will to live life in the army. The roles of the girls vary from being actual soldiers through to serving as porters, cleaners and cooks. In many countries, they are forced to serve as sex slaves or 'wives'.

China Keitetsi became an international campaigner against the use of child soldiers (Amnesty International, 2005b). In her autobiography (Keitetsi, 2004) and on her website (http://xchild.dk), she reports on the systematic raping and violence inflicted on children recruited into Uganda's armed forces. She had suffered from this herself; she was enlisted into the Ugandan Government's National Resistance Army (NRA) at the age of 8 in the 1980s. Girl soldiers in the NRA were used by officers in their own army for sex as well as being used to fight: 'When I was 14 years old, I gave birth to my son, and when I was 15 years old, I could not count how many Commanders had already used my body' (Keitetsi, 2006).

She argues that this abuse by her own people was turned into rage on their enemies. That is, her feelings of anger, shame, and dehumanisation meant that killing could be normalised even for a child. China Keitetsi has admitted that she has killed so many people from the age of 8 to 17 years that she has lost track of the number (Amnesty International, 2005b).

That was in the 1980s. In the 2000s, the Ugandan Government has been fighting an internal war with a fanatical cult based in the north of the country called the Lords Resistance Army (LRA). The LRA's forces have been strengthened by tens of thousands of kidnapped children. This later internal war has caused huge humanitarian problems with large refugee camps being set up because villagers are fearful for their lives and also scared that their children will be abducted.

Hence, in Uganda child soldiering has been both legitimate and illegitimate. Perhaps children are used to kill in unstable countries out of military necessity when adults are not available in the required numbers (casualties of that or previous conflicts), or useful because they can be exploited in other ways. However, it is worth remembering that it is not only struggling states or ethically dubious insurgents that militarise young people. Some Western governments have a policy of recruiting boys and girls under the age of 18 to fight in their army. The USA, Australia, Austria, the Netherlands and the UK used 16- or 17-year-olds in their armed forces.

Harold Shipman

A British medical practitioner was probably the world's most prolific serial killer. Harold Shipman killed at least 250 patients between 1971 and 1988. He started killing not long after qualifying at the University of Leeds, England.

The Shipman case has had serious implications for the autonomy of the medical profession. A long-term inquiry into Shipman's killing career was set up following his trial and provided a series of reports under the Chair of Dame Janet Smith. The final report was published in 2005 (Shipman Inquiry, 2005). The outcome of the inquiry has led to criticisms of how the British medical profession supervises itself. In particular, the way in which death certificates have not been thoroughly inspected by the doctor who counter-signs the attending doctor's diagnosis of death, and the lack of a specific reason for death, have been altered. The closed nature of the General Medical Council, the governing body of the medical profession, has also been attacked.

Shipman's known victims were nearly all women. Although he did kill a 41-year-old woman, the rest were elderly (the oldest being a 93-year-old woman). Most were killed whilst he worked as a general practitioner in a single-doctor practice, but prior to becoming a general practitioner, he may have killed 15 patients at a local hospital where he worked after qualifying.

Smith's report was unable to provide a conclusive motive for his crimes. There was no sexual or financial benefit to his killing. However, although the police had been informed earlier of suspicions by the undertakers with whom he dealt and by other doctors working in the same area, it was the last of his murders that led to his arrest. Moreover, it was this killing that had an obvious financial gain. The forging of this victim's will was not only amateur in style (he had deceived two of his patients into counter-signing the will, which had a poorly counterfeited signature and was received by her solicitor soon after her death). More problematic for Shipman was that the deceased woman's daughter was a solicitor and the executor of a will already prepared by her mother. Naturally, the daughter queried the new will, and then reported her concerns to the police.

Shipman refused to undergo formal psychiatric-psychological assessment. When interviewed by medical experts, he would answer curtly or remain silent. However, this did not stop the speculation on his motives by the public, media and professionals. Four psychiatrists from the Institute of Psychiatry, London, reviewed the details of Shipman's life. The psychiatrists told the inquiry that Shipman's arrogance and over-confidence were probably masking low self-esteem. Shipman had become addicted to the analgesic pethidine during his early career, for which he had been prosecuted and rehabilitated in a private psychiatric hospital. The psychiatrists conjectured further that Shipman had for most of his adult life almost certainly been angry, deeply unhappy and chronically depressed (Whittle & Ritchie, 2004).

However, Shipman's murders, unlike the killings of most serial killers, were not violent or sadistic. Nor did he choose victims at random, although there was a randomness of opportunity to kill in that he didn't kill everyone who was defenceless or irritated him. Serial killers do tend to have themes. That is they may become fixated with killing a certain type of person. They may concentrate on the killing of young girls, prostitutes, hitchhikers, or people from particular ethnic groups. Most serial killers do not know their victims, but Shipman knew all of his (Carole, 2005).

It has also been suggested that Shipman became desensitised to death through his work, and that the effect of his mother dying a painful death when he was young furnished a compulsion to kill (Carole, 2005). But this line of speculation comes unstuck when the question is raised about all those medical practitioners who have experienced loss at an early age but who do not kill anyone illegally (euthanasia aside).

Shipman does demonstrate some of the features of the intelligent psychopathic killer. He was aloof, cold, conceited, grandiose and calculating. His favourite put-down was to describe someone as 'stupid' if his antagonist didn't come up to his own intellectual standard. Of course, this seems a banal verbal strike, but if used regularly and with venom, it implies arrogance and a lack of empathy, perhaps the arrogance to believe that the medical practitioner has the right to eradicate obtuseness.

Furthermore, Shipman already had a criminal record for an offence that can indicate a personality disorder: serious abuse of illegal drugs. Possibly whilst still a student, but certainly shortly after qualifying, he became addicted to the heroin derivative pethidine, used commonly as an analgesic. He was convicted in 1976 on three charges of unlawful possession of the drug, and two of forging prescriptions. Shipman asked for 74 other charges to be taken into account. This was no minor form of addiction. He was fined but not struck off the medical register.

Shipman had a penchant for murdering people who had recently been bereaved, and patients whom he may have perceived as over-using his time and resources. Patients who were vulnerable, demanding or a nuisance, were particularly susceptible to an early death. Whilst accepting that Shipman's motives remain a puzzle, Keith Soothill and David Wilson (2005) observe that the characteristics of Shipman's victims demand sociological consideration. They argue that the structural position of the elderly in British society, whereby they are socially marginalised, provides the context for their exploitation by powerful figures in the community.

Shipman, the respected and popular family doctor, committed suicide in the early hours of the morning of Tuesday, 13 January, 2004, by hanging himself with a bed sheet whilst serving life sentences in Wakefield Prison in Yorkshire for murdering 15 of his patients.

Stanley 'Tookie' Williams

Stanley 'Tookie' Williams became a children's author and four times Nobel Prize nominee for peace and literature. He spent nearly a quarter of a century on death row in San Quentin, north of San Francisco, USA. A Californian judge signed his execution warrant for December 2005 after the US Supreme Court, the Federal Appeals Court, and the Supreme Court of California declined to consider his petitions. All legal avenues exhausted, his only hope of saving his life was to gain clemency from Californian Governor, Arnold Schwarzenegger.

Williams was convicted of four murders and he was also the co-founder of one of America's most violent street gangs, the Crips. Williams's autobiography *Blue rage, black redemption: a memoir* (blue is the Crips's colour and black because Williams is the quintessential black African-American gang leader) was published in 2004. He became a writer of books for children, and on the inhumanity of prison life and its internal crime, and a campaigner against gang culture, violence and drug use. Claiming that black Americans too often fall into criminality because socially acceptable opportunities for a successful life are closed to them, he recommends that their energy would be better placed challenging the factors that prevent this success. For Williams, it is racial discrimination, poverty, illiteracy and unemployment that must be dealt with so that black Americans do not need to become criminals. Specifically, Williams has argued in television and radio recordings, in his books and on his website, that young people should not join gangs. A film was released in 2004 portraying his life, called *Redemption: the Stan Tookie Williams story*, which starred Jamie Foxx.

At 17 years of age Williams co-founded the Crips with Raymond Washington in South Central Los Angeles. From inception in 1971, the Crips then spread to dozens of other US cities and towns, as well as to Canada, South Africa and Germany. It has even attracted white members, largely from impoverished rural areas of the southern USA. The Crips and their bitter gang rivals, the Bloods, are infamous for the number of people who have been injured and killed because of their criminal activities. Thousands may have died, and many hundreds of members of the two gangs are, or have been, imprisoned. Washington was killed in 1979. Williams was imprisoned in 1981. He was convicted and sentenced to death for killing a man during a robbery, and three people in another robbery two weeks later. Only a small amount of money was netted from the robberies that cost four lives.

However, Williams denied that he was a murderer, claming that the witnesses produced by the prosecution had been interrogated using illegal means. A substantial amount of the decades he has spent in prison were in solitary confinement. Williams never divulged any details about how the Crips operated before he was sent to prison, or indeed how they operated subsequently. Nor has he assisted the police to gain convictions against any of the gang's members. He does, however, offer an apology for the mayhem unleashed by his gang:

> [W]hen I created the Crips youth gang with Raymond Lee Washington in South Central Los Angeles, I never imagined Crips membership would one day spread throughout California, would spread to much of the rest of the nation . . . I also didn't expect the Crips to end up ruining the lives of so many young people, especially young black men who have hurt other young black men . . . So today I apologize to you all . . . who must cope every day with dangerous street gangs. I no longer participate in the so-called gangster lifestyle, and I deeply regret that I ever did.
>
> (Williams, 1997)

The Criminal Justice Legal Foundation (CJLF) in the USA countered what it views as Williams's disingenuous campaigning. Set up in 1982, the CJLF challenges civil liberties groups that want to stop the death penalty. It lobbies to restore the rights of victims and the criminals, arguing that the guilty should receive swift and constitutional punishment. The CJLF aims to rid the USA of its unnecessarily prolonged, complex and costly appeal system, which means a convicted murderer may, as with Williams, spend many years awaiting death. Their position is that an efficient and effective justice system is the most powerful deterrent to criminality. For example, it wants police investigations to be improved.

With reference to Williams, the CJLF points out that he committed multiple cold-blooded murders, allegedly laughing about them later, and showed no genuine remorse. The CJLF argues that he should not have been glorified in the media, receive public sympathy, or be nominated for Nobel prizes as the crimes for which he was convicted, let alone all of those for which he may have been responsible, were horrific. It was, points out the CGLF, whilst robbing a late-night store at gunpoint that the first victim, the store worker, died. He was shot in the head whilst he knelt on the ground. In the second incident, wife and husband motel owners and their daughter were shot.

> After unsuccessful attempts to rob a liquor store and a restaurant, the group robbed a 7-Eleven store at gunpoint. After ordering the clerk to his knees, Williams killed him with a gunshot to the head. He later laughed as he told his friends how the victim gurgled as he lay dying. Two weeks later, Williams murdered a motel owner, his wife and daughter during a robbery that netted $50, bragging to fellow gang members about how he 'blew them away'.
>
> (Criminal Justice Legal Foundation, 2005)

The implication from the CJLF is that Williams worked steadily on a campaign to gain sympathy for his vicious deeds to avoid being executed. That is, rather than being sincerely redemptive, Williams became expertly calculative.

Californian Governor, Arnold Schwarzenegger made the decision not to grant clemency. Schwarzenegger's justification for his decision was that Williams's claim of redemption had not coincided with remorse. Shortly after midnight on Tuesday, 13 December, 2005, the process of killing Williams by lethal injection commenced in the execution chamber of San Quentin Prison. Thirty minutes later, Williams was pronounced dead.

Rami Arafat

> A woman is like an olive tree. When a branch catches woodworm, it has to be chopped off so that society stays clean and pure.
>
> (Jordanian tribal leader quoted in Murphy, 2003)

In Jordan, 1997, 17-year-old Rami Arafat shot his sister, 21-year-old Rania Arafat, four times in the back of the head and once in the front. She had been persuaded by her two aunts to go with them for a walk through the suburbs of Amman. Reaching open land, the aunts moved physically away from Rania, and then she was murdered by her brother. She had refused to marry an arranged bridegroom, and instead had planned to elope with her Iraqi boyfriend (Borger, 1997). Rania had dishonoured the family. She had to be 'chopped off'.

In Jordan, honour killings take place apparently with the connivance of the law. Certainly, men who kill women who have been suspected of dishonourable behaviour are treated very leniently, perhaps only receiving a sentence of a few months in prison. Even when a woman has been raped she may be killed by her family for the 'dishonour' this brings. Premarital, extramarital relationships (usually involving sex, but not necessarily), refusing an arranged marriage, attempting to gain a divorce, even merely talking with a man or not carrying out domestic duties properly, may result in death.

Islamic culture perpetuates the mores that it is a woman's responsibility to maintain her honour and not bring dishonour on her family. She needs to be beyond reproach. Rape is seen, generally, as her failure, not only that of the man. Patriarchy, however, is still central to the honour killing tradition as a woman who shames a man undermines his social position. Moreover, other female family members join in with the castigation and planning of killings because they are dependent on the man/men.

Honour killings have taken place in a diverse range of countries such as Bangladesh, Equador, Brazil, Egypt, Israel, India, Italy, Pakistan, Morocco, Sweden, Turkey, Uganda, Afghanistan and Jordan. Women are a commodity to be bought and sold. Men own the commodity (women), and have absolute authority over its fate.

Such killings are also undertaken by followers of the 'honour' tradition in non-Muslim countries such as Britain. In 2005, Oxford, England, a father and his two sons were found guilty of murdering a university student, Arash Ghorbani-Zarin. 'To vindicate the family's honour' the father, Chomer Ali, ordered his two teenage sons, Mohammed Mujibar Rahman and Mamnoor Rahman to kill his daughter's boyfriend. The daughter had rejected an arranged marriage and was pregnant. Her boyfriend was stabbed 46 times (Gillan, 2005). London's Metropolitan Police force in 2004 began re-examining 120 deaths (over a 10-year period) on the suspicion that they may have been honour killings amongst the Asian communities. Europol (the European-wide police agency) is also examining the issue of honour killings (Bennetto & Judd, 2004).

Women are killed by their families for the shame having a daughter brings. But there are a number of causes of this shame. For example, a family can be affronted at the low financial reward for taking a daughter, a financial liability. That is, they haven't been given what the in-laws consider to be a full dowry. Dowry is practiced throughout Africa, but it can be the man who pays the woman's family in the form of livestock, clothes, valuables, gold or money. In most other regions it is exclusively families of the bride who have to subscribe goods, money, or property.

Dowry is illegal in India but is still common practice. Money or goods are usually passed over at the time of the marriage by the bride's family. However, later more may be demanded. If these demands are delayed or refused the wife may be killed, possibly dowsed in kerosene and set alight. Veena Talwar Oldenburg (2002) argues that the custom has its origins in the period of British rule in India. For Oldenburg the British increased patriarchy, replacing communal land rights with private property land rights. Men became the owners of land not women. Far from condemning the dowry system however, Oldenburg argues that the problem is in gender relations that have changed allowing men's reward for marriage to be the domination of women.

Pakistan's National Assembly passed a bill in 2004 that prescribes the death penalty for those who kill women in the name of family honour (Haider, 2004). But people living in communities where honour killings are practised do not usually report them to the police. This may simply be because most people in these communities still have a commitment to honour killings, or because they are afraid of reprisals. Moreover, the police may be unwilling to make charges against a family who have committed such a killing.

Furthermore, the *Hudood Ordinances* remain as legal edicts in Pakistan. These are interpretations of Islamic laws covering theft, drug trafficking, consumption of alcohol and sexual misdemeanours. One of these ordinances, *Zina*, makes inappropriate but voluntary sexual intercourse (that is, before marriage or adultery), as well as rape, punishable by *Hadd*: the miscreant could be whipped a hundred times, or stoned to death. For a Muslim woman to establish that she has been raped rather than having agreed to (illicit) sexual intercourse (thereby avoiding being killed for honour, although still susceptible to a whipping or stoning), courts demand that either: (a) the accused confesses; or (b) at least four Muslim adult males give evidence as eye-witnesses.

Jordanian honour killings became infamous worldwide through the publication of *Honor lost: love and death in modern-day Jordan* by Norma Khouri early in 2004. Khouri's book sold more than 250000 copies worldwide. Khouri told the story of how she and her Muslim female friend ran a unisex hairdresser in the capital of Jordan, in the early 1990s. Her friend began a relationship with a Christian man, and then was stabbed to death by her father in 1996. Khouri claimed she fled Jordan after this honour killing because she was afraid she too might be killed. She was granted asylum in Australia, but then the author herself became infamous. Australian investigative journalists (from the *Sydney Morning Herald*) made the accusations that the story was a fake. There are, apparently, a multitude of mistakes in the book about Jordanian society. Moreover, it was suggested that she didn't live in Jordan at the time of the events (and hadn't done so since she was three years of age). Khouri continued to defend the 'facts' of the story. However, her publisher (Random House) announced in August 2004 that Khouri had been unable to produce enough evidence to support her position that this was a true story of an honour killing and the book was withdrawn from sale.

CORPORATIONS

I can never forget THAT NIGHT. We were in this very house. I was asleep. The sound of coughing woke me, my neighbour next door was choking. I opened the door and was hit by smoke that seemed to be burning red chillies. Gas billowed into the house. My wife was unconscious. I lifted her and carried her. My daughter Leila, who was twenty years old, took Habib and we ran. It was panic, sheer terror, the clouds of gas were so thick, lamps looked like pin pricks. The street was a river of people, running, falling, not getting up, dying. In the crush our family got separated. Afterwards, like all the others who survived, we were horribly ill. It has been twenty years since that filthy night, but pains, breathlessness, fevers, coughs, never for a day have they left us.

(Bhopal survivor quoted in an advert for the Bhopal Medical Appeal, *The Independent*, 25 September, 2004)

In 1984, an extremely poisonous chemical (methyl isocyanate, MIC) leaked from an industrial plant in Bhopal, India. The plant, owned by the American-based company, Union Carbide, was set up in 1969. It was supposed to be the answer to struggling Indian agriculture. It was supposed to offer reliable employment to India's lower castes and skilled classes alike.

Dominique Lapierre and Javier Moro (2003) recorded that at five minutes after midnight on 3 December, 1984, one of the MIC tanks exploded and a green cloud of lethal gas began poisoning thousands of people, many dying as they slept, or running away. The areas first affected were the shanty camps near the factory, with their residents of migrant rural workers attempting to find jobs in Bhopal. Those living in the nearby town were then beset by the poison because the wind was blowing in their direction. The stinking fog was to envelop $20\,km^2$. Babies and children were especially vulnerable as families fled. The gas, heavier than air, descended to their level as they were pulled along by their parents.

The lobby group for survivors of the Bhopal disaster, the International Campaign for Justice in Bhopal (ICJB), records the awfulness of that night:

There was no warning, none of the plant's safety systems were working. In the city people were sleeping. They woke in darkness to the sound of screams with the gases burning their eyes, noses and mouths. They began retching and coughing up froth streaked with blood. Whole neighbourhoods fled in panic, some were trampled, others convulsed and fell dead. People lost control of their bowels and bladders as they ran. Within hours thousands of dead bodies lay in the streets.

(ICJB, 2006)

The prolonged effects of MIC poisoning have resulted in many of those who seemingly escaped from the immediate threat then enduring serious illness and early death. About 3000–8000 people died during that night and shortly afterwards. The ICJB refers to a death toll of 20000, whilst Lapierre and Moro (2003) suggest it could be as high as 30000 dead.

Union Carbide's insecticide Sevin, made from MIC, was not selling as well as it had been because of droughts within India, and the suggestion is that the company was saving money through reducing its commitment to the overseeing of safety (Lapierre & Moro, 2003). On the night that MIC fell on Bhopal, safety precautions at the factory were allegedly not working at all or not operating properly. Flares installed to burn off any escaping gas were not lit; caustic washers that could have been used to neutralise the escaping gas were not in operation. The mechanism installed to audibly warn people in the town of such a failure was seemingly not switched to its correct level (that is, a volume that could be heard in the town). Lapierre and Moro (2003) argue that the company put the factory on 'care and maintenance status' and therefore reduced safety systems. This, for Lapierre and Moro, was a criminal act. However, Union Carbide, whilst regretting the 'terrible tragedy' in 1984, has stated that it suspects sabotage:

Shortly after the gas release, Union Carbide launched an aggressive effort to identify the cause. A thorough investigation was conducted by the engineering consulting firm Arthur D. Little. Its conclusion: The gas leak could only have been caused by deliberate sabotage. Someone purposely put water in the gas storage tank, causing a massive chemical reaction. Process safety systems had been put in place that would have kept the water from entering into the tank by accident.

(Union Carbide, 2005)

Twenty years later the factory remained contaminated; Bhopal's water supply continued to be suspected of being dangerous to drink; little compensation has been paid to the survivors; legal wrangling continues over who was ultimately responsible for the release of the poison, with Dow Chemical, the company which took over Union Carbide in a merger, wishing to draw a line under the disaster, whilst the ICJB calls for a judgement of culpable homicide (ICJB, 2005).

Anushka Asthana (2004), explaining why her family is still fighting for justice in Bhopal, observes that Union Carbide's US parent has claimed that the Bhopal factory was managed by Union Carbide India Limited. The latter was a company owned and financially supported by investors from within India. Union Carbide sent a million dollars for relief funds and medical equipment after the incident, as well as compensation. The Indian local government with jurisdiction for Bhopal (the State of Madhya Pradesh) then took over what remained of the factory and its land. Subsequently, Dow Chemical merged with Union Carbide. Union Carbide is viewed by Dow Chemical as a separate company.

As Asthana remarks, within three years following the 11 September terrorist attacks in New York, the US government was compensating survivors and using the judicial system to prosecute those responsible. But a US corporation had been able to avoid meaningful moral and financial adjudication where many more people have lost their lives than did in New York.

Are corporations homicidal? Are their executives murderers? The Dow Chemical Company is a global corporation, describing itself as leader in science and technology which provides innovative chemical, plastic and agricultural products and services across 175 countries, and employing 43 000 people. In 2005, its sales were worth US$40 billion. It declares a vigorous commitment to 'social responsibility', setting up a charitable foundation to distribute US$18 million annually throughout the world for philanthropic projects and humanitarian aid (Dow, 2005).

In the book *The corporation: the pathological pursuit of profit and power* by Joel Bakan (2004) (which was made into a film by Mark Achbar, Jennifer Abbott and Joel Bakan), global corporations are branded as 'psychopathic'. Bakan argues that they are psychopathic because they have a disregard for the effect of their business operations on human life. Corporate psychopathy extends to murder indirectly through wide scale environmental damage, the effects of low wages of employees and the shedding of jobs, and endemic materialism that leads to a quality of life conquered by consumerism.

> Over the last 150 years the corporation has risen from relative obscurity to become the world's dominant economic institution. Today, corporations govern our lives. They determine what we eat, what we watch, what we wear, where we work, and what we do. We are inescapably surrounded by their culture, iconography, and ideology.
>
> (Bakan, 2004, p. 5)

Corporations directly murder thousands through such incidents as Bhopal, and are potentially omnicidal because of the threat they pose to all living organisms. Furthermore, no government can control this pathological pursuit of power. When governments attempt to do so by insisting on preventative and reparative measures for the environmental and human harm caused, the response of the corporation is to up-sticks to a part of the world where they do not have to abide by such impositions to their business. Alternatively, the global corporation donates a minimum amount of its resources to tokenistic 'socially responsible' programmes.

Robert Hare, an expert on psychopathic behaviour, was asked in the book to apply a checklist of psychological traits to the way in which corporations operate. According to Hare, if corporations were people they would be psychopaths. Corporations, driven by profit, are unconcerned about the seriously negative consequences of their business (for example, the exploitation of already impoverished workers, pollution and global warming) unless media, political and public criticism threatens to undermine their market dominance. Concern expressed by corporations about these ill-effects is only at a superficial level compassionate and magnanimous. At root, corporations are uncompromisingly selfish. People, cultures and even the planet are subjugated to corporate needs.

Tobacco industries can very obviously be attacked for their reckless disregard for health in their desire to maximise revenue by targeting sales of cigarettes to young people in the West and new markets in developing countries. However, companies that ostensibly have a role in maintaining health can also be accused of immoral practices. Drug companies are amongst the ranks of the global corporate elite, making profits bigger than the gross national product of many countries. They operate in the most lucrative (Western) markets but minimally in developing countries where huge numbers of people die from diseases that are controlled, have been eradicated, or don't crop up, in the West. But corporate income is considerably higher from treating miserable, bald, impotent, fat, or wrinkled rich Europeans and North Americans than the infested, contagious and malnourished of sub-Saharan Africa or South-east Asia. Moreover, new personalised drugs (pharmacogenetics) will only focus on diseases in the developed world, whilst the 'old' drugs' will be dumped in the Third World just as 'unapproved' and out-of-date medicines may have been (War On Want, 2002).

Indeed the medicalisation of everyday life in the West is rampant. New syndromes and diseases are discovered (or 'invented') daily with concomitant treatments, many of them drugs. The medical and pharmacology professions have colonised large areas of our lives with the creation of a never-ending list of diseases for which pills and potions are offered (most of which come at the price of iatrogenesis and dependency). Whether it is adult gloom and worry, childhood hyperactivity, 'jogger's nipple', 'Chinese restaurant syndrome', pre-menstrual tension and the menopause, or 'irritable male disorder', we are offered healing that is probably pharmaceutical.

However, attempts to alleviate human suffering are skewed towards those 'problems with living' that can provide the biggest profit (with particular attention paid to the rejuvenation of happiness, hair, breasts, genitals, teeth and faces, and the renovation of cholesterolised arteries and flabby thighs). If you live in a Western country and have HIV/AIDS you are more likely to have available life-prolonging treatments – and can afford to buy them – than in the developing countries, where their cost will be prohibitive (Medecins Sans Frontieres, 2005). India has been one of the biggest producers of 'generic' drugs, which are much cheaper copycats of patented medicines, distributing these to its own poor and poorer regions of the world. However, due to the backlash from the original manufacturers of the drugs and the need for the Indian Government to obey the rules of the World Trade Organisation, the generics may be taken off the market (Adiga, 2003).

For Hare, despite the psychopathic traits of corporations, their employees are rarely really psychopaths. Even the most driven Chief Executive Officer is likely to show affection and loyalty towards others at the end of the business day (that is, their family and friends). It is the corporation as an institution, with its unremittingly manipulative, selfish, predatory and anti-social traits that is the psychopath. This may be anthropomorphic, but with reference to social responsibility Hare states the connection between the psychopathic behaviour of people and that of institutions can be made:

> Human psychopaths are notorious for their ability to use charm as a mask to hide their dangerously self-obsessed personalities. For corporations, social responsibility may play the same role. Through it they can present themselves as compassionate and concerned about others when, in fact, they lack the ability to care about anyone or anything but themselves.
>
> (Hare quoted in Bakan, 2004, pp. 56–57)

The ultimate expression of corporate self-interest can be seen in the account given in Bakan's book by Carlton Brown (Bakan, 2004, p. 111), a commodities broker, in New York on 11 September, 2001: 'It was one of the worst things I have seen in my lifetime . . . All I could think about was getting them the hell out . . . Before the building collapsed, all we were thinking was, let's get those clients out.'

Where Brown wanted to get his clients out of was not the burning building, but the gold market. Once the World Trade Center was no longer able to trade, the gold markets would close. His clients had to be able to keep trading in order to profit from the steep rise in the value of gold because of the uncertainty created by the terrorist action. All his traders doubled their money within a few days. In Brown's words, 'In devastation there is opportunity' (Brown quoted in Bakan, 2004, p. 111). Most murderers are brought to justice. However, few murders committed by corporations get to court.

Few if any corporations are put into receivership because they perform as psychopathic killers.

GOVERNMENTS

International and intra-national inequalities in education, employment, wealth, living conditions and health generate huge variations in lifespan. The gap in lifespan between those with and those without personal skills and financial resources (that is, social and material capital), may be anything from one to three decades. People with low social and material capital in developed countries have increased their lifespans substantially. But many developing countries as well as Russia and some of its former European and Asian colonies, have seen lifespans shorten considerably (United Nations, 2005a).

Social epidemiologist, Richard Wilkinson (2005), using evidence from all over the world, argues that levels of inequality correlate precisely with life expectancy. Inequality universally is damaging to society precisely because it shortens lives. Paradoxically, however, if the inequality is minimal within an impoverished society then people are healthier (and happier), says Wilkinson, than people in richer but widely unequal societies. The perception that you are at the bottom of the social hierarchy is what is linked to ill-health. Unhealthy habits and especially anxiety and depression provoked by low self-esteem and low control of life conditions combine to reduce lifespan.

For Wilkinson, the cross-cultural constant factor is social respect. If you do not have respect from society for the job you do or because you have little money then this is the key factor in shortening your life. Moreover, not only are those in a lower socio-economic position exposed to higher levels of violence and thereby risk an early death, but murder rates correlate with inequality. That is, posits Wilkinson, unfair societies have more murders than poorer ones where the latter have high degrees of social trust. That is, a culture of fairness generates less killing. This phenomenon is true for countries and for subsections of a country that have a strong conviction that fairness exists, such as particular states in the USA.

There is a wealth of data available linking early death with social disparity. Governments that do not diminish inequalities are guilty of murder. It is culpability through malice aforethought then through negligence.

Governments authorise killing through the instigation of war. They also wilfully supply the means for others to kill. The USA, France, Germany, UK,

Russia, China, Poland, Czech Republic and Netherlands are the major arms producers. A report by an organisation campaigning for tighter regulations in arms industries (Control Arms, 2004), laid bare the unscrupulous practices of governments which pledge the ethical selling of armaments. Supported by Amnesty International, Oxfam and the International Action Network on Small Arms, the report refers to how the major manufacturers, with their government's connivance, manage to circumvent the official rules by selling arms components, which then can be bought and assembled by a third-party and passed on to banned states. These states are banned because they have dire human rights records, and may be using the very weapons sold by 'ethical' states to conduct torture and kill their own citizens.

What makes matters worse points out Control Arms is that many of the countries buying arms can only do so by diverting money from health care, education and infrastructure. This could hardly not be known by the manufacturing countries, making their culpability all the more great. These countries are part of the rich developed world, which is already resistant to an effective redistribution of wealth, an unrestricted cancellation of debt and fairer trade agreements, in order to decrease global poverty.

Mark Curtis argues that governments have been responsible for clandestine murdering across the globe. Using the example of the UK, he suggests that whenever it is in the interests of the government it has connived in killing through supporting coups and helping to install dictators in many countries. He points out how the very two governments that invaded Iraq for 'ethical' reasons (along with an espoused fear of 'weapons of mass destruction') secretly instigated a change in regime in Iraq during the 1960s. This caused the death of one thousand people, and led to the Ba'athist Party gaining power in Iraq. The Ba'athist Party later came under the leadership of Saddam Hussein. The UK and the USA then invaded Iraq in 2003 to remove the Ba'athist Party and Saddam Hussein, costing thousands more lives.

Then there is genocide. 'Genocide' is a neologism from the Greek 'genos', meaning race or tribe, and the Latin 'cide', which means to kill. The term was coined in 1943 by the Jewish-Polish lawyer Raphael Lemkin (Hickey, 2003). It was given a legal definition, after the Second World War's Nazi holocaust, in the 1948 Convention on the Prevention and Punishment of the Crime of Genocide (Krug et al., 2002). In that convention, any act committed that is intended to destroy, in whole or in part, a national, ethnic, racial or religious group is considered to be genocide. For Irving Horowitz (2002), the key to understanding genocide is not the examination of individual perpetrators but the organisation of the society in which it takes place and specifically how the state orchestrates killing systematically:

> More strongly than ever, I believe the best way to deal with the awful truths of genocide is through an analysis of state power and social systems, rather than through analyses such as the earlier psychiatric or biographic accounts of the perpetrator and the victim of genocide.
>
> (Horowitz, 2002, p. 5)

The International Criminal Court (ICC) was established in 2002 as a permanent tribunal. Its aims are to prosecute perpetrators of genocide, crimes against humanity and war crimes. By 2005, one hundred countries had ratified or acceded to the ICC Statute guaranteeing ICC jurisdiction over the most serious crimes when national authorities cannot or will not prosecute. To date (2006), the USA has not joined the ICC.

Apart from the Nazi holocaust, other unequivocal examples of genocide include the 1994 conflict in Rwanda when 800 000 Tutsis and moderate Hutus were slaughtered by Hutu militia and the Rwandan military. However, the international community was very slow in recognising what was happening in Rwanda, and only intervened after the carnage had become unmistakenly genocidal. Moreover, in some scenarios, although there may be blatant evidence of methodical and widespread killing, there can be disagreement about whether or not the concept of genocide is applicable. Caution is exercised by international agencies and national governments because if genocide is designated this has consequences such as military intervention. Public opinion may, at times, also impede the labelling of massacres as genocide, because of the stigma attached to their country or national heroes. A book written by the French historian Claude Ribbe, *Le crime de Napoleon* (2005), claimed that the emperor paved the way for the Nazi holocaust by exterminating 100 000 rebellious slaves in San Domingo (known today as Haiti) using the poisonous gas, sulphur dioxide. Ribbe's thesis was not appreciated in France where Napoleon is still regarded highly.

Sudan has had a civil war lasting 21 years. More than 1.5 million people have lost their lives in the conflict between northern Sudan, which is predominantly Muslim, and the Animist and Christian rebels of southern Sudan. Various groups have been involved in the rebellion, but principally the Sudan People's Liberation Army (SPLA) and the Sudan People's Defence Force (SPDF). In 2002, these two groups joined together against the government based in Khartoum. A peace deal between the south and the north was signed in 2005 and a 'Government of National Unity' installed. Sharing of the nation's potential wealth from oil is agreed. However, whilst this deal was being brokered, a further rebellion broke out in Darfur, western Sudan, late in 2003. Early 2004 saw the Sudanese army move to quell the new rebellion. Tens of thousands were killed in and around Darfur. At least a million were displaced, with many entering neighbouring Chad (Prunier, 2005).

Subsequently, the pro-government Arab African Janjaweed militias, who are incontrovertibly linked with the Sudanese Army according to Amnesty International (2005), carried out a campaign of ethnic cleansing against black Africans in the region. The Janjaweed killed, raped, and looted persistently and on a large scale:

> The Janjawid militias and the soldiers arrived on market day in Abu Jidad. The soldiers cordoned off the market and the Janjawid got inside to take the money and the cattle. They killed several persons. I saw the bodies of those killed. Some were killed by the gun, others by bayonet.
> (Ercouri Mahamat, Koranic student, from the village of Abu Gamra, near Kornoy town, in North Darfur, quoted in Amnesty International, 2005c)

Although the Sudanese government's exact role in the slaughter in Darfur is disputed (by the then government), the United Nations was highly critical of official efforts to control the area and resettle those living in make-shift camps (without sufficient water, food and medicine) who were particularly susceptible to mistreatment (United Nations, 2005b).

Gerard Prunier (2005) is unambiguous in deciding that Darfur is a case of genocide. Given how many people were being killed, how those killed had a specific cultural identity, how systematic the killings were, and the role of state (either directly or by not disarming the militias – although a small army from the African Union did enter Darfur), it is hard not to conceive of Darfur as genocide.

However, major disagreements existed over whether or not Darfur was genocide. In 2004, the then US Secretary of State Colin Powell, speaking to the US Senate Foreign Relations Committee stated categorically that the atrocities in Darfur were genocide (CNN, 2004). The United Nations, the British Government and the European Union on the other hand have all refused to describe the Darfur mass deaths as genocide.

If the murderous actions of the Janjaweed and the culpable inactions of the Sudanese government are not describable as genocide, genocide is still happening in Darfur according to Martin Bell (2004). For Bell, former war correspondent and British member of parliament, and presently UNICEF ambassador, Darfur can be viewed as the first example of 'climatic genocide'. Darfur is an arid region, and much of the conflict appears to be over water supplies between non-Muslim Africans and the Arabs. The Arabs have been encroaching on the farmland of the non-Muslims to gain access to their watered land. The reason this has become necessary is because of creeping desertification. The reason for creeping desertification is global warming. The reason for global warming is government policy over industrial output and transport.

Lord Alton of Liverpool and Rebecca Tinsley (2004) of the Jubilee campaign (a human rights pressure group, lobbying to protect children's rights and the 'persecuted church') argue that not declaring Darfur as genocide allows the international community to stand by idly as the killing continues and continue trading with the country. Any country signed up to the Geneva Convention Against Genocide must act to prevent and to protect and subsequently bring to justice those who commit crimes against humanity if genocide is recognised. Alton and Tinsley suggest that the rate of death from murder, malnutrition and malady is comparable to the death rate at the peak of the Rwandan Genocide in 1994.

Governments also 'murder' their citizens in ways other than through genocide. A legal method of killing is the death penalty. The death penalty may be used for murder convictions, but some countries (for example, China) execute other types of criminals such as drug dealers and rapists, as well as political dissidents or merely those that stand in the way of 'progress'. The defunct Union of Soviet Socialist Republics (USSR) killed millions of its citizens in the twentieth century, primarily when Joseph Stalin was in power, because they were perceived to be impeding a socialist economic transformation.

Some states execute their young people. Iran, in 2005, publicly executed two teenagers. They were lashed two hundred times each and then hanged for 'being homosexual'. The Iranian Government stated that sexual assault, alcohol consumption and public disorder had been the real reason for killing them. In the same year, Iran executed two other homosexual older men. They were in their 20s (Human Rights Watch, 2005). Iran punished occurrences of homosexual contact using Sharia law. Under Sharia law the crime of 'lavat' is penetrative and non-penetrative sexual acts between men. Whereas non-penetrative sex between men has as punishment the lash, Iranian law punishes all penetrative sexual acts between adult men with death. If non-penetrative perpetrators are caught indulging four times, then they too would be killed. China, the Democratic Republic of Congo, Pakistan and the USA did or still do execute juveniles. It was only in 2005 that the US Supreme Court decided that the death penalty for juveniles was unconstitutional.

Historically, the death penalty has been accomplished by various means: stoned, bludgeoned, beaten, broken on the wheel, drawn and quartered, eviscerated while alive, buried alive, burned alive, drowned, garrotted, beheaded, hanged, shot by firing squad, electrocuted, poisoned by lethal gas or drug. Contemporary methods of state killing include: beheading (Saudi Arabia and Iraq); hanging (for example, Egypt, Iran, Japan, Jordan, Pakistan and Singapore); lethal injection (for example, China, Guatemala, Philippines and Thailand); shooting (for example, Belarus, China, Somalia, Taiwan,

Uzbekistan, Vietnam); and stoning (Afghanistan and Iran). Unless a particularly high-status social group is targeted specifically, such as the middle classes and intelligentsia were under Khmer Rouge rule in Cambodia (1975–1979), the death penalty is a punishment directed at those in the bottom segments of the social order. Eric Hickey (2003) commented that those found on death row in the USA are in the main the poorly educated from low-income backgrounds. There is a further social bias of death row inmates in the USA as ethnic minority groups are overrepresented (blacks and Latinos), although overall more Caucasians are death row inmates and more are executed.

Amnesty International (2005d) recorded that during 2004 nearly 4000 people were executed in these 25 countries: Afghanistan, Bangladesh, Belarus, People's Republic of China, Egypt, India, Indonesia, Iran, Japan, Jordan, North Korea, Kuwait, Lebanon, Pakistan, Saudi Arabia, Singapore, Somalia, Sudan, Syria, Taiwan, Tajikistan, USA, Uzbekistan, Vietnam and Yemen. In the same year, over 7000 had been sentenced to death in 64 countries.

Although dozens of countries retain the death penalty, most of the executions in 2004 took place in only a few of them. In 2004, 97% of the executions took place in China, Iran, Vietnam and the USA: Iran executed 159 people, Vietnam 64, and the USA 59. However, for Amnesty International this is an underestimate of the actual number as governments do not always broadcast their killing rate. International criticism of 'sensitive' cases that might provoke public hostility towards the state may mean that executions are performed clandestinely, only known after the event or never disclosed. Moreover, downtrends in the global statistics on executions (as happened in 2005) have to be treated sceptically. For example, although officially China executed 3400 people in 2004 and 1770 in 2005, this, according to Amnesty International, is a massive underestimation. Amnesty International refers to a 'Chinese legal expert' who has calculated, using information from local officials and judges, that the true figure for executions each year in China is approximately 8000. However, data about the death penalty remains classified as a state secret (Amnesty International, 2006).

Thirty-eight states of the USA in 2005 retained the death penalty, although two (New York and Kansas) were declared unconstitutional in 2004 by the Supreme Court. The US federal government and military also can implement the death penalty. Lethal injection, electrocution, gas chamber, hanging and firing squad are the legal killing methods.

Amnesty International monitors where executions are taking place worldwide and in what circumstances. It cooperates with other human rights organisations and governments, aiming for the abolition of the death penalty. Amnesty International argues that the deterrent effect of the death penalty has not been proven. It cites Canada where, following the abolition of the death penalty in 1975, an already falling homicide rate continued its decline. Moreover, Canada's homicide rate is very much lower than its neighbour's, the USA.

There are organisations that campaign for the opposite situation. For example, the Pro-death Penalty group of the USA, as its name suggests, wants legal executions to be retained as a penalty against murder. It regards the criminal justice system as favouring the culprit, not the victim, and uses a quote by John McAdams of Marquette University/Department of Political Science in support of their case:

> If we execute murderers and there is in fact no deterrent effect, we have killed a bunch of murderers. If we fail to execute murderers, and doing so would in fact have deterred other murders, we have allowed the killing of a bunch of innocent victims. I would much rather risk the former. This, to me, is not a tough call.
>
> (Pro-death Penalty, 2005)

This approach misses the point that retaining the death penalty also risks killing innocent people. Amnesty International points out that from 1973 to 2005 more than 120 prisoners had been released in the USA because of faulty evidence and judicial procedural failings. Many had spent years on death row. There is also an absence of awareness about how authoritarian, totalitarian states can use the death penalty for political reasons, to quell opposition to their rule or to employ drastic policies that would otherwise be defied. Democratic countries such as the USA are not immune to the politicising of execution as local politicians (for example, US state governors) may have the power to pardon doomed felons and could be tempted not to do so if votes are in jeopardy.

SUMMARY

So, people commit murder. So do corporations. So do governments. But in a sense we all are complicit in murder. We all know, through the vivid images and expansive literature on our television screens and in our newspapers that people are dying unnecessarily. Many of us overeat whilst digesting another famine in front of our televisions. Hoards of us holiday whilst our hosts succumb to disease. Well-off Westerners conspicuously spend whilst most of the global village's population cannot buy adequate amounts of nutrition, medicines and education.

This is murder through mass complacency, but how can the deaths of millions as a consequence of global inequalities be compared with the corporate murder of tens of thousands, the 'final solution' strategy to ethnic cleansing, the murder of a cheating wife by her jealous husband, the killing of children by other children, or the judicial use of the death penalty? That is, in what ways can murder be categorised? On a moral basis, with some killings deemed worse than others? If so, would this be focused on the victim, the culprit, or on circumstances? Should the numbers of murders be used as a classifier? Would numerical classification mean that one murder would be in a different grouping to two, would two be in a different section to five? Where would the numerical cut-offs be, and how would time, space, and motive be taken into account? Each murder has particular antecedents, behaviours and consequences: the history of the participants, just who is included in that history, the accounts of the event, what constitutes the event, and the perceptions of the killing portrayed by the police, defence and prosecution lawyers, judges, juries, press, film makers, authors and script-writers and journalists.

This is not to argue that there aren't structural trends in assessing 'who commits murder'. Men kill more than women do, but most men don't kill. Dispossessed people kill more than well-heeled people, but powerful people can kill whole communities with impunity. Murder happens in all societies, but with different quotients and with different connotations. There are, therefore, unmistakable social trends in deciding who commits murder, but the murdering event is also idiosyncratic. The Pierre Riviere killings in nineteenth-century France, and the killing of Tim Parry in twentieth-century England (whose killer has yet to be brought to justice), were inexorably associated with wider socio-political events. But they were also personal tragic events.

CHAPTER 3

WHY COMMIT MURDER?

Knowing what murder is and who commits murder is problematic. It follows that formulating theories about why murder is committed must also be tricky. Not that this trickiness prevents the public and the press from being amateur detectives in real and fictional cases, with ascertaining the *motive* behind a murder the customary hub for their sleuthing endeavours. The question of motive is also central to police investigations. Although a conviction is possible without a motive being discovered, finding a specific reason makes it much more likely.

Motives for aggression generally can be divided into two forms, expressive and instrumental. Expressive aggression is the outburst of anger as a reaction to, for example, an insult, and physical assault. Instrumental aggression is intended to make a gain for the perpetrator, either in terms of social status or materially. Both expressive and instrumental aggression can be either premeditated or spontaneous. However, it is more likely that expressive aggression has not been pre-planned to a prolonged extent, and may be an immediate and seemingly uncontrollable response that becomes self-defeating rather than rewarding.

Motives for murder can also be condensed into four sets of 'ls', lust, love, loathing, and loot:

- *Lust*: someone is killed because they stand in the way of sexual gratification (perhaps a wife who has discovered her husband's adultery); a lover ends a sexual relationship and is killed by their resentful ex-partner; there is a yearning for fame and killing is a method to gain a celebrity status perhaps by murdering a celebrity; the 'thrill-killer' who loves murdering people because of the emotional and sexual pay-off for him or her.

- *Love*: the killer believes that they are freeing the victim from present or future pain and low-quality of life, such as the 'mercy killing' of a baby with a major deformity or partner with incurable cancer.

- *Loathing*: hate and/or resentment directed towards one person (for example, an abusive parent), group (such as homosexuals), culture or nation (for example, Palestinians towards Israelis and vice versa).

- *Loot*: killing for financial gain through inheritance or insurance pay-outs; a murder occurring during a robbery, or gang-warfare over the control of drug markets; employment as a contract killer or mercenary.

Finding a motive for murder does not go far enough to elucidate, for example: why this person's lust led to murder when others sublimate their lust, say, into sport or find a more accessible sexual partner; why does love preclude rather than precurse killing in most relationships; what is it that catapults loathing between certain communities into mutual massacre, whilst others have resolved to live in multicultural harmony or at least co-exist without killing?; how is it that this gun-toting mugger pulls the trigger when his prey resists but another street-robber would flee?

If the public, press and police only look for superficial answers to why murder is committed, are criminologists any better? Conventional criminological thinking about why people kill one another has also been narrow and naive. Murder theorists use retrospective deduction to fit killing events with an explanation that coincides with a discourse with which they are familiar. Neurobiologists rarely mutate into structuralist sociologists, and experimental psychologists seldom metamorphose into neo-evolutionists.

Murder theories are, therefore, the expected conjectural offspring of their parental paradigm. Most are also teleological. That is, effect (murder) and cause (either individual or societal pathology) are bound in a self-serving explanatory cycle. These theories then offer generalisations and predictions: the identified faults in one or a few humans and cultures will produce the same result in other humans and cultures (fatal violence). Each such theory is a *gratis dictum*, dogma without robust empirical and/or conceptual evidence. Furthermore, whether a theory is of the *faulty individual* or *faulty society* variety, there is a tendency towards determinism. That is, there is an overemphasis on biological, psychological, neo-evolutionary and sociological predisposition to murder at the expense of what precisely precipitates a killing, or alternatively what prevented a killing taking place.

I suggest that human behaviour needs to be acknowledged as a convoluted matrix of predispositions and precipitations than cannot be encapsulated by a single theory. Before reviewing critically these theories, however, I comment on the two reasons for committing murder most favoured by my students and a level of analysis beyond just finding a motive: *madness* and *badness*.

MADNESS

In September 1966, at 3pm, Demitrios Tsafendas walked up to South Africa's Prime Minister Hendrik Vervoerd in the parliament building and stabbed him four times. Tsafendas was overpowered and disarmed. Verwoerd died shortly afterwards. Verwoerd was one of the architects of the apartheid system in South Africa. Tsafendas could be regarded as one of its economic victims, confined to either unemployment or the low-paid work of a messenger in South Africa's parliament.

Born in Mozambique, Tsafendas' father was Greek and his mother a black African. His father deserted his mother, and married a Greek woman. Tsafendas moved with his father and mother-in-law to South Africa. In South Africa he was accepted as white, but became estranged from his family and became an itinerant, travelling around the world. He suffered from mental illness throughout his life. He was treated for mental illness in different countries; he believed that he was possessed by a huge tape-worm, and was paranoid. His madness saving him from execution; Tsafendas spent about 30 years in prison before being sent to a psychiatric hospital where he died in 1999. Henk van Woerden, a Dutch artist brought up in South Africa during the Verwoerd years, has written an account of Tsafendas's life (van Woerden, 2000). Van Woerden comments that nothing that occurred at this time in South Africa can be separated from the racial tensions that dominated people's lives, not even the madness of this assassin.

Tsafendas, an immigrant to South Africa, had assassinated another immigrant. Verwoerd was born in Holland, and as a child his family had moved to South Africa. But Tsafendas was in a worse predicament than merely that of an immigrant. He was of mixed racial origin, a *métique, mulatto*, half-blood, Creole, bastard. As such, his social position in South Africa within a political system that rigidly demarcated people on the basis of race, was ambiguous. He was neither fully white, nor black. Nor did he want to be included in the third major racial category of 'coloured'.

As a parliamentary messenger, a job he had held only since the month prior to the killing, he was to see daily some of the most powerful people in the country. His responsibilities were menial, taking drinks to members of parliament and journalists, and to carry bundles of papers between offices. Tsafendas had detested the Nationalist Party for a long time, presumably because it created the system that put him in a social no-man's-land. Now, through no design of his own beyond needing to earn money after years of travelling around the world, he was in close contact with its senior protagonists and its leader, whom he especially hated.

Four hours after the murder, Tsafendas told a psychiatrist why he killed the Prime Minister:

> I'm against Verwoerd. He's a foreigner . . . He is a Nationalist and he hasn't got the people behind him. I see no progress for the African people. There is

> something spiritual in me . . . I thought this thing had gone too far, they have made an ideology of it. The sexual part of it too – the Immorality Act, telling you who you can't marry . . . The only girl who wanted to marry me did not have the right identity card. I could not keep changing my identity card.
>
> (Tsafendas quoted by van Woerden, 2000, pp. 114–115)

In October 1999, 33 years after he killed Vervoerd, Tsafendas, already suffering from chronic heart disease and susceptible to pneumonia, became very ill. He died a week later, aged 81 years. Tsafendas's death became the lead item in national news broadcasts.

More than a century earlier, there was another assassination by a madman, but this time it was in England. That murder had the greatest impact on the law relating to insanity. Daniel M'Naghten, a carpenter from Glasgow, suffered paranoid delusions directed toward members of the Tory political party. He was charged in 1843 with the homicide of Edward Drummond, whom he had shot by mistake, intending instead to kill the Tory Prime Minister Sir Robert Peel (1788–1850), to whom Drummond was the private secretary. After the presentation of medical evidence, the trial judge indicated to the jury that he believed the case for the defence to have been established so as to leave no doubt as to M'Naghten's madness. M'Naghten was found 'not guilty on the ground of insanity' and became an inmate of Bethlem Asylum.

Subsequent to the M'Naghten trial, to succeed in a claim of insanity, three points had to be substantiated. First, the accused must have been suffering from a 'disease of the mind' at the time of the unlawful deed. What are excluded as 'diseases of the mind' for the purpose of the M'Naghten rules are those mental disturbances that come about as the consequence of external factors such as violence, drugs, alcohol, hypnosis and hypoglycaemia. Second, the disease of the mind must produce a 'defect of reason' beyond simple moments of absentmindedness or confusion. Third, this reasoning deficiency means that the offender either did not know the nature and quality of their actions or, if knowing this, was unaware of the wrongfulness (in the 'moral' rather than merely 'legal' sense) of these actions.

The M'Naghten rules remain, in the twenty-first century, the implicit or explicit reference point for laws on 'mad murder' that originate from English law, including those of South Africa. But there has never been unadulterated acceptance of these rules. Medical expert opinion and mental health laws have gradually grown in significance. Expert medical opinion was to displace attempts to obtain universal rules governing mental disorder offenders. Moreover, such defences as diminished responsibility, both guilty and not guilty because of insanity, and unfit to plead, have become available instead of murder convictions.

Both Demitrios Tsafendas and Daniel M'Naghten were blatantly mad, but attempting to define madness poses a major problem for the criminal justice system. The quandary involves, at one level, the courts making decisions about personal responsibility, free will, self-control, maturation, legal liability and punishment and/or treatment. At another level, the frequently contending and internally discrepant beliefs and practices of the law and psychiatry cause further confusion and irresolution.

For Michel Foucault (1988), psychiatry helped to resolve a paradox over the 'intelligibility' of criminal acts from the early part of the nineteenth century onwards. The growing commitment to rationalism and individualism, as a consequence of industrialisation, meant that the criminal justice system focused on the personal responsibility of the miscreant. In this setting, a discourse of 'disclosure' is demanded. By the nineteenth century, courts were interested in the criminal as well as in the crime and the penalty. Judges, jurors and lawyers expect to be provided with details not only of the infraction and the immediate circumstances, but also of the personal and social history of the accused.

Foucault refers to a case in a French court of a man convicted of kidnapping and killing a child. The man's defence lawyer made a plea against the death penalty, arguing that little about the man had been forthcoming from the interrogations of the police or the court; he asked the question, 'Can one condemn to death a person one does not know?' (Foucault, 1988, p. 127). The inference here was that only when the crime was made intelligible (through the presentation of 'understandable' aspects of the criminal's biography) could the discipline of the court be justified.

'Unintelligible' crime (in which no motivating factors have been disclosed by the accused or discovered by the court) is to be conceived as not being the responsibility of the perpetrator, and is thereby 'excused' as an act of madness. Recategorised as such, insane murders became the province of psychiatry. Trials of 'monstrous crimes' such as the killing of children for no apparent purpose have allowed psychiatry successfully to penetrate the criminal justice system. Medical experts adjudicating over such crimes have justified the legitimacy of their interventions by demonstrating that no 'reason' could be explicated. Foucault cites two other infamous murders of the nineteenth century:

> In the case of Henriette Cornier, who had decapitated her neighbour's daughter, it was carefully established that she had not been the father's mistress, and that she had not acted out of vengeance. In the case of the woman from Selestat, who had boiled up her daughter's thigh, an important element of the discussion had been, 'Was there or was there not a famine at the time? Was the accused poor or not, starving or not?'
>
> (Foucault, 1988, p. 132)

Presumably, if Henriette Cornier had been known to be sexually consorting with the victim's father, and the cannibal from Selestat had been in a state of abject hunger, the court would have had no hesitation in taking the 'reasonable' course of killing them both.

BADNESS

In Iraq, October 2004, 59-year-old Margaret Hassan was kidnapped at gunpoint in Baghdad. Forced by her kidnappers, she appeared in a series of videos that were broadcast on the Arabic television news station Al-Jazeera. Hassan was shown becoming increasingly distraught over a period of weeks in these videos. Pleading for her life in one video, she said that she didn't want to meet with the same fate as Ken Bigley, who had been beheaded seemingly by the same kidnappers. She asked, presumably voicing the wishes of her kidnappers, for foreign troops (that is, the 'coalition' of countries that had invaded Iraq in 2003, led by the USA and the UK) to leave the country.

Margaret Hassan was born in Ireland, but had spent much of her life in England. She had married an Iraqi, and the couple moved to his home country in 1973. Following Iraq's annexation of Kuwait (1990), and the consequential first Gulf War (1990–1991), the United Nations imposed economic sanctions on Iraq in 1990. Margaret Hassan was to become the Director for Iraq of Care International, an aid agency working to alleviate the negative effects on the health of Iraqi civilians due to these economic sanctions. Children in particular endured deficient medical care at that time, although the Iraqi authorities may have been duplicitous by restricting even further the limited supplies in order to gain international support for ending the sanctions. Robert Fisk, an eminent armed-conflict journalist from the British newspaper *The Independent*, knew Margaret Hassan, and commented about her tenacity and philanthropic zeal:

> I remember her arguing with doctors and truck drivers when a lorryload of medicines arrived for children's cancer wards . . . She smiled, cajoled, pleaded to get these leukaemia drugs to Basra and Mosul.
>
> (Fisk, 2004)

Margaret Hassan spoke Arabic and had become an Iraqi citizen. She had also spoken at the United Nations and to the UK government, trying to get the economic sanctions rescinded as they were leading to hardship and ill-health of innocent Iraqis. They were, she reasoned, not effective against Saddam Hussein's leadership, which they were aimed at undermining. She was, therefore, an illogical choice of victim for kidnappers demanding the end of the military occupation of Iraq that began in 2003.

The last video shows her apparently being shot in the head by the kidnappers. A year later her body was still not found. Her killers had appeared heavily disguised in the videos. Abu Musab al-Zarqawi, apparent killer of Ken Bigley, has been associated with Margaret Hassan's death, although he was not amongst the many suspects arrested in the year following the killing. By 2006, only one person had been found guilty of involvement in the murder (al-Zarqawi was killed in an air-strike by US forces north of Baghdad). Mustafa Salman al-Jubouri, was sentenced to life imprisonment for aiding and abetting the kidnappers by an Iraqi court.

Can the killing of Margaret Hassan be considered to be anything other than having been committed by evil (that is, bad) people? Moreover, is this murder not so atrocious, so un-understandable, so incomparable, so inhumane compared with most other murders as to invite an exceptional label beyond that of ordinary evilness? Is this such a heinous crime that it deserves the tag of 'barbaric', and the perpetrators must be barbarians?

The term 'barbarian' has an ancient Greek pedigree. Originally, it denoted people of another nation or language (that is, non-Greeks), but came to mean much more than being merely non-Greek. By the second century AD in the Roman Empire, barbarian became applied specifically to the tribes from Northern Europe that made incursions into their territories. The hubris of the Greeks and Romans during the height of their military and cultural dominion, reconceptualised foreigners as uncivilised, cruel, brutal, inhuman, savage, ruthless and 'atrocious' as they are capable of carrying out atrocities. Barbarians (and their acts) must therefore be exceptional.

Joanna Bourke (2000) adopts a Freudian approach to analyse the interconnections of eroticism, cruelty and the mad desire to destroy (that is, to be 'atrocious'). Bourke claims that humans actually enjoy killing. She sees these as intimate elements of human psychology. Reviewing a selection of twentieth-century wars involving the USA, UK and Australia, she asserts that humans (especially men), are essentially barbaric. The corollary of Bourke's thesis is that the killers of Hassan are not exceptional, but exposing a human attribute, which for the most part is hidden in the unconscious or, if conscious, is not divulged.

It is also a matter of social perception and moral judgement who can be included and excluded from the category of barbarian. When do terrorists become so dreadful that they can be described as barbarians? Was Margaret Hassan's murder barbaric but Ken Bigley's not? What non-political murders could be regarded as barbaric? As with the identity of 'terrorist' and 'murderer', 'barbarian' may be applied by the powerful (mainly governments and their institutions, and triumphant armies) against those attempting to undermine the authority they represent. Barbaric acts, terror and murder are conducted by legitimate governments and victorious soldiers, but even in democratic societies can influence the interpretation of killing events in their favour.

Moreover, some notorious terrorists, if their movement achieves its aims, become legitimate politicians or perhaps leaders of their country as has happened in Europe and the Middle East. As Noam Chomsky, the radical polemicist, argues, the USA has been 'the covert terrorist' in many parts of the world, instigating such brutal regimes as the 1973 change from democracy to dictatorship in Chile (Chomsky, 2004; Mitchell & Schoeffel, 2003).

Furthermore, are those of us who reside in rich countries or belong to the elite elements of poor countries not the barbarians? Is the avarice or simply complacency shown by the privileged stratum in a global society towards the majority who endure health and wealth hardship not atrocious? Millions of people die each year directly through HIV/Aids, malaria, malnourishment, drought, war, genocide and indirectly through climatic change. All of the killing causes are known, and frequently televised in vivid detail. How does that compare with the terrorist who beheads or shoots his victim on video?

Christopher Hitchens (2004) describes the terrorists responsible for initiating and enacting such attacks as that on the Twin Towers in New York in 2001 as 'theocratic fascists'. He focuses on the actions of the Taliban in Afghanistan, and al-Qaeda internationally, which is underpinned by an extreme religiosity. Hitchen's examples are Islamic fundamentalists, but it could just as easily be Christian fundamentalists. Gregory Paul (2005), reviewing a large-scale survey, concluded that homicide rates (along with sexually transmitted diseases, youth pregnancy and marital breakdown) were much higher in highly religious communities than in secular communities. Theocratic fascists, argues Hitchens, wish to create closed societies in which the general population is servile, and women are subjugated to rule by men. For Hitchens, this is one of the ugliest forms of totalitarianism without historical precedence. Theocratic fascists want people to exist in dire poverty as a purifying measure in the spiritual sense. Homosexuality and alternative belief systems are not tolerated. Neither is free speech nor a free press. Theocratic fascists are barbarians, explodes Hitchens. Political and military intervention in such countries as Iraq is morally acceptable to prevent the development of a theocratic fascist empire, states Hitchens. Similar to the threat to the Roman Empire, the barbarians are threatening Western civilization.

The description of barbarian may fit the killers of Margaret Hassan (and Ken Bigley), but, does 'barbarian' fit, for example, those responsible for the suicide bombings of London on 7 July, 2005 when over 50 commuters and tourists died? These killers were young Muslims whose families and friends were astonished that they could have conducted this carnage. Mohammed Sidiqe was a father and teaching assistant; Hasib Hussain was described as a 'nice lad' who belonged to a loving family; Shehzad Tanweer was a sports science graduate; Germaine Lindsay was also a father and viewed as intelligent. As Michael Bond (2005) comments, none was bad or mad (that is, they did not have criminal records or any diagnosed mental disorder), nor were they particularly poor or uneducated. They were, states Bond, 'ordinary'. All of the research into suicide bombers, observes Bond, affirms that they tend to be better off materially and educationally than average for their community, most are sane, and do not have histories of drug or alcohol abuse. Moreover, suicide bombing cuts across communities. Contemporary suicide-homicide originated as a political weapon in Sri Lanka with the Marxist-Leninist Tamil Tigers, and has been used by other secular groups as well as Muslims.

It is not the individual pathology of the suicide bomber that holds the key, suggests Bond, but the way in which terrorist organisations recruit and train the usually young men or women to take their own lives and those of others: people who have sympathy with the organisation's aims (possibly because they have experienced what they feel is an injustice by the intended target) are selected and placed in small groups; they are then indoctrinated by the organisation's leaders into believing that the aims of the organisation are justifiable and self-sacrifice is noble as it may be the only method available to achieve these aims; in this psychological condition of moral outrage at the injustices of the targeted enemy, and heroism, members of the group are encouraged to make a pact with each other to die for the cause. It is the intense peer pressure and peer bonding that ensures that the majority of suicide bombers execute the pact.

Both evilness and barbarity (extreme evilness), whether attached to an individual (for example, Adolf Hitler, Joseph Stalin, Abimael Guzman and Mao Tse-tung) or collectivity (for example, some acts of the Third Reich, Soviet Union, Peru's Shining Path, and the Chinese Communist Party), are subject to disagreement. Moreover, describing someone as evil begs the question 'so what is good?' Hitler, Stalin, Guzman and Mao are still viewed by some as national heroes and role models for fanatics although they were responsible for the deaths of tens-of-millions of people, many of whom were their fellow citizens. Suicide bombers are frequently inculcated with the idea that their killings are so meritorious that they will be lavishly rewarded in the afterlife, and are martyred in the present life by their communities. Convicted killers, even those who have been found guilty of multiple murders, make friends and even get married whilst in prison to people who presumably find decent qualities in them.

Perceptions of evilness also depend on who is considered responsible. Is it the individual who actually performs killings such as executions and suicide bombings, the person who gives the orders, or both? In countries where the death penalty operates, it is not the morality of the executioner that is scrutinised, but that of government and legal officials who endorse its use or do not utilise their powers of compassion.

Is evil inherited or inculcated? If evil people are born that way, is their evilness a somatic aberration whereby a specific gene or genes have mutated dysfunctionally, or an evolutionary ('atavistic') throwback where in some pre-historic cave it performed a use for the individual and their cave-dwelling clan? On the other hand, is evil the result of unfortunate experiences and iniquitous associations? That is, being in the wrong location (for example: a child in an abusive family; a soldier caught up in a spate of rape and mutilation), or having dubious friends (for example: belonging to a street gang or political party that increasingly indulges in violent conduct under the influence of a charismatic leader; having a series of intimate partners whose own attitudes and behaviours model malevolence).

Whether bad people have a genetic/evolutionary drive or are socialised into evilness, the implication is that their thoughts and actions are determined (by biology or culture). However, the notion of a free will to be bad or good is enshrined in virtually all religious faiths and criminal laws as a 'moral choice'. But morality, and therefore evilness, is not an absolute. The suicide bomber or terrorist who maims and murders innocent bystanders, the army general or government leader who accepts 'collateral damage' of non-combatants during war is judged as immoral by those affected by their actions but ethically principled by their supporters because they are fighting a 'just cause'. The powerful describe their enemies as 'evil' to justify war.

What makes any moral dilemma for the powerful, and those who conduct killing on their behalf, more palatable is modern warfare. The management of morality is much easier from a distance, perhaps only viewing the death scene virtually, than being next to one's adversary when life is extinguished. As the former British war correspondent and independent Member of Parliament Martin Bell observes:

> The sole remaining superpower [the USA] seeks out its enemies and blasts them with the firepower of its missiles, drones, long-range bombers and carrier-based aircraft . . . Too bad about the collateral damage and the needless taking of life. The higher the warplanes fly, the harder it is for their pilots to distinguish between a friend and a foe, an allied and an enemy reconnaissance vehicle (Iraq), a tank and a tractor (Kosovo), a terrorist cell and a wedding party (Afghanistan).
>
> (Bell, 2003, p. 4)

Bell comments that the powerful use opposing terms to separate their morality from that of their enemies (for example, the USA carries out 'surgical strikes' within cities whereas al-Qaeda conducts 'atrocities' against harmless civilians).

The labels of 'goodness' and 'badness' can, therefore, be interchangeable for political reasons. Moral hierarchies of nations can be reformed, with some deemed atypically good or bad. In the US President's State of the Union Address in 2002, George W. Bush redeemed former 'bad' regimes, Afghanistan (which was helped along the road of redemption by Western military might) and Pakistan (which was rewarded with the promise of increased trade and political recognition by the West), but degraded others:

> States like these [Iraq, Iran and North Korea] and their terrorist allies, constitute an *axis of evil*, arming to threaten the peace of the world. By seeking weapons of mass destruction, these regimes pose a grave and growing danger. They could provide these arms to terrorists, giving them the means to match their hatred. They could attack our allies or attempt to blackmail the United States. [Emphasis added]

It is also incredibly easy to override biological and cultural predispositions when morality is constructed by an authority figure. Stanley Milgram (1963, 1974) conducted social psychology experiments at Yale University on obedience and aggression that have become famous for demonstrating how easy it is to induce 'evil' behaviour. Ordinary men and women were recruited to help in what they were told was a study of memory. The recruits were instructed by an authority figure (that is, the experimenter) that they were to play the role of a 'teacher', and every time the 'pupil' (a stooge) made a mistake, they had to give him an electric shock. This the teachers did. The majority of teachers went on to increase the voltage to a lethal level despite the protestations of the pupils and their sincere belief that they were inflicting great pain. Electric shocks continued to be administered in some cases after the pupil was thought to have died.

Dave Grossman (1996) makes the point that if this kind of obedience could be obtained by someone wearing a laboratory coat and holding a clipboard (who has been known for only a few minutes), then military techniques of conditioning and bonding will be far more effective. When, in 1968, Lieutenant William Calley during the Vietnam war ordered the soldiers under his command to enter the village of My Lai and kill women and children, the order was at first not obeyed. Calley then went with his men back to the village demanding that they open fire and commenced the massacre himself of five hundred civilians. As with suicide bombers, argues Grossman, it is the powerful sense of accountability to their comrades that gets soldiers to fight, endanger their own lives and, occasionally, behave atrociously.

The ordinariness of evil is underscored by Hannah Arendt's interview with the Nazi Second World War criminal, Adolph Eichmann (1963). Arendt's assessment of Eichman was that, as a bureaucrat in the Nazi systematised murder of millions, he was not a monster, nor a fanatic, nor even aggressive. She found him banal. His excuse for the mass butchery of human life was also mundane. In what has become a discredited defence cliché, Eichmann maintained that he was only 'following orders'. Arendt's conclusion is that everyone has the potential to behave as heinously as Eichmann.

Philip Zimbardo's (1971) social-psychology experiment did provide evidence of how otherwise decent people can be transformed into persecutors. Zimbardo's work goes some way to explain how the ideologues of the Third Reich instilled cruelty into otherwise ordinary Germans. Goldhagen (1997) estimates that half a million Germans became 'Hitler's willing executioners', exterminating six million Jews. A group of everyday university students were divided, and told to role-play either prison guards or prisoners under gaol-like conditions. In less than half of the two-week period the researchers had allotted for the experiment it had to be abandoned. The 'guards' had become tyrannical and sadistic, and the 'prisoners' depressed and anxious.

Accepting that there isn't unanimous agreement over what is evil, and demonstrating how effortlessly people can be socialised into evilness, does not preclude the possibility some people really are evil. Michael Stone (reported in Leake, 2005), Professor of Psychiatry at Columbia University in New York, attempted to discover why 500 US and British serial killers committed murder. Stone concluded that madness could be verified for some of these serial killings, but for others, no extenuating reason could be found. These killers fantasised about killing. They rationally decided to kill. They gained pleasure from killing. They are evil.

The psychopath, however, transcends and thereby muddles the boundary between madness and badness. Psychopathy is a medicalised idiom for a series of traits, including: selfishness, cruelty, an absence of empathy, manipulativeness, impulsiveness, no remorse for actions taken, or fear of their consequences. As Robert Hare (1999) illustrates, these symptoms occur in a range of characters, not just the infamous murderer. For example, artists, confidence tricksters and sexual predators (ranging from violent male rapists to women deliberately setting out to get pregnant without consulting their chosen mate) could be considered psychopaths.

Psychopathy for Blair, Mitchell and Blair (2005) is at root an emotional disorder that can lead to extreme and instrumental anti-social behaviours. They calculate that psychopathy is prevalent in about half of male prisoners and a third of female prisoners throughout the world. The incidence of psychopathy in the community is approximated at 0.75% of the male population (data on females is unreliable). However, Blair et al. acknowledge the inadequacies of contemporary diagnostic tools and systems of classification for psychopathy (for which there are a number of competitors), and their own claim for a biological cause is less than definitive:

> While we are confident that there is a genetic basis to the emotional component of psychopathy, which genes are involved and what they are specifically affecting remains basically unknown.
>
> (Blair et al., 2005, p. 155)

The main problem, however, with the concept of the psychopath is that no matter how scientifically based it is, it remains a descriptive label for patterns of emotions and behaviours, not a robust explanatory genus of human pathology. These patterns, whether they relate to recurrent self-centredness or to excessive aggression, occur in the population at large. But they usually only become noticed when something catastrophic happens like a murder. Then a psychological assessment might be made that could throw up a high score on the psychopathic checklist of choice. If brain scanning is also possible (that is, if the subject agrees to participate in medical assessment and the technology is available) a neurological pathology may be spotted.

However, neither the checklist nor the scanner can prove causation. Nor can any results from checklists and scanners of a limited and skewed sample group be generalised to the global population of psychopaths.

Besides these difficulties, there remains the controversy over whether or not psychopathy is a bona fide madness, and hence subject to psychiatric intervention in the form of treatment and/or incarceration (Morrall, 2000). The psychopath is not deranged by psychosis or disabled by neurosis, and nor is psychopathy necessarily part of the dubious grouping of madnesses it is usually associated with, 'personality disorders' (Blair et al., 2005).

But psychopaths are not normal. Crucially, they are 'without conscience' (Hare, 1999), and humans usually have a conscience along with consciousness. That's largely what makes them human – animals do not have ethical codes (certainly not ones that they have bothered to write down, or chat about openly). What, therefore, is the psychopath? Idiosyncratically mad or unpalatably bad? Or mad *and* bad?

It is not, however, sufficient to describe a murderer (whether psychopathic or not) as mad or bad in order to resolve the question of 'why commit murder'. Just as ascertaining a motive doesn't go far enough and leads to consideration of madness and badness, so reasons for the madness and badness need to be explored.

FAULTY INDIVIDUALS

Biology

An interesting but in retrospect bizarre beginning to the study of biological causes of criminality came from the anthropologist Cesare Lombroso (1876). Lombroso argued that normal humans during their life-time experience all of the stages that the species has undergone in its process of evolution. Abnormal behaviour was thus a throw-back to a previous primitive juncture in the history of humankind. According to Lombroso, atavism can be observed in individual physiognomy (sloping foreheads, oversized jaws and cheek bones, protruding ears, oversized arms, large orbital cavities, abnormal genitalia, excessive hairiness and extra toes, fingers and nipples) and in certain extreme habits (excessive indolence, tattooing and a love of orgies).

Whilst someone with an atavistic body and an odd lifestyle may still be stereotyped by the public as mad or bad, contemporary biological criminology looks for abnormalities in brain structure, biochemicals, and genes. Biological explanations have been rejuvenated through spectacular scientific advances in genetic mapping, brain scanning/imaging technology and biochemistry.

The primitive limbic structures of the human are the sites for innate aggression. When a response to an aggressive stimulus (for example, a physical or verbal attack) commences, specifically in the amygdala, it is normally 'supervised' by the higher-order areas of the frontal lobes. Impulsive behaviours, such as those of predatory or violent nature, are blocked, moderated or, after inspection, allowed to continue. Primitive urges may, after inspection by the frontal lobes, be allowed to surface if their effect is socially acceptable (for example, during certain sports aggression is indispensable) or necessary for self-protection (Hickey, 2003).

Damage to the frontal regions, has been linked to serious sexual abuse or murder (Ashcroft, 1999). Evidence from experiments on animal and brain scanning of humans, demonstrate that damage to and disease of this part of the cerebrum increases impulsivity, anger and anxiety. On the other hand, if the neurological ties from the amygdala to the frontal lobes are severed, this can lead to blunting or complete absence of emotion.

There is, for Daniel Goleman (1996), 'emotional hijacking' by the amygdala of the cerebral emotional control mechanisms. This can lead to, for Goleman, emotional outbursts with horrendous consequences. He cites a burglary that became a murder at the time in 1963 when Martin Luther King was giving his 'I have a Dream' speech. Unexpectedly, one of the two young women who owned the apartment being robbed by chronic heroin user Richard Robles was at home (Janice Wylie), and the other (Emily Hoffert) was to return during the robbery:

> As Robles tells the tale years later, while he was tying up Hoffert, Janice Wylie warned him he would not get away with this crime. She would remember his face and help the police track him down. Robles . . . panicked at that, completely losing control. In a frenzy, he grabbed a soda bottle and clubbed the women until they were unconscious, then awash with rage and fear, he slashed and stabbed them over and over with a kitchen knife . . . Robles lamented 'I just went bananas. My head just exploded'.
>
> (Goleman, 1996, pp. 14–15).

It is the amygdala, acting as a neurological tripwire, that springs preconscious and hence non-premeditated reactions to threats. Of course, instantaneous reaction is required where the threat is grave. Fright and flight mechanisms are essential in an unsafe world. But, for Goleman, these survival techniques are used too often and inappropriately in our daily lives, leading to difficulties in personal and social relationships. Exceptionally, and thankfully, only when the brain has been seriously traumatised, catastrophe such as murder can be the outcome of our primal (limbic) brain bypassing our civilised (frontal) brain.

Empirical evidence for the effect on emotion of one of the body's neurochemicals, serotonin, is strong. A reduction of serotonin increases the likelihood of spur-of-the-moment and hostile impulses. Low serotonin is also related to the occurrence of depression. Research has correlated testosterone, the male sex hormone, with competitive and assertive behaviour. Alterations in the breakdown of glucose in the body also appear to affect mood and deeds. Both hyperglycaemia and hypoglycaemia can lead to aggression. Alcohol in the bloodstream undermines higher-order control exercised by the cerebral cortex. Environmental pollutants circulating in the body (for example, pesticides and lead) are linked to heightened aggression (Hickey, 2003).

What became known as the 'Speck theory' (after Richard Speck who murdered eight student nurses in the USA in 1966) pointed to an extra 'Y' sex chromosome in men (whose normal sex chromosome make-up is XY) causing increased violence. Unfortunately for the Speck theorists, their conclusion came out of research on only violent men. When a valid sampling procedure was used by later researchers the prevalence of violence amongst men with XYY was no higher than that of XY men (Pincus, 2002).

The mapping of the human genome began earnestly in the late twentieth century and was completed early in the twenty-first century. Its potential to offer a causative bond between virtually all human thoughts, actions, dispositions and medical conditions has been hyped by the media and scientists. Martin Rees (2005), President of the Royal Society, declared: 'Probably the most significant scientific development of the 21st century so far has been the mapping of the entire sequence of human genes.'

The expectation is that a gene, or blend of genes, can be found that triggers off, for example, homosexuality, schizophrenia, depression, alcoholism, most cancers, heart failure, optimism and pessimism, intelligence and criminality. As yet, much of the promise of a 'genetic theory of everything' is unfulfilled with even Rees (M. Rees, 2005) accepting that it will be many years before the genetic revolution will materialise.

Certainly, some habits and diseases do run in families. Studies of twins and adopted children have assessed the relationship between genetic inheritance and criminality. However, after decades of research, evidence of this relationship is inconclusive, and due to the small number of available subjects to study has to be treated circumspectly. Some people may inherit criminality from their biological parents, but the impetus to actually become a criminal is either curbed or encouraged by their social environment (Brookman, 2005).

The brain cannot be conceived as empty of genetic influence at birth, a *tabula rasa*. But this does not mean that genes cause violence in any linear and easily understood fashion. There may be genetic risk factors in an individual. However, these will interplay with their biochemical as well as psychological aspects (such as a cognitive ability to reason that violence is not appropriate) and the social environment.

It is accurate to state that men kill far more commonly than women, and their biology (and psychology) may play an important part in why this happens. But, there is little if any difference between the brain structure, biochemicals and genes of men across the world (as well as any inherited aspects of the male psyche). Why then is there such a massive difference in the murder rate from one country to another? This must be largely accountable for by cultural variation (Hickey, 2003).

The evidence for serotonin as a source of violence is not conclusive, notwithstanding the hundreds of studies that have been carried out on the topic. People who have low serotonin levels may not be violent. Nor does every excessively belligerent (or exceedingly miserable) individual have low serotonin levels. Furthermore, how can low serotonin levels cause violence *and* depression? They are poles apart as human conditions. Significantly, the question over cause and effect has not been answered adequately (Pincus, 2002). Whilst violence may be correlated with low serotonin, does the low serotonin cause the effect of violence (and depression), or does violence lead to a decrease in serotonin, or are they simply idiosyncratic biological bedfellows.

Neo-evolution

> 'Boys are made to squirt and girls are made to lay eggs. And if the truth be known, boys don't very much care what they squirt into'. Crude though it may be, Gore Vidal's pithy quote neatly sums up the argument for evolutionary psychology.
>
> (Malik, 1998, p. 1)

Charles Darwin's theory of evolution has been applied to contemporary human behaviour by psychologists, and rebranded as 'evolutionary psychology' (it is also known as neo-evolutionary theory). Evolutionary psychology is entwined inexorably with biological presumptions about human existence (socio-biology was its epistemological ancestor), because the mode of transmission of human traits for supporters of this perspective is either primarily or wholly genetic inheritance. Hence, evolutionary psychology is distinguishable from the social evolutionary approach, which focuses on how human behaviour is transmitted through culture, and shares the pitfalls of biological determinism.

The broad neo-evolutionary perspective is underpinned by the biology of criminality. The premises of evolutionary psychology are: human behaviour has ancient biologic origins; the psychological attributes of humans have undergone natural selection over thousands of years; human behaviour today is the outcome of prolonged adaptive improvement; any behaviour that helps reproductive success is selected and carried over into the next generation (Hickey, 2003). Some behaviours (for example, murder), however, are maladaptive, as they would seem to mitigate an individual's genetic graduation.

David Buss is a radical and zealous evolutionary psychologist. He has applied his version of evolutionary psychology to a number of behaviours: mating, desire, jealousy, happiness and murder. In Buss's intriguing book *The murderer next door* (2005), he extols the neo-evolutionary approach to understanding murder to the exclusion of all other perspectives, and turns round the customary question about humans killing humans from 'why commit murder?' to 'why commit so few murders?'. In doing so, he is claiming that far from murder arising from a defect in the individual, it is a normal trait.

Buss begins by revealing that in cross-cultural research he conducted involving thousands of respondents, the vast majority of people (more men than women) fantasise about killing other humans. These fantasies, according to Buss, are vivid, detailed and frequently erotic. For Buss, killing is a core element of human nature because in evolutionary terms it serves a purpose. Specifically, it is advantageous to reproduction. It is an adaptive strategy. Murder, therefore, is inherently logical. The mind is designed to murder.

The gains for killing, argues Buss, are: the killer has not been killed and therefore can reproduce; augmenting his (and it usually is a man) own survival and the death of a reproductive rival, he can have sex with the dead man's mate, and take his property; it scares the hell out of any other would-be antagonist; he is immediately converted into a sexually attractive partner for admiring females; he has displayed another attribute that these doting but vulnerable women need, protection from predatorial males (presumably, also from dinosaurs and other marauding beasties).

Buss is, in the end, debunked by his own proposition. He argues vehemently that murder is evolutionarily functional and should be more common than it is. But the fact that it isn't common, and humans have progressed biologically and culturally so radically without it being common, means that the proposition is probably wrong, not probably right. That is, he can't have it both ways. Murder can't be necessary to evolution if evolution continues so effectively without it being much more prevalent. Murder is maladaptive not adaptive.

More damning to Buss's theory is his simplistic assertion that most murderers are clinically sane and hence they understand that what they are doing is morally wrong and illegal. Most murderers may not be insane according to strict psychiatric diagnosis. But the majority (besides exceptions such as the highly instrumental contract killer), are in a state of emotional turmoil and/or are cognitively impaired when they murder. Young men killing young men in a street fights, mothers killing their children, lovers killing their lovers, may be aware that what they are doing is unacceptable morally and legally, but are in the main not acting rationally. The psychopath is also emotionally disordered – the emotions are absent or inappropriate.

Buss does try to get round this dilemma for his theory by asserting that the rationality in murder is genetic success. The murderer is making a calculation about the risks of being constrained reproductively versus reproductive gains. Presumably, given the high conviction rate for murder, there is need for further evolutionary development so that assessing this risk becomes more accurate or the ability to get away with murder becomes more finely tuned.

Yet another fallacy in Buss's evolutionary-psychology of murder is his unjustified conflation of two separate phenomena, fantasy and reality. Buss's link between occasional rumination about killing by everyone to actual murder by a few is an *exaggeration ad absurdum*. Moreover, why is the reverse not true? Couldn't the prevalence of thoughts about killing be the reason why the murder rate is low (low as far as this evolutionary psychologist is concerned).

Nancy Friday (1976, 1993, 2003) has argued that vivid, violent and morally dubious sexual fantasies that occur in both men and women are not related to what then becomes sexual practice. Sexual fantasy is both a release to sexual tension and a stimulus to socially acceptable sexual activity. Although excessive and lurid ruminating about killing has been found amongst certain murderers (Hyatt-Williams, 1998), murder fantasies for the majority of people may well serve the same purpose as erotic thoughts. Furthermore, ruminating about murder for the majority of humans can only be one of the countless trillions of thoughts they have during their lives. Virtually all human thought, therefore, is not about murder. As a consequence, the absence of both murderous thoughts and murderous actions has assisted evolution, not the opposite.

Lastly, unlike many other evolutionary psychologists, Buss doesn't account for the evolutionary function of altruism. The existence of altruism has, even within his discipline, always constrained those who would otherwise reduce all human behaviour to primary selfish drives. Humans cooperate with other humans far more often than they fantasise about trying to kill them. The individual's evolutionary propulsion is to maintain their life form, either through direct self-protection measures or by ensuring that their genes are propagated. To do so, humans compete with other humans (as well as the natural world), but also have to collaborate with others. That is, there exists in the human condition both selfishness and altruism.

Peter Singer, director of the Centre for Human Bioethics at Monash University, describes the predicament of individuals when they have to decide whether or not to cooperate (the so-called 'prisoner dilemma'):

> The prisoner dilemma describes a situation in which two people can each choose whether or not to cooperate with each other. The catch is that each does better, individually, by not cooperating; but if both make this choice, they will be both worse off than they would have been if they had not pursued their own interest. The individual pursuit of self-interest can be collectively self-defeating.
>
> (Singer, 1998, p. 29)

Singer goes on to illustrate how many of us have to contend daily with a version of the 'prisoner dilemma'. When travelling to work by car, we are participating in behaviours that affect detrimentally fellow commuters and the community at large. That is, we help to create traffic jams, pollute the environment and collude with others in an inefficient method of conveying people from home to their place of employment. If we were to make the decision to use public transport, the road would be less congested and the air cleaner. However, not only do we wish that all of our fellow car drivers would use buses and trains so that our journey by car would be made easier, but we also recognise that unless a substantial number of commuters switch to public transport, there will be little investment in these services to make them a suitable alternative. We are all, therefore, caught in a trap of waiting for the other person to make the move. Human existence, therefore, requires a balance to be struck between the survival of the gene-formulations of the human subject and the social relationships and institutions that assist that survival. Survival is dependent on being helpful and being helped. This is especially necessary in a globalising world where cultural, economic and technological interdependence is exacerbated.

Turning the question 'why commit murder?' into 'why not commit more murder?' has not neutered the quest for an answer to human destructiveness. Human violence would seem to be far too risky for genetic survival than aspiring to peaceful co-existence.

A more temporate strand of evolutionary psychology than that formulated by Buss is offered by Martin Daly and Margo Wilson (1988, 1999). From their analysis of who kills and who gets killed, they have produced what they describe as 'conflict typologies'. These conflict typologies consider the relationship between the victim and the killer. Murders are, for Daly and Wilson, invariably about young men attempting to gain dominance over each other, women attempting to gain independence from proprietary partners or ex-partners, and the disposing of children by those entrusted with their care.

Like Buss, Daly and Wilson postulate that violence is not necessarily a pathological behaviour. Humans, along with many other animals, are designed to deal with, and enact, violence. This they do for self-protection and to survive in situations where resources and breeding opportunities are scarce. Challenging the sociological structural theories of crime (which predicate murder on such factors as economic disparity, social strain and social disorganisation), Daly and Wilson argue that, in some societies (for example, tribal communities), it is those at the top of the social hierarchy who are the most violent. Here, violence is used to maintain dominance for an elite and stability for the community, rather than as a reaction by the disempowered to social inequality and decay.

Although not wishing (as Buss does) to posit that murder is intrinsically and wholly an evolved behaviour that enables humans to adapt to their environment and reproduce successfully, Daly and Wilson do claim that violence is connected to self-interest. That is, murder *may* assist the murderer's genetic survival rather than *does* give the murderer reproductive advantage. In that cautious vein, they provide an evolutionary account for some common murders. Specifically, they argue that the presence of step-parents in 'reconstituted' families increases the risk of child abuse and killings as the result of an imbalance in the investment/benefit ratio. That is, unlike the case with biological parents, step-parents have no genetic pay-off for their material and emotional input into the rearing of dependent children.

Moreover, for Daly and Wilson, murder between sexual partners is more likely when there is evidence or suspicion of infidelity. This is especially the case when it is the woman who has been seen by the man to have undermined his genetic potential by engaging in sexual activity with other men.

Men killing unrelated men, for Daly and Wilson, occurs quite obviously (to the neo-evolutionist) because of competition between men over mating and mating related acquisitions. That is, murder may be the outcome of contests concerning sexual partners, or elements of social status (for example, material possessions and money) that enhance sexual attraction. These conflicts may be immediate or long term. A fatality may be the result of a 'spontaneous' nightclub brawl between men over a prospective girlfriend, or the higher rate of murder amongst people at the lower end of the social system may be grounded in feelings of retribution aimed at an unfair society.

However, the reduction of human behaviour to evolution (or biology) ignores the differences in cultural manifestations of behaviour and contexts for behaviour. Moreover, concentrating on any one behaviour (for example, murder) amplifies the significance of that behaviour:

> Crimes of violence are more frequently carried out by men than women . . . One may argue that this says something about the Y chromosome, carried by men and not women, but the overwhelming majority of men are not violent criminals . . . Violent crime is much higher in the USA than in Europe – higher, for instance than in Britain, and much higher than in Sweden. Could this be accounted for by some unique feature of the American genotype? Well, possibly, but pretty unlikely, since much of the American population originated by migration from Europe. But also the rates of violent crime change dramatically over quite short time periods.
>
> (Rose, 1997, p. 298)

Crucially, evolutionary psychologists and their biological bed-fellows erroneously conflate male violence with violence per se. Bjorkqvist and Niemelä (1992) argue that if a less a male-orientated view of violence is taken, then women may be as aggressive as men. In particular, they argue women are more verbally hostile than men (using put-downs, rumour and gossip as their weapons). Historical examples of female violence equivalent to that of men include: the semi-naked 'Amazons' who fought French foreign legionnaires during the Dahomey expedition in the nineteenth century; the Vietcong women who fought US soldiers in the Vietnam War in the twentieth century (Grossman, 1996); the guerrilla and revolutionary wars of both nineteenth and twentieth centuries that have had women fighting (and killing) alongside men (Dyer, 1985).

Most indicted war criminals have been men. But there are examples of villainous women whose behaviour during conflicts resembles the worst of men's callousness. Irma Grese is one of these women. Grese was born in Germany, 1923. She became a Nazi. In 1943, at the age of 19, she was sent to work first at the Ravensbruk Concentration Camp, then later that year to Auschwitz, and finally to Bergen-Belsen early in 1945. At Auschwitz, Grese became a senior supervisor in charge of about 30000 female prisoners, who were mainly of Polish or Hungarian origin. Here she beat with a whip and stick, tortured, sexually abused, set dogs on to and murdered prisoners in cold-blood, and helped in their selection for the gas chambers. Grese was convicted of war crimes in a British military court held at Luneburg and hanged in December, 1945.

To date, female aggression has, notwithstanding the above examples, been less physically violent than that of men. But this may not be an unalterable constant. As women gain male privileges in terms of power and freedom then they may take on other male patterns. This masculinisation of women in the West has affected rates of smoking and alcohol consumption, so why not violence?

Psychology

There is a wide variety of theories that attempt to detect defects in the psychological disposition of the individual which may lead to violence, although most offer only tangential insights into murder. Such is that variety that contradictions abound, and some have a far greater level of intricacy than others. A few are so convoluted that their veracity is doubtful or at least unverifiable. The most implausible (psychoanalytical) is one that has theorised the most directly about murder.

At the more straightforward end of the spectrum are those that attribute violence to faulty learning. For example, behavioural psychology posits that humans (and animals) learn how to respond to others and the environment through 'reinforcers' and 'eliminators' (Smith, Nolen-Hoeksema, Fredrickson & Loftus, 2003). These act to encourage or discourage behaviour. They help to formulate 'learned responses'. For example, reinforcers could be: a parent smiling at each developmental accomplishment of their child; extra remuneration given to an employee from their boss for completing a task well; a cigarette given to a psychiatric in-patient in the days of institutionalised care after they have got out of bed. Eliminators include: simply ignoring 'bad' behaviour; punishments like smacking, verbal attacks and imprisonment. This, argue the behaviourists, is how violence becomes a learned response. An individual may behave violently because of the reward it brings, such as affirmation by significant others (for example, parents and peers). The 'aggressive' tantrum of the child in the supermarket is quelled for the moment by the parent with the prize of a chocolate bar. This then provides the incentive to behave in the same way over and over again.

Moreover, the 'frustration-aggression hypothesis' suggests that this is how some children, who in later life may become violent, have not learned to cope with the delays, disappointments and dissatisfactions of life. Their immediate reaction is the equivalent of the child in the supermarket. They scream, punch, and perhaps go as far as kill if their needs are thwarted. As adults, however, certain cognitive stages may be gone through after the frustration induces anger but before violence is the outcome: preparation to use violence, which might entail selecting a weapon; mulling over of how much the person perceived to be responsible for the frustration meant to cause that frustration; further deliberation over the amount of harm to inflict and the possible consequences (Berkowitz, 1989).

'Social learning theory' is wonderfully straightforward. Social learning theory assumes that we learn from other people – now that's what I call a theory! By observing and listening to, for example, our parents, siblings, friends and characters in the media, we pick up behaviours and make them our own. If your parents, siblings, friends and idols are all criminals and your favourite television programmes, films and computer games contain criminal heroes, then you might adopt a number of criminal habits. The higher the status of the person who is modelling the behaviour, the more that behaviour will be reinforced. This reinforcement would then be exacerbated if you were sent to prison because the models for you are largely fellow criminals. Prisons therefore aren't very appropriate places to try to rehabilitate criminals. Social learning theorist Albert Bandura (1983), who argues that socialisation has the biggest influence on human behaviour, states the blindingly obvious when he comments that humans also think. He accepts that humans make decisions for themselves, albeit within a social context. A person can therefore 'think' that murder is not such a good idea, despite having read about it and watched it happen thousands of times as entertainment and experienced violence regularly in their community.

It is the 'thinking' element of being human that is the greatest weakness in these 'learning' theories (that is, behaviourism, frustration-aggression and social learning). Lip-service is paid to thought but overall humans are viewed as being conditioned by their social environment. This under-accounting of human free will to determine how to behave is challenged from within psychology by cognitive perspectives.

One cognitive perspective is Lawrence Kohlberg's (1969) 'moral development theory'. This is a six-stage model identifying the progress of decision making over what is right and what is wrong as humans grow up. Kohlberg's six stages of moral development are:

1. What is right is to be obedient to those in power, and avoid punishment.

2. What is right is taking responsibility for oneself, as others must do so for themselves.

3. What is right is having good motives, and being able to be empathic towards others.

4. What is right is respecting the rules and needs of a society.

5. What is right is based on a balance between individual rights and the needs of society (the social contract).

6. What is right are universal principles of justice and equality for all, and respect for all human life.

Criminals, argues Kohlberg, get stuck in the 'selfish' stages of moral development, particularly the second stage. However, at each stage an individual chooses what the consequences are to engagement with crime. These may be punishment or approbation from family and friends. However, how accurately these stages correspond with criminal careers is debatable. Any measurement of this relationship would have to accept the soundness of the model in the first place. But then it is probable if moral development and criminality does correlate, then this is no more than a tautology. What other than immoral are criminals? It isn't much of an insight to find that people who steal, rape, and kill think mainly of themselves unless the penalty for not doing so outweighs the benefits. Nevertheless, cognitive psychology does address thinking (and that's another tautology). However, it doesn't propound explanations about murder.

Cognitive-behavioural psychology brings thinking, behaviour and emotion together. The ways in which we perceive our experiences and behave towards them, the cognitive-behavioural therapist argues, produce either helpful or destructive behaviours, including emotions (Smith et al., 2003). Changing our thinking alters what we do and/or how we feel about what we do. As a psychotherapy, cognitive-behaviourism can reduce the possibility of violence being the outcome of anxiety-provoking circumstances. For example, a young man who feels angry because another young man is seemingly being hostile towards him, can, with training, re-adjust this perception so that the evidence for apparent hostility is assessed. In doing so, he may feel and act very differently to otherwise becoming angry and starting a fist fight. Cognitive-behaviourism is underpinned, therefore, by the functioning of the brain, specifically, the amygdala and frontal lobes, as identified by Daniel Goleman (1996).

A psychological approach that doesn't revere 'behaviour' or 'thinking' (in the sense that neither behaviour nor expressed thought can be taken at face value), but has very much attended to murderers' emotions, is psychoanalysis. Psychoanalysis has commonality with evolutionary psychology because both consider that primary drives, such as sexuality and violence, have innate origins (Smith et al., 2003). To appreciate the psychoanalysis of murder, the conceptual framework of the founder of psychoanalysis, Sigmund Freud (1856–1939), has first to be understood. Freud reasoned that the mind had abstract structures. This interplay between the abstract structures of the mind becomes the personality of an individual. These structures are:

- The id (the unconscious biological drives for survival – food, elimination, sex and aggression); the id operates on the 'pleasure principle', wishing to avoid pain, and satisfy and enjoy the primitive drives instantly and violently if necessary, without heed to the needs of others; it is also the site of the 'death instinct', which can be regarded as the urge towards self-destructiveness although neither Freud nor his disciples have organised a clear description of this concept.

- The ego (the 'reality principle' that develops in childhood); this is the real 'self' that controls the drives of the id by responding to the needs of others and social conventions.

- The superego (the conscience and 'idealised self image', like the ego, it develops during childhood); this is the collection of moral standards handed down to the child from significant others and society.

Freud had a lot to say about violence, as did his followers. Humans for Freud are basically evil because primary drives have to be satisfied, which will be through violence unless, or until, they are conditioned by society to behave otherwise. The precept of psychoanalysis, and its broader offspring psychodynamic therapy, is that to comprehend an individual's behaviour, emotions and thinking, deep-rooted (probably emanating from early childhood) experiences have to be uncovered. This means long-lasting therapy, possibly years, unlike cognitive-behavioural therapy, which may last only hours. Somehow the id, ego, or superego is deficient (Hickey, 2003); a weak ego is not controlling the impulses of id; the conscience of the superego is either immature or absent (Hickey, 2003).

Melanie Klein (1932), one of the post-Freud gurus of psychoanalysis, argued that violence stemmed from distressing and unresolved childhood experiences. Klein concentrated on Freud's idea of humans having not only a 'pleasure principle' but also a 'death instinct'. Anxieties that can be manifested as serious psychological disorders and violence (both to others and to oneself) can be located in the destructiveness of the death instinct.

Not learning how to control destructiveness in early childhood is taken up by Duncan Cartwright (2002). He argues that a particular sort of personality is vulnerable to extremely destructive attacks of rage. This is the seemingly conventional, conservative and controlled individual who has another 'split' side. In this person there is the idealised 'real' self that they believe themselves to be, as do most of their family, friends and associates. But there is also a 'false self' that rarely gets a public airing, but when it does it contrasts tremendously with the usual way in which they behave. Rage-type murder, for Cartwright, has happened because of the perpetrator's explosive and unregulated anger. He suggests that rage-type murders often are unprovoked. They appear to be motiveless and senseless. But, significantly, the killer has 'dissociated' their 'true self' during what can be a particularly malicious killing. That is, the murderer seems to switch off from their 'real self' whilst killing and stand outside themselves, unable to recognise the 'false' self.

Cartwright gives an example of rage-type murder in which he suggests splitting and dissociation has taken place in otherwise 'ordinary' people:

A man on his way home from work became enraged with another motorist who had accidentally cut in front of him. He managed to stop his victim and after a brief exchange of insults, bludgeoned him to death with a hockey stick. The victim's skull bore the signs of repeated powerful blows to the head. In another incident, a loving father of two repeatedly stabbed his wife to death with a kitchen knife after she had refused his embrace. The report claims that the couple had decided to separate a week prior to the murder. In a final example, a successful businessman turned his gun on his family after a quarrel with his wife. He shot all but one of his family members in a spray of bullets and then attempted to turn the gun on himself.

(Cartwright, 2002, p. 4)

Cartwright points out that in the cases he cites, none of the perpetrators had a history of violence or mental disorder. All were considered psychologically balanced. No motives or levels of provocation could be found to readily excuse the murderers. Cartwright concludes that it is the collapse of 'narcissistic defences' which best explains rage-type murders. The over-controlled personality is intensely shamed by what to others would seem like either a minor infringement of the integrity of the true self, or not sufficient to warrant an excessively violent reaction to protect that self. The disproportionate response of murder is the false self annihilating a threat that might otherwise annihilate their true self. It could, therefore, be regarded as 'self defence'.

Cartwright has been influenced heavily by the work of Arthur Hyatt-Williams (1998), who began the psychoanalytic examination of 'rage-type' murder. Although Hyatt-William's overuse of jargon is worse even than Cartwright's, he has made a stimulating contribution to theorising about murder which is born out of 30 years of dealing with violent offenders. Hyatt-Williams believes that whilst these murderers appear normal, going further than Cartwright's concept of a dual personality, they have a 'criminal personality'. The criminal personality exists in a psychological position between neurosis and psychosis. The neurotic element is unduly narcissistic and protective, and the psychotic element unduly dehumanising of others. When the individual shifts towards psychosis (entering what Hyatt-Williams calls 'paranoid-schizoid crisis'), then a violent attack on a now dehumanised victim might transpire. What Hyatt-Williams found in the murderers he treated was that they had intra-psychic 'constellations of undigested murderous fantasies':

> Some years ago I was asked to give dynamic psychotherapy to a man who had been convicted of murdering another man. The patient had been sentenced to death and reprieved, with the sentence commuted to life imprisonment. Later I was asked to treat several more men serving life sentences for murder. What struck me most was the presence in the mind of the convicted murderer of a constellation of fantasies, dreams, thoughts, impulses, and ruminations to do with killing, annihilating, and obliterating.
>
> (Hyatt-Williams, 1998, p. 25)

What he also found was that these constellations were, in cruel and violent individuals, associated with the 'indigestible fear of death'. These undigested fantasies and indigestible fears formed a 'latent murderousness'. The latent murderousness became actual murder whenever the individual experienced extreme persecution. That is, whenever the person with the criminal personality had feelings of impending death at the hands of another person, then that person would be killed. The killers were terrified of death, and to avoid their own death they had to precipitate death in others:

> Murderousness as an evacuation of an indigestible fear of death began to crystallize in my mind. The battered baby who became the killer of a man who threatened to annihilate him physically (not his father, but a substitute) acted in panic and fear of his own death, but his reaction was potentiated by anger and revenge displaced upon somebody standing in the place of his cruel father.
>
> (Hyatt-Williams, 1998, p. 43)

However, all varieties of psychoanalytical-psychodynamic theory have the same deep-seated problem arising from Freud's work. That is, there is a basic circularity of reasoning. For example, Hyatt-Williams (1998) accepts that having a criminal personality does not need to lead to murder. Employing our old friend teleology again, he suggests that if the relevant factors do not 'constellate' in a seriously threatening way to the individual then a dangerous emotional outburst will not ensue. Moreover, although Freudian ideas are commonplace in Western thought long after the death of their creator, there remains a paucity of proof available to support these ideas. Some are widely accepted as having veracity (for example, the role of the unconscious in human thinking, behaviour, and emotions). But most remain inspired but decidedly obscure abstractions (Smith et al., 2003).

FAULTY SOCIETY

Social Evolution

Neo-evolutionary theory has biology as the driving force for individual and cultural change. Anthropology, however, takes a different causative root, that of culture being the predominant influence on how people behave and on their ways of living in groups. Culture becomes both the expression of collective life and the catalyst for social change. For example, the spread of Western capitalism, along with mass electronic communications and entertainment systems, has had the effect of globalising culture. The concomitant values of capitalism (principally, state-organised education, the work ethic and material possession) are to be found in the vast majority of countries, either already in place or as essential for economic and social survival.

What the social evolutionists have observed is that aggression and violence differ greatly across cultures. This variation is dependent on the level of social evolution of that culture. However, unlike the neo-evolutionists, who see humans becoming more adept at adjusting to their social and physical environment in a progressive direction (that is, modern humans are biologically 'better' than cave dwellers), the social evolutionists try to avoid making prejudicial judgements about which culture is superior. A 'primitive' tribe is not automatically inferior to twenty-first-century USA just because its people are hunters (including fishing) and gatherers rather than 'sophisticated' consumers of a never-ending catalogue of commodities. This is also true for violence (Hickey, 2003).

Some hunters and gatherers are tremendously violent, for example the Yanomamo of the Amazon rainforests in Brazil and Venezuela live in a constant state of warfare with other tribes (Hickey, 2003), and the Waorani of Ecuador rainforest, who killed not only their enemies and outsiders, but also regularly murdered their own people (Robarchek & Robarchek, 1998). But hunting and gathering societies generally, unless serving a specific and contained ritualistic purpose, tend to abhor violence (especially murder). Today's Western societies, particularly the USA, would seem to revel in violence. What early human groups (and those few still in existence) required to survive was peaceful cooperation not fierce competitiveness. Examples of those that have been studied by anthropologists and found to have low levels of violence are: the Fore of New Guinea, the Semai of Malaysia and the !Kung Bushmen of the Kalahari Desert. These tribes have no social hierarchy or division of labour, minimal wealth creation and personal possessions, a dislike of anger and non-violent mechanisms for sorting out interpersonal disputes (Hickey, 2003).

The intricate rules of tribal society ensure that people work together in order to obtain food, water, shelter and to procreate. It is largely only when faced with a depletion of these resources, because of the growth in their own numbers and those of nearby tribes, that warfare might be embarked upon. As human groups became more complex, inter-group rivalry became more necessary as well as more possible to organise. What also happened was that the status of violence became enhanced because it was an effective (cultural) strategy to ensure that the group's existence continued. As the status of violence rose, so did the prestige of those who were effective at being violent as well as organising violence. That process of increased complexity eventually (over tens of thousands of years) turned into political and military bureaucracies of the modern state, some of which have violent capacity to obliterate the world's population.

The temptation to criticise the violence of industrialised/post-industrialised societies whilst romanticising about pre-industrial tribes misses the point that like is not being compared with like. This is so whether the comparison is between the broader cultural contexts or the enactments of violence within those contexts.

Furthermore, the 'anthropologist's dilemma' of coming from one culture to study another, which because of its very difference makes it worthwhile to examine, has never resolved. How can, for example, a Western researcher really understand the meanings given to violence (or the lack of it) by !Kung peoples? Methodological nuances may be added to traditional techniques such as participant observation, but a series of cultural translations still have to be made, starting with what is observed and ended with the anthropological essay perhaps years later, which inevitably re-interpret what were the original events. If, and this would be rare, there was complete validity in such research (that is, the meanings given by the !Kung people to their actions and the reporting of the actions overlap), that may mean that the !Kung, in twenty-first-century countries such as Botswana, have become too much in cultural orientation like the researcher.

Social Structure

Social structure refers to the enduring configurations and divisions in society. In capitalist societies it is economic class, wealth, ethnicity, gender and age that in the main give differentiations in power. This hierarchy of power affects what is considered a crime and who is labelled a criminal (Reid, 2006). Society's elites manipulate the making of laws and how the criminal justice system works to protect their interests and to ensure that it is not they who are targeted by the police. 'Anti-social behaviour', so much the target of politicians and police in twenty-first-century Western societies, is largely associated with deviancy at the lower end of the hierarchy, not deviancy within the elite groups. Moreover, deviant acts that are possibly traceable to the conflict that exists between those with power in society and the disempowered (for example, public drunkenness and street violence) are observed using vast numbers of CCT cameras and punished more vigorously compared with the crimes of the powerful (for example, corporate homicide and environmental damage, or instigating illegal wars).

Social structural theory also comments not only on how social divisions but different social systems furnish criminality. Sandra Bloom (2001) argues that Western societies, particularly the USA, are essentially 'sick' and that this sickness is exemplified in an addiction to violence. It is society rather than individuals that propagates violence. Although enacted by individuals, the aggressive act is a consequence of the values that a society generates. Values such as those associated with actual physical violence, or competitiveness in sport and at work, are inculcated into the individual via, for example, the educational system and the media.

The long-standing debate about the effects of violent images from television, film, videos and computer games has swayed towards the side of the argument that reasons they must have an effect (Reid, 2006). However, the evidence for causal relationships between violent media images and criminal behaviour (such as homicide) is not strong. Kevin Browne and Catherine Hamilton-Giachritsis (2005), examining results from studies conducted in North America, found that regular bombardment of violent images produced a substantial if short-term negative effect on younger children. The effect was not associated with socio-economic status, family behaviour, or intelligence:

There is consistent evidence that violent imagery in television, film and video, and computer games has substantial short term effects on arousal, thoughts, and emotions, increasing the likelihood of aggressive or fearful behaviour in younger children, especially in boys.

(Browne & Hamilton-Giachritsis, 2005, p. 710)

Erich Fromm (1963) argues that it is the capitalist nature of Western society that is inherently insane. Capitalism, for Fromm, has insuperable faults that indicate social pathology: the huge social and financial cost of conducting wars to protect markets; high levels of unemployment occurring regularly as a result of the vagaries of the economic system; the 'dumbing down' of human activities, and the displacement of face-to-face relationships because of mass entertainment; the propagation of a culture of materialism and commodity fetishism; a loss of meaning to life; and an out-of-control level of crime.

From Fromm's perspective, homicide can be seen to be the outcome of specific flaws in the social and legal rules of a society. For example, the USA (and the same can be claimed of Brazil and South Africa) is, because of its lax gun controls, more prey to multiple killings and a higher rate of suicide. Moreover, it is the brand of rampant capitalism that occurs in such countries as the USA that is ultimately responsible for encouraging the possession of guns. Excessive value is placed on individuality, ownership and an unregulated market (which allows large profits to be made on the manufacturing of weapons). Furthermore, the freedom to carry arms is sanctioned not only through the values of the capitalist system, but also in the constitution of the USA. Of course some countries (and the exemplar is Switzerland) manage to have a lot of guns without these being used unduly to kill their own citizens.

Feminist ideas have added to structural analysis of violence, focusing on gender relationships. Violent acts by men against women are viewed as being contained within unequal relations of power between men and women. Feminists argue that gender-based power relations underscore all social institutions, including economic, political, educational, social, religious and familial. Moreover, when wars, civil unrest and other forms of military intervention take place (including liberation and peace-keeping) women are often subjected to exploitation and extreme violence. Women's bodies become sites for territorial conquest. They are forced into prostitution, raped, mutilated and murdered (Hickey, 2003).

The problem with social structuralism is that it is very deterministic. The individual's structural position is viewed as dynamic in the shaping of their life chances and beliefs. Personal volition is for the most part discounted. There is the implicit notion that murderers kill and victims die because of their lack of power, and there isn't much that can be done by either to avoid this scenario except wait for society to reform. Furthermore, a postmodern conceptualisation of society considers lifestyle choice, rather than social structure, as the mark of personal identity.

Social Ecology

Elie Godsi (2004) offers an explanation for violence and murder that is similar to the structuralist approach, concentrating on powerlessness in society. However, Godsi pays attention to a particular mode of powerlessness, the abuse of children. Those adults who are abusive towards others may have been abused when they were young. Neurologist, Jonathan Pincus (2002) examined and probed into the family and medical history of about 150 murderers (many of whom were serial killers) and other violent criminals to analyse what creates and triggers the violent instinct. He discovered that virtually all suffered severe abuse as a child, as well as brain damage and mental illness.

Children can themselves display cruelty. Those who deliberately and regularly harm animals may be training themselves to indulge in interpersonal violence (possibly murder) at a later age (Ascione, 2005; Lockwood & Ascione, 1998). Older children who were abused when younger may abuse other children for whom they may have temporary responsibility (for example, if left to baby-sit while parents work or go out socially).

People who are abusive, suggests Godsi, are searching for control in their lives which had been taken away from them as children through the ill-treatment they received. Emotional, physical abuse, but especially sexual abuse, could turn the abused into a schizophrenic, psychopath, or killer. Godsi looks at the life histories of violent people, and refers to the abuse experienced by a number of infamous British murderers (Mary Bell, Ian Huntley, Robert Thomson and John Venables), but he also comments on global violence, claiming that violence enters all of our lives. To understand fully interpersonal violence, he argues, what has happened to the individual perpetrator *and* what is happening in society has also to be understood as humans are affected profoundly by the social and political environment.

Godsi agrees, however, with the constructionist view on social phenomena. That is, definitions of what constitutes a violent act are not static. The meanings ascribed to particular events depend on the culture and the historical epoch in which they occur. During periods of war for example, violence is legitimised by the warring states and vicious killings may be accredited as heroic. Moreover, during wars other killings take place that are sanctioned by the state other than carried out by soldiers against the enemy. For example, during the First World War, hundreds of soldiers were executed by their own side under the directions of officers who perceived them as traitors because they refused to go on fighting. In retrospect, most of those killed in this way were probably suffering from 'shell shock' (that is, post-traumatic stress disorder). They were not cowards, but mentally ill.

Godsi's main emphasis is, however, on how the violent acts of the powerful are concealed, whereas the violence of the powerless is revealed. The powerful have, with some success, covered up their social and economic policies and corporate decisions that have resulted in serious disease and multiple deaths. For example, governments and businesses are responsible for Creutzfeldt-Jakob Disease (CJD), asbestosis and methicillin-resistant *Staphylococcus aureus* (MRSA). The tobacco and arms industries alone brought about millions of deaths in the developed countries, and continue to do so in the developing countries. For Godsi, the powerful and the governments get away with large-scale murder, whereas the dispossessed and the poor, even if they commit a small crime, and certainly if they commit violence, are considered as undermining the fabric of society.

Godsi describes his theoretical approach as 'social ecology'. But again he makes a structuralist point: if a society has an economic system based on competition this will promote aggression and suppress cooperation. A social ecological solution to violence is to recognise that the treatment of offenders is important to prevent the repetition of violence, but society also needs reforming. What Godsi particularly wants to be reformed are socially dysfunctional families. He argues that the effects of parents divorcing or separating, particularly where that has been vitriolic, are profound on children, as they are if children are brought up in unstable families. Godsi condemns single mothers who have multiple male partners because of what he considers to be their harmful child-rearing practices:

> Typically their fathers will be completely absent or else they will have little or sporadic contact with their children. Any other male figures in these children's lives will tend to be transient; for example, their mother's various lovers who move in, live with them for a time, and then leave again as quickly as they came . . . The mothers in these family set ups are likely to have had several children, each by a different father.
>
> (Godsi, 2004, p. 78)

Godsi's argument that violence in adults can be traced to abuse in childhood may go some way to explain some murders, but childhood abuse cannot explain fully the brutality of the sadistic totalitarian leader, the barbarian terrorist, or the Nazi concentration-camp guard. Have they had in their childhoods a megalomaniac parent, or one who liked to indulge in the equivalent of beheading people, or one who acquiesced to the commands of the other parent no matter how excessively cruel?

Moreover, Godsi falls off his structuralist perch when he suggests that the cycle of abuse for children can be broken if they are given love and professional help. Surely the influence of society cannot be so easily overridden? Abuse in childhood is but one factor in understanding why people become 'mad' or 'bad' in later life.

Social Strain

Robert Merton (1938) applied Emile Durkheim's (1858–1917) concept of 'anomie' to the issue of antisocial behaviour. Anomie is the state of 'normlessness' that an individual may experience when confronted by profound and rapid transformation in the way in which society is organised, and in the belief systems and moral guidelines it propagates. In situations in which the orderly administration and integration of social institutions is irresolute, the consequential social disorder may cause (some) people to experience debilitating feelings of aimlessness, insecurity and despair, leading possibly to suicide.

For Merton, there is, however, a particular problem when the norms and expectations of the individual do not correspond with the reality of their social existence. For example, in the West, material wealth and occupational advancement are given high value, and their achievement is portrayed as the inevitable outcome of the effort of the individual. But, if despite application and diligence, an individual does not reach these goals, illegitimate strategies may be used. That is, when the means to fulfil the values of society (economic success and promotion) are severely hampered by social disadvantage (for example, inequalities in schooling, racism, sexism and ageism), 'strain' occurs in both the individual and society.

According to Merton (1938), people react to this strain in a number of ways:

1. Conformity. There is an acceptance of both the values and means of achieving these values, notwithstanding the fact that most will fail in their endeavours as there is only limited 'room at the top'. The majority of people follow this route.

2. Ritualisation. Here people acquiesce to the means of achieving 'success', as determined by social norms, but do so without an end game in sight in terms of achievement – for example, the employee who 'plods' through their working life.

3. Retreatism. Both values and means of achieving what is regarded highly in society are relinquished in favour of an alternative lifestyle – for example, 'new-age travellers' and employees who opt for demotion in order to concentrate on their social and personal interests.

4. Rebellion. A critical view of the social system is taken, and its means and values are rejected, but instead of 'retreating', attempts are made to introduce radical amendments to its structure and ideology. For example, social campaigners may set up their own political party to gain power and thereby change society, or alternatively they may instigate a revolution.

5. Innovation. The attainment of socially decreed outcomes such as wealth is accepted, but the means used are not within the moral or legal framework of society's norms. Criminals are therefore innovators.

The innovators, aside from opting for criminal careers such as burglary and robbery which could bring a degree of material benefit and heightened social status, may become part of organised criminal sects and networks. In doing so, their innovative techniques to obtain wealth and high social status may include violence. For example, various mafia crime syndicates have murdered thousands of people in order to reach and maintain power and prestige.

For Merton, increased strain generally in society will lead to higher levels of violence. Frustration at widening inequality (as is occurring within and between societies in a globalised world) could be the reason behind the rise in both instrumental *and* expressive murder (Miethe & Regoeczi, 2004). People kill for specific outcomes but also because they are angry with their low position in global society from which they have little potential to escape. This frustration is exacerbated because of the imagery of ostentatious privilege that appears globally on television and in films. The poorest community has access to images of conspicuous consumption.

Certainly Merton's theory does resonate with what is happening in the twenty-first century global village. Violence is growing and conceivably the strain could become a break, producing widespread dissent and calls for a different world order. But, it is more probable that the powerful people of the rich nations, in league with the elites of the poor nations, will pre-empt such a threat to the present world order. The hegemonising effect of global capitalism backed up by the military might of the leading capitalist countries appears to be either smashing or containing ideological and physical rebellions. State socialism has gone from Russia and Eastern Europe, communist China belongs to the World Trade Organisation and has a burgeoning capitalist economy, Islamic fundamentalism is being fought head-on, and uncooperative countries are or could be invaded. Those with interests in the status quo are the real innovators, and the vast majority of the population of the world are conformists or ritualists (and that includes most criminals, even murderers).

Social Disorganisation

Society may experience strain not only because what is deemed 'success' cannot be achieved by many people (perhaps the majority), but because parts of it, mainly inner-city localities, are in disarray. Areas of social disorganisation are associated with a high population turnover, multiple ethnic groupings, significant levels of material disadvantage and unemployment, and single parent families. Such socially disorganised environments are also associated with domestic violence and the murder of intimates, as well as street violence (Reid, 2006).

For social disorganisation theorists, such as Robert Faris and Warren Dunham (1965), the city can be broken down into a number of 'concentric zones' whose characteristics either enhance 'normality' or boost deviancy. In their model of the city, the zone at the geographical centre is the commercial sector, containing shops, offices, small factories and places of entertainment. Today, this area may also be occupied by the homeless, within whose ranks the mentally disordered will be disproportionately represented. Those people without permanent residence take shelter in the nooks and crannies created by a mix of architecture (industrial, modernist and postmodernist).

The next zone identified by Faris and Dunham is typified by slum housing, ghettos and rented accommodation. In this area reside various groups of new immigrants, the lower working class (semi-skilled and unskilled workers, many of whom are only partially employed), and sections of the 'underclass' (the permanently unemployed, criminal recidivists, drug users and dealers, and prostitutes). If and when the members of these groups are successful in terms of running businesses or finding employment, they have the opportunity to enter the third zone, which accommodates the 'stable working class' as well as former immigrants who are now more established within the social system.

In many Western cities, these last two zones have become to some extent 'gentrified'. That is, relatively young and well-off, single or cohabiting people without children occupy 'executive apartments', and mini 'town houses' built on 'brown field sites' (that is, places that previously had dilapidated buildings on them or were unused). Living in these busy and polluted sections of the city gives the advantage of easy access to the centre of the city for work and entertainment.

Finally, situated on the edge of the city, there are the residential suburbs, the main habitation of the middle class. Today, however, a growing number of people travel to the city from the countryside. Villages have seen the process of gentrification occur within their environs in the same way as it has occurred in the unfashionable regions of the inner city.

Robert Faris and Warren Dunham (1965) argue that it was not the personalities and behaviour of the inhabitants that created the distinguishing features of these zones, but the other way round. That is, it was evident that the environment dictated how people behaved as each location maintained its specific identity despite the movement of groups (for example, Jewish immigrants being replaced by Hispanics in the USA, Irish immigrants replaced by Afro-Caribbeans in Britain) through its parameters. Moreover, even though high rates of mobility occur within the most unstable area (found principally in the second zone, but also in the first and third zones), a significant level of officially recorded crime and deviance continues. In fact, the pace of population movement causes the anonymity and social isolation that then produces the conditions under which crime and deviancy (including mental disorders such as schizophrenia) will flourish.

Interestingly, although criminal activity had grown to be a problem in the 'core' areas of the modern city, electronic surveillance may eventually reduce this and move crime to other sections of the city not under the gaze of the authorities. It is also worth noting that it is the perception of lawlessness in these highly mutable zones that appears to increase the fear of crime, rather than the issue merely being one of social instability. Moreover, many disturbances in these so-called disorganised sections are not crimes of the dispossessed any more. They are the 'anti-social behaviours' of people further up the social hierarchy who have enough disposable income to spend on binge drinking, which might then lead to street brawling and even murder.

Social Situations

Miethe and Regoeczi (2004) compare murder situations for different sorts of people in the USA (for example, men, women, teenagers, adults, strangers, intimates, blacks, whites and Hispanics). They point to the fallibility of murder groupings. They also criticise conclusions reached about causes of murder based on these groups. For them, most murder theorising is both limited and circular (that is, it is teleological). Hence, when references are made to 'serial killers' or 'infanticide mothers' there is already a set of meanings attached to these acts of killings that influences how they are perceived, the style of criminal investigation and potential outcomes of the trials.

For Miethe and Regoeczi, different social groups commit killings under different circumstances. They argue, therefore, that criminologists need to rethink traditional conceptualisations of murder. Miethe and Regoeczi's analysis of the situation of murder involves the nexus of offender, victim and the crime as defined through time and space. They conclude that there are specific situational issues in murders (in the USA) that have to be recognised. For example, they suggest that murders committed using guns revolve around issues of gender, race, class and urban locations.

People 'make sense' of what they experience in different ways; that is, the same circumstances will mean different things for different people. Individuals bring with them understandings to situations and gain understandings from these situations that have specific meanings for them. For example, a husband entering his bedroom and finding his wife with her lover may murder them both, one of them, attack them verbally, or just leave depending on what meaning this circumstance has for him and how the other two react (Birkbeck and LaFree, 1993).

'Bad situations' (neighbourhoods with low social control) foment violence. Violence is also correlated with 'hot spot' situations such as parking lots, bars/pubs, night clubs, accident and emergency hospital units, psychiatric acute services, sex shops and 'red light' areas, drug-buying locations, and shelters for the homeless (Birkbeck and LaFree, 1993). Evenings are more dangerous (in terms of violence and homicide) than daytime. Summertime is more dangerous (people are in bars, on the street, or attending crowded public venues such as music festivals) than wintertime (although domestic violence might rise). The home offers a viable killing arena, not only because of the relationships within it, but because it is shielded from observation and creates its own rules of conduct. Easily entered and exited areas, such as alleyways and train stations, offer greater opportunity for killing.

The situationalist approach does have the merit of debunking typologies of murder. By implication, no two murders are the same as the people in the murder scenario have created their own unscripted drama in which their performance will be adjusted as they interact with each other. However, there are pre-written elements of the script that this theory underestimates. For example, social structure and social learning offer parameters that restrict what meanings can be attached to any situation. Biology and evolution inhibit the physical and emotional possibilities that can be expressed by the actors.

SUMMARY

The IRA members who planted the bomb that ended Tim Parry's life, Pierre Riviere, Demitrios Tsafendas, Abu Musab al-Zarqawi, Adolf Hitler, Joseph Stalin, Abimael Guzman, Mao Tse-tung, Lieutenant William Calley and Richard Robles are all murderers. Why did they commit murder? Can their reasons be collated under one or another theory of murder? Can finding a 'motive' be sufficient to answer this question? Does finding a motive then require an assessment of the killer's disposition as mad or bad, psychopath or barbarian? Or can a solution to the question be found, and only be found, by exploring the faults in that individual or the faults in society?

Eric Hickey (2003) argues that the causation of violence cannot be understood by adding specific factors together in a linear fashion. Biological, psychological and social elements interact and produce many possible outcomes. For example, Jonathan Pincus (2002) observes that the biology of the brain is shaped not only by genetic influences. The brain 'senses' the social environment and changes accordingly:

> The sensory systems of the brain detect sights, sounds, odours, tastes, pain, touch, temperature, pressure, motion and position. The development of the synapses between brain nerve cells is very sensitive to the outside environment, including the psycho sensory environment.
>
> (Pincus, 2002, p. 120)

Hickey points to evidence from animal experiments (rats and hamsters) that the individual's biology and 'psychology' is altered by social environmental stimuli such as prolonged physical threats. Neurochemical changes occur (for example, to levels of serotonin), and as a consequence the threatened animal appears more fearful and alters its behaviour by taking evasive action. There is, therefore, reflexivity between social factors and the individual's constitution.

As Pincus admits about the link he believes he has identified between murder and sexual abuse, most people who have undergone sexually damaging childhoods do not become murderers. Pincus argues that neurological disorder (and possibly illegal drug use) has to be present before the likelihood of violence increases. This is true for all other correlations that seem to offer a clear-cut tie between one biological, psychological, or social phenomenon and murder. What Pincus also accepts is the role of society in 'releasing' the potential to murder created by awful personal experiences and cerebral pathology. Governments and media give backing to violence by initiating 'moral panics' about certain groups (for example, paedophiles and refugees), as well as starting wars and indoctrinating the population to view a former friendly neighbouring country as an enemy. For Pincus, abused and brain damaged people are more likely to become willing perpetrators of violence and atrocity if the context for brutality has been set by society.

Certain mental illnesses (for example, paranoid schizophrenia) do precipitate violence in comparison to the rest of the population (Taylor, 2003). But most mentally disordered people are not violent, and if they are it is probable they will take the route of self-injury and suicide rather than hurting or killing someone else. There is, suggest Krug et al. (2002), a complex interplay of qualities and events on a number of levels concerning individuals, relationships, communities and societies. I would add to this list, factors arising from globalisation especially, as Ulrich Beck (2005) has written, the power games that are played out between transnational corporations, governments and other interest groups.

Miethe and Regoeczi (2004) advocate a synthesis (what they call 'conjunctive thinking') of both macro (sociological) and micro (biological, evolutionary and psychological) theories to understand the cause of each murder. Tim Parry's killers, Pierre Riviere, Demitrios Tsafendas, Abu Musab al-Zarqawi, Adolf Hitler, Joseph Stalin, Abimael Guzman, Mao Tse-tung, Lieutenant William Calley and Richard Robles committed murder because their faulty genes, neurochemicals, brains, learning, thinking and emotions emerged in 'faulty' social settings that were structurally and ecologically dysfunctional, strained and disorganised.

However, does such a synthesis offer a realistic tool for solving the riddle of why commit murder? Can each killing be wrapped up so neatly? Is it possible to extract from a murder the relevant issues and weigh up their relative contribution? Does this analytical fusion offer anything better than just finding a motive or labelling the murderer 'mad' or 'bad'? I am sceptical.

CHAPTER 4

WHY IS MURDER DEVASTATING?

Pol Pot, the Bad Man

(Mr Hong, taxi driver, Phnom Penh, Cambodia, January 2004)

Mr Hong's was a truly awful story. With some prompting from my friend and travelling companion in Cambodia, Dr Gordon MacDonald, Mr Hong explained his life as a teenager whilst driving us to one of the all too numerous Cambodian museums of genocide that have become de rigueur for tourists.

Mr Hong's mother (because she was a teacher), his sister (because she was student), and his grandmother (because she was a doctor), had been executed by the Khmer Rouge. They were regarded as part of the intelligentsia. The Khmer Rouge government *devastated* the educated class in their attempt at national re-invention. Some were targeted for extermination merely because they had the most rudimentary schooling or wore spectacles.

Prince Norodim Sihanouk (the on-and-off Cambodian head of state following independence from France in 1953) had allowed the Viet Cong (north-Vietnamese communists) to use Cambodia as a base during the Vietnam War (1954–1975). A civil war erupted in the country in 1970 between the USA and south-Vietnamese-backed forces of Cambodian General Lon Nol (who had in 1970 deposed Sihanouk) and Cambodian communists, the Khmer Rouge.

Victory came in 1974 to the Khmer Rouge. The winning regime decided to install a Maoist social order directed by its leader, Pol Pot. For the Khmer Rouge, Pol Pot was 'Brother Number One'. For Mr Hong, Pol Pot was 'The Bad Man'.

This brave new world was to commence in what the Khmer Rouge declared as 'Year Zero', 1975. Year Zero was so named because everything that had gone before, the political, educational, health, financial, legal and hierarchical systems (and the people working within those systems) would be devastated to make way for a communist state unshackled by the country's past. Cambodian history would be erased. Those people who represented that history would also be erased. During less than four years of rule approximately 1.7 million people died at the hands of their fellow citizens or through malnutrition and disease.

Oddly, Mr Hong spoke of the loss of his close relatives without any overt signs of sorrow or embitterment. When Gordon (an expert in public health and therefore as interested as me in the effects of traumatic experiences) and I questioned him about his lack of emotion, he didn't appear to understand what we meant. Every time we had a query he responded monosyllabically or with an answer that didn't relate to the topic we had raised. This could have been a problem of language as our taxi driver spoke only a modicum of English and we had no grasp whatsoever of Khmer. It could have been that there were differing cultural expectations about grief between the three of us (Gordon and me as Europeans and Mr Hong a south-east Asian). Alternatively, was Mr Hong repressing the terrible events in his youth, his mind not able to face memories of how his close relatives, along with millions of others, had been killed by 'ordinary' Cambodians (many of the executioners were peasant workers indoctrinated by a murderous ideology).

In a prescient report, Janet Ng writes:

> There are thousands of Khmer Rouge survivors who, everyday in the United States, relive the terror they endured in Cambodia. These survivors of one of the worst holocausts in history rarely speak about their experiences, however. Instead, many sit silently in their homes, reluctant to emerge because their minds are riveted on the horrors they witnessed in their homeland.
>
> (Ng, 2001)

Survivors of the Khmer Rouge period explain in Ng's report that a climate of fear was created deliberately amongst communities to control dissent. Silence was the result.

There are three levels of victimisation with violence. There are the primary victims, those people who have directly suffered from an act or acts of violence (Mr Hong's mother, sister and grandmother). Next are the secondary victims, the 'significant others' of both primary victims and perpetrators (Mr Hong's remaining family and friends of the family), and close associates (for example, the work colleagues, peers and neighbours). 'Murder survivors' and 'co-victims' are other terms used to describe secondary victims.

Unlike Mr Hong, some Cambodian secondary victims did eventually find their voices. Theanvy Kuoch, who went to Thailand (and subsequently the USA) with her young son to escape probable death did 30 years later:

'I lost everybody,' Kuoch says, her voice strained. 'I only had my son, but I was separated from him.' The Khmer Rouge murdered 19 members of her family. Kuoch, who now resides in Connecticut, barely speaks of the horrors she has witnessed in Cambodia, but they remain fixed in her memory.

(Ng, 2001)

However, there is also a tertiary level of victimisation. The wider social networks of primary and secondary victims, their communities and societies, and ultimately the 'global village' (that is, the cultural unification of the whole of the world's inhabitants through mass media: McLuhan & Powers, 1992) are damaged by the 'ripple effect' of murder. The millions of deaths in Cambodia, as with every other killing, have consequences for humanity.

Sandra Bloom (2001, p. xiv) uses the notions of 'vertical' and 'horizontal' rippling in society from violence:

The effects of violence are infectious – they spread down through the generations, from person to person, from family to family, from nation to nation. And as we become more globally interconnected, the reverberations of human rights violations in one corner of the world are felt throughout the entire global network.

What Bloom is referring to is the accumulation of large numbers of people from violent societies who have had a death by murder of a family member, friend or associate, and the multitudes who are exposed to regular reporting of killings in the media. Whether you live in Lima (Peru), Hamilton (New Zealand), Toronto (Canada), or Windhoek (Namibia), globalised and electronic information is available readily. Moreover, 24-hour international news broadcasting (for example by the BBC and CNN, on television and the internet) and news-storage (filed in electronic form and retrievable by anyone with access to the internet) provides a constant diet of killings. A selection of murders from all over the world can be viewed and read about, and one murder event will be reported repeatedly. As Godsi (2004, p. 32) remarks, violence has become pervasive:

Violence is a part of all of our lives whether it affects us directly as victims and perpetrators, whether we know or care about others who have been victimized or who have themselves been violent, whether we have lost friends or relatives through murder or violence or simply because we are aware of violence in the world around us.

But the knock-on effect from murder will impinge on secondary victims in different ways. A murdered son or daughter will probably not feel the same as losing an uncle or aunt, or a murdered sibling as a workmate. Nor is secondary victimisation equivalent to tertiary victimisation. But, they are part of the same process. The flow and pervasiveness of violence converts personal suffering into social suffering.

PERSONAL SUFFERING

Mr Hong may have suffered (and still be suffering) but he wasn't willing or able to elaborate his story for his overly inquisitive passengers. Nor were we trained to gauge the non-verbal signs of suffering that had its roots in events some 30 years previously. Even if we had been so skilled, delineating these signs from any other tragedies in his life, or indeed from the everyday miseries stemming from a hand-to-mouth existence in the socially indigent city of Phnom Penh, would not have been easy. But in other cases the personal suffering is all too obvious.

Georgy Farniyev was, in 2004, 10 years of age. An inhabitant of the Russian town of Beslan and pupil of Middle School Number One, he survived an atrocity that destroyed much of the physical structure of his school and many members of his school's community (BBC News, 2004b).

This child had watched as many of his fellow pupils were slaughtered, and then hid amongst their dead bodies or what remained of them. The killing occurred when male and female Chechen separatists (or from the point of view of the Russian government, terrorists) took over the school and held hostage its occupants, a mixture of children, teachers and parents. Farniyev became known across the world when a video shot by the hostage-takers inside the school was given to the media and broadcast; it showed him sitting with his hands on his head beside the dead with a gunman standing over him.

A Russian soldier helped Georgy Farniyev escape. The soldier was part of the security services' attempt to contain the siege, and then manage the unfolding calamity of the rescue attempt. But his mother was not aware that he had been saved and was searching for him amongst the dead:

> It was the worst imaginable torture each time I looked inside the bags containing the remains of children, the ones with the most space inside . . . Each time I thought I was about to see the face of my dead son – and each time I felt the most incredible relief before moving down the line to do it again.
> (quoted in BBC News, 2004b from interview in *The Sun* newspaper)

The separatists had murdered a number of people in the school but appeared to be settling down for a prolonged negotiation over their assumed demand for Chechnya to become independent from Russia. But, believing they were under attack they detonated a series of bombs, some of which caused the school's gym roof to collapse, killing more people, and then began shooting the remaining children. At that point, the Russian security services entered the school. However, yet more innocent people were killed in the cross-fire between the Russian forces and the separatists. Some of the terrorists then blew themselves up, causing the deaths of more hostages because of their proximity to the explosions. The only surviving hostage-taker out of thirty-two was Chechen carpenter, Nurpashi Kulayev. He was sentenced to life imprisonment in 2006 by a Russian court for murder and terrorism.

Diana Gadzhinova, aged 14 at the time of the siege and held hostage in the school gym, records what happened:

> It took us all by surprise, we were told there would be talks and we were ordered to lie face down (in the Gym) . . . Then there was an explosion in the yard. Then there was shooting . . . (My sister and I) stayed where we were, lying on the floor. But suddenly there was another explosion above us and part of the ceiling fell in. People were screaming, there was panic. I looked up and saw some children lying on the floor covered in blood and not moving. There was a dead lady lying beside me. Torn off arms and legs were lying everywhere. There were bombs hanging on the rope they had strung up between the basketball hoops across the gym and now these bombs began going off, one after the other, coming closer and closer to us.
>
> (Diana Gadzhinova, quoted in BBC News, 2004c)

With her sister Alina, Diana Gadzhinova got away from the carnage through a nearby window. The siege lasted 52 hours. Over 300 people were killed, about half of whom were children. Chechen warlord Shamil Basayev admitted, during an interview on USA's ABC Television on 29 July, 2005, planning the occupation of the Beslan school. He has also been linked with other terrorist activities in Russia, specifically Moscow theatre siege in 2002. Russian special forces had stormed the theatre to end the siege by Chechen separatists. But 120 of the hostages (and most of their captors) were killed, poisoned by gas that was pumped into the auditorium by the authorities with the intention of making the hostage-takers become unconscious.

There are two overlapping concepts used commonly for the fall-out from murder, which have been applied by support groups and professionals to secondary victimisation. These are *bereavement* and *post-traumatic stress disorder* (PTSD).

Bereavement

Bereavement is a 'normal' psychological state that applies to many types of life's occurrences where there is a loss of something or someone. For example: leaving behind familiar people and places through emigration; the 'empty-nest syndrome', when children leave the family home to go to university or to make homes of their own; a family pet goes missing; personal belongings are stolen through a mugging or burglary; an individual's community is fractured because of natural or human-made disaster.

Bereavement encompasses many emotions: disbelief and denial, numbness, anxiety, vulnerability, depression, confusion, shock, anger, vengeance, emptiness, isolation, helplessness, humiliation, blame, sorrow, guilt, fear and grief. These may be grouped together in stages, or one emotion dominates for a period of time before being replaced by another (for example, the phase of refutation may turn to a period of resentment).

But murder, either of individuals or communities, produces a variation of bereavement that can be distinguished from other forms of grieving (Rock, 1998). Moreover, bereavement after murder is discernible when compared with the loss of human life from illness and accidents.

> The experience of bereavement by homicide is emotionally and psychologically *devastating*. The traumatic grief which follows homicide is unlike the grief that accompanies a death by natural causes: those affected experience intense and overwhelming emotions over a long period of time, which can make normal functioning in everyday life difficult. [emphasis added]
>
> (Victim Support, 2006, p. 9)

Jane Alexander of the victim support group Citizens Against Homicide (CAH), based in California, USA, describes from her own experience and that of other victims with whom she has contact the difference between the death of a loved one from natural causes and from murder:

> My husband died twenty-five years ago of a heart attack. At the time it was very *devastating* to me and our six children. However, we all recovered, the children finished college and went on to be successful citizens with nice homes, families etc. I now have twelve grandchildren. The homicide I still live with, all the time. Rarely a day goes by that I don't in some small way think about it. It's just there. I spend a lot of time talking to victims, and especially those who do not have closure, it never goes away. [emphasis added]
>
> (Alexander, pers. comm.)

Secondary victims of murder are more angry, more anguished, and more stigmatised (Redmund, 1989; Rynearson, 1984, 1994). The Beslan children who escaped the massacre at their school are reported by clinical staff, who are helping and offering them support, to have become fearful and aggressive (Lavrentyeva, 2004).

Victoria Cummock (1995), ironically an activist working in the field of aviation security and counter-terrorism, lost her husband in the destruction, by terrorists, of the airliner PAN AM 103 over the Scottish town of Lockerbie in 1988. Altogether, 270 passengers were killed. Cummock argues that for secondary victims of murder the suddenness and intentionality of the act heightens their suffering. Generally, if a loved one dies because of a cancer or AIDS then, as heartbreaking as it is, the expectedness and comprehensibility of the death does not equate with the abrupt and (at least in the short term) perplexing style of murder. Sudden bereavement through murder is compounded if the killing has been vicious. The profundity of the loss is also made severe because of the feeling of 'unfinished business', and because the killer may not be known, or if known not apprehended, if apprehended not convicted, if convicted subsequently released by appeal, re-trial or pardoned.

Cummock points out that murder survivors' anguish is exacerbated yet further because of the various official processes that have to be undergone. Near relatives will, in all probability, have to sort out the financial affairs of the victim, and make the funeral arrangements. These responsibilities, whilst having a ritualistic function (and therefore perhaps reducing the anguish for a short time), add tangible realities to the sense of privation. Georgy Farniyev's mother's searching for hours the lines of body bags (a process partly required for bureaucratic reasons, enabling the dead to be officially recorded) may have mollified her agony because her son was not in one of the bags. But every time she opened one she was faced with some other parent's dead child and the possibility that her child could be in the next bag. Even when the last bag was opened, there may still have been undiscovered bodies in the ruins of the school. Her angst about her son presumably remained until she was reunited with him.

Social scientist Deborah Spungen (1998, p. xix), whose own daughter was murdered at the age of 20 years, vividly describes the feeling of desolation on the news that a loved one has been 'unlawfully killed': 'the blackest hell accompanied by a pain so intense that even breathing becomes an unendurable labor.'

However, as Spungen explains, beyond the instantaneous emotional turmoil, the distress that accompanies the bureaucratic procedures surrounding modern death, and the reactivation of these emotions during the trial, there quite conceivably lies a lifetime of bitterness and heartache. Moreover, Spungen records that secondary victims can undergo an illogical sense of guilt about the murder, which may be increased by the reactions of others. That is, a not infrequent response from associates of the victim, which may be implied rather than stated openly, is to hold the secondary victim in some way or another culpable. Witnesses to murder and onlookers (who also can be considered secondary victims) may similarly feel guilt, with either the real or imagined social approbation raising questions of 'why didn't you intervene' and 'how could you watch'. That is, there can be double jeopardy from secondary victim-hood, both personal distress and social disgrace.

As the officials (primarily, the police, lawyers and judges) become involved, families of the primary victim are not able to control events affecting their lives. At worst formal processes can last years, and secondary victims may feel that they cannot get on with their lives until they are over. Various investigations into the 1988 bombing of the PAN AM 103 airplane flying over Scotland have gone on so far (in 2006) for nearly two decades. The bomb was hidden in a radio cassette recorder and on detonation the plane exploded over the town of Lockerbie in Scotland. A total of 269 people were killed. Libyan Abdelbaset Ali Mohmed al-Megrahi was convicted in 2001 of the atrocity, but in 2004 lodged an appeal against his 27-year sentence, and in 2005 the prosecution evidence was brought into question by the Scottish Criminal Cases Review Commission (due to report in 2006).

Cummock suggests that dealing psychologically with a murder begins with secondary victims hoping that their loved one hasn't been murdered at all. But for Cummock, denial following murder is far more intense than in other forms of bereavement. This is especially so if the discovery of the murdered person's body is delayed or never found. After terrorist bombings in crowded markets and packed buses (during 2005 alone bombs planted in buses or markets were exploded in countries as far apart geographically and politically as: Israel, Indonesia, Iraq, Afghanistan, Egypt, Burma, India, Pakistan, the Philippines, Turkey, Nepal and London), the dead may be so mutilated that they cannot ever be identified. This gives impetus to the desire to reject the possibility that a loved could be one of dead, even if there is strong circumstantial evidence (they were likely to have been buying food in that market at that time, or travelling to work on that bus). Cummock points out that, after the Oklahoma City bombing (in which 168 people were killed by Timothy McVeigh and Terry Nichols), the families of people working in the destroyed building were sombre and emotionally flat. When families of the dead were notified that their loved ones had definitely been killed, the grieving process ensued but was profound. There was, according to Cummock, a 'generalised release of emotions' amongst the affected families.

Cummock goes on to argue that the grieving process is further complicated by the intrusiveness of the media. Of course most murders do not attract media involvement, but when they do, families may be left with extreme feelings of disorientation and vulnerability. This is particularly so if media images are repeated of scenes of carnage.

The media is always interested in new stories and can be quite ruthless, argues Cummock, in their sensationalisation of tragedy. Rod Liddle (2005) takes up this point. He observes that the public's tastes have changed from the diet of mildly eroticised and quasi-puzzling killings that reached the press prior to the liberalisation of social mores during the 1960s. Liddle argues that today in order to gain the English media's attention and feed the more salaciously sophisticated appetite of the public, murders have to have lots of gore, utterly defenceless victims and murderers with incomprehensible, highly sexualised, outstandingly deranged, or fervently cannibalistic motives. Such media hype and public prurience adds to the personal suffering of the families who are still at the time grappling with the facts of what has happened, let alone dealing with dramatically lurid versions of the murder.

Whilst bereavement is part of everyday understanding of suffering following loss, as a human condition it has been reconceptualised and taken over by professionals. There are, for example, 'bereavement counsellors' who specialise in therapies that offer their therapeutic skills to help people deal and come to terms with death. That is, as with most types of personal suffering, bereavement has been accommodated with a professional (psychotherapeutic) discourse.

Not all of the psychological states of bereavement are experienced by those who are bereaved; their intensity will vary between individuals, and loss itself may not in some people provoke any psychological change. However, the emotional effects of bereavement have physiological consequences. For example, anxiety and depression incite a multitude of alterations in the physical stasis of the human body, some of which, if prolonged and severe, can be life-threatening. Apart from those murdered, millions of people are left injured as a result of violence and suffer from physical, sexual, reproductive and mental health problems (Krug et al., 2002).

CAH (2006) publishes statements presented to the courts by those who have lost loved ones. The statements refer to how words cannot describe the feelings that follow the death of a son or a father, mother or sister who, for example, has been shot during a robbery. The secondary victims mention the agony of knowing that their loved one has been killed, and the subsequent re-living of those feelings when important events (for example, a birthday or wedding anniversary) or belongings of the dead person are noticed. Specifically, CAH records the loss of peace of mind, insomnia, feelings of insecurity, loss of innocence, loss of trust and faith in people, remorse about feeling happy, and the perpetual anxiety associated with not knowing what is going to trigger memories of the deceased and recreate subsequent feelings of loss. That is, when these memories are triggered, the feelings of pain experienced when first learning of the death are rekindled and on top of that is the pain associated with the second-stage realisation of loss at a later date.

Some relatives of murder victims are reported as being very dissatisfied with the criminal justice system, which they argue, adds to their suffering.

> [T]raumatic grief is complicated by involvement in the criminal justice system whose processes can inhibit and hamper grief reactions, and exacerbate feelings of rage and powerlessness.
>
> (Victim Support, 2006, p. 9)

For many homicide survivors, watching the trial of their loved one's alleged killer may be their first experience with the criminal justice system, which may be a disorientating and frustrating experience. What they complain of in particular is the dehumanising of their loved one. In the trial process, the primary victim becomes 'evidence' rather than a bona fide (if dead) person. As such they are tossed between prosecution and defence lawyers (in adversarial legal systems), each side attempting to win their case without due respect to the deceased or sensitivity towards the attending relatives. Medical experts may appear especially callous as they refer to the intricacies of the post-mortem examination. The accused may provide statements that the relatives find offensive and believe are untrue. Moreover, the accused may have family members and supporters in court. These supporters may on occasions deliberately set out to intimidate the primary victim's family in and outside of the courtroom, or can inadvertently intimidate the victim's relatives by their mere presence in court. Sometimes there may be intentional intimidation. Lucy Cope's tragedy was intensified when, in 2004, the case against the man charged with her son's murder was dropped due to a lack of witnesses willing to testify: 'I am *devastated*. Nothing can heal my broken heart' (Cope, 2004 [emphasis added]).

The relatives of the victim may also feel that the accused is given far more rights than they deserve, and that they, the relatives have few. For example, whilst in many US courts relatives have a say in the trial process, this remains limited in British courts (pilot studies of victim 'impact' statements were taking place in 2006). The involvement of victims in court procedures, however, may have little or no bearing on the outcome of the trial. Their 'right' being a 'rite' through which bitterness can be discharged. Testimonies from relatives of murdered loved ones can be heart-wrenching to read, and often very detailed. They go into the day-to-day minutiae of loss, illustrating how the murdered person was entwined in their lives and how at home in their personal lives, and indeed in their working lives, the loss of the person is far-reaching.

The newsletters of CAH (February, 2005) contained this story from the wife of Flake Marty Wakefield:

On July 19, 1995, my husband, Flake Marty Wakefield and three of his fellow supervisors were victims of workplace violence. Flake, James Walton, Neil Carpenter and Tony Gain, had been employed by the City for many years. Mr. Gain had the distinction of working for the city longer than anyone else at that time. Four families were *devastated*, four women became widows, their dreams shattered . . . In five minutes, the evil subhuman [killer] changed my entire future and that of three other women who also had long time marriages, love and devotion from our husbands. The evil one used only eight bullets, every one was a fatal shot and now none of us get valentines, anniversary cards, or birthday cards. I don't have anyone to love and touch and care for, and there is no one to love and care for or touch me . . . [emphasis added]

Post-traumatic Stress Disorder

The combination of psychological, physiological and lifestyle aspects of loss through murder has become encapsulated by what is now known as PTSD. PTSD is a medical syndrome that previously described what happened to some soldiers who, during wartime (particularly if they had undergone heavy bombardment, partaken in killings, and had seen their comrades die), became so terrified that they refused to fight again.

During the First World War, military psychiatry focused on what was known variously as 'shell shock', 'battle fatigue', 'combat stress' and 'war neurosis' as thousands of soldiers appeared incapable of fighting both emotionally and physically. If examined by a medical military officer (not all were) and found to be 'malingering', they were shot as cowards or deserters. If, on the other hand, they were considered to be ill they may still be shot (the medical officer's opinion ignored by army commanders), but could be hospitalised until they recovered or were discharged (Wessely & Jones, 2005). Since then, PTSD has become widened to take in psychological and physical symptoms resulting from ordeals ranging from observing brutality to being caught up in a tsunami.

PTSD represents the thorough medicalisation of the suffering surrounding aggression and violence in their broadest senses. It is defined exhaustively in the American Psychiatric Association's (APA, 2000) *Diagnostic and Statistical Manual of Mental Disorders (DSM-IV-TR)*. Under Section 309.81 the disorder is described as occurring when a person has been exposed to an extreme stress in which both of the following were present:

- The person directly experienced an incident or incidents that involved actual or threatened death or serious injury to themselves or to another person, or has been told about or witnessed such an incident(s).

- The person's response to the incident or incidents was one of intense fear, powerlessness or horror.

The traumatic event(s) referred to by the APA cover physical attack, sexual assault, being kidnapped or taken hostage, terrorist attack, torture, natural and man-made disasters and accidents, and other unexpected deaths (for example, the sudden heart attack of a loved one). For a diagnosis of PTSD, the traumatic event(s) has to be relived persistently through conscious thoughts, dreams or 'flashbacks'. These can occur because of certain 'triggers', such as a woman passing the location where she was raped, or a man who has been beaten up coming across someone with a similar ethnic identity to his assailant. On the other hand, a person with PTSD may 'dissociate' from the trauma consciously or unconsciously, not willing or able to remember what had occurred. There is, in psychiatric jargon, 'psychic numbing'. Drug, alcohol, gambling, extreme sports, sex, or pornography addiction may become a way of trying to remain dissociated from the trauma.

Other persistent symptoms of PTSD include:

- difficulty falling or staying asleep

- irritability or outbursts of anger

- difficulty concentrating or completing tasks

- hyper-vigilance

- being easily startled.

The good news is that, true to its internally consistent discourse, the medical profession is offering a treatment for a condition it has 'manufactured'. As an element in the progressive medicalisation of everyday life, harrowing episodes of violence are re-interpreted as *wholly* pathological conditions (both for the perpetrators and their prey) rather than either partly or predominantly socially contextualised events in which some of those implicated *may* have faulty psychological or biological constitutions. Psychiatrist Roger Pitman, from Harvard University, has argued that medication can reduce the likelihood of PTSD after trauma and could possibly be curative for those with who have enduring PTSD (reported in Cromie, 2006). What Pitman is trying to achieve is the removal of long-term memories concerning the PTSD-causing incident. Pitman's research (a pilot-study) consisted of administering the blood-pressure lowering drug propranolol, a beta-blocker which acts on the memory-storing receptors in the brain. He selected 20 people who had been in accidents or had undergone abuse decades previously. Compared with the participants who received dummy drugs, those who received propranolol were less anxious when memories of the relevant episodes were reactivated through sessions with counsellors.

Hence, if there is a pill for the personal suffering that is brought about by violence, perhaps the aspects of human relationships and social conditions that foment violence need not be revised. Why bother to ameliorate humanity and global society when the pharmaceutical companies have the answer? There needs to be no revolution in interpersonal communication and social processes to diminish aggression (or even genetic interference to rearrange evolutionary drives), only a relatively slight amendment to the status quo: for example, better tax-breaks and the removal of profit controls to allowing the drug peddlers to research and generate a magnitude of production that will deal with the aftermath from all the millions of injuries and deaths that happen each year globally. After all, despite political rhetoric to the contrary, most health systems in the world remain 'illness' not 'health' services, therefore the provision of *disease treatments* rather than *health promotion* is a coherent policy. But then the people most vulnerable to violence are those who may not be able to afford to buy these PTSD-stopping pills.

Furthermore, secondary victimisation after murder can be oblique. For example, a study of birth rates amongst women in New York after 11 September, 2001 linked a higher than average number of male foetal deaths to the bombing of the Twin Towers (Catalano, Bruckner, Gould, Eskenazi & Anderson, 2005). A similar change in sex ratios was found after Slovenia's 1991 ten-day war (Zorn, Šučur, Stare & Meden-Vrtovec, 2002). Infants born of women who witnessed the destruction of the Twin Towers had low levels of the stress hormone cortisol, as did their mothers. Low cortisol is a sign of PTSD (Yehuda et al., 2005).

Long-term health problems have been reported amongst some of those who survived the destruction of the Twin Towers, those who continued to work and live nearby, rescue personnel, and the workers on the clearing of the site. About half-a-million people may have been contaminated by lead and mercury, asbestos, pulverised concrete, powdered glass and jet fuel, emanating from the site, which became known as 'Ground Zero'. Allegedly, this has caused a range of symptoms, as well as chronic heart and respiratory disease. Class action lawsuits have been filed against the federal authorities (Shulman, 2006).

Another example of the anomalous fall-out from murder comes from Hazel May's (2000) research into families who had been accused of murder. May argues that they undergo a process of stigmatisation instigated by what they assumed is or actually experienced as the reaction of others in their communities. May labels the sense of shame expressed by murderers' relatives as 'moral failure'. Furthermore, sociologist Susan Sharpe (2005) has posited that families of those waiting on death row for execution are also (secondary) victims of the murder their loved one has been found guilty of committing.

SOCIAL SUFFERING

> As a nation, we are all so *devastated* . . . and we all grieve so for those who actually lost loved ones . . . It absolutely breaks my heart to know how many thousands are so shattered by our tragedy, and their homes and lives are now so empty . . . they have to carry on, caring for children, going through all the motions we all go through, but having lost their beloved life partners . . .
>
> (email sent to *New York Metro* by US citizen Joanna Lilly, 24 September, 2001)

In New York, on 11 September, 2001, when the airplanes hit the Twin Towers, there was an audience of millions who were really or virtually at the scene of murders. There were those who escaped the Twin Towers, those in the immediate vicinity fleeing from the wreckage, and the police, ambulance crews and firefighters helping to save lives. There were also the people who were not near enough to be in danger and stood watching the drama unfold. Then there were the millions of TV audiences across the world watching live or soon after as death and destruction ensued. The film footage of the striking by the terrorist-controlled airplanes and the collapse of the Twin Towers was shown over and over again. Later, conversations by some of the passengers on the airplane who used their mobile phones to talk with their relatives about their impending deaths were retrieved and transmitted frequently by the media.

Together with those who lost loved ones, friends and colleagues, the observers of the attacks and listeners to the primary victims' conversations can be viewed, to a greater or lesser extent, as secondary victims. Not everyone aware of the attacks of course was sympathetic to the USA. Leaders from the UK, Germany, France, Russia, Colombia, Mexico, China, Israel, Canada, Japan, Malaysia, Italy, as well as Iran and North Korea, expressed their outrage. But there were celebrations reported in the Palestinian territories and Lebanon. On the first anniversary of the attacks, extremist Islamists held a conference in London in which support for the terrorist action in New York was the theme (Shaikh, 2002). Nevertheless, the people globally who experienced PTSD symptoms must run into the tens if not hundreds of millions.

The World Health Organisation has projected that by 2020 one million people per year globally will be murdered (Krug et al., 2002). As Mercy and Hammond (1999, pp. 297–298) state: 'There is overwhelming evidence that homicide and nonfatal and assaultive violence are major contributors to premature death, injury and disability in the United States and around the world.'

Eric Hickey (2003) suggests that a murdered individual may have hundreds if not thousands of contacts whose lives are impinged on by that person's death. If those killed have family, friends, and associates totalling the very conservative sum of 100 each, then at least 200 million people will be susceptible to PTSD every year. As PTSD may last for many years, and assuming a conservative estimate of a three-year average for PTSD morbidity, this will lead to 600 million people suffering from the side-effects of murder at any point in time.

This is the wider consequence of murder. Murder is like waves hitting land. As with water against the shoreline, the effects of murder vary greatly. The sea, immense and powerful, nevertheless can wash the beach with trifling swells, hardly altering the surrounding land. In some instances, society may not register a murder at all, or if it is recorded then it is dealt with ritualistically, a routine event: a vagrant dying in some dark and lonely corner of a European metropolis, attacked by drugged-crazed teenagers; an unruly prostitute working from a hovel in a crime-ridden locality of Washington DC, Pretoria, Bangkok, or Lima, 'punished' by her pimp; a street-child in Bogota 'socially cleansed' by local police. The deaths of such socially marginalised people usually have a minimal disruptive outcome for society or possibly any other human. Their anonymity makes it easier to kill them and to escape punishment as there is less hue-and-cry about their death and less resolve by the authorities to 'waste' resources on investigations. Their deaths in a macabre sense may be considered by local communities, media and politicians, to benefit society. The removal of those who have attracted the tag of social deviant (vagrants, prostitutes, street-children) can be perceived to reinforce the moral code of that society and increase the safety of its 'good citizens'.

On the other hand, the murder of high ranking people or the whole-sale killing of innocents can set off in the immediate aftermath (and potentially for many years) serious disruption to a society if not to world order. To return to the metaphor of waves, the sea in a hurricane or a tsunami may be enormously destructive to land in its path but it also has unforeseeable consequences.

The Nazi holocausts of the Second World War, in which not only Jews were systematically exterminated but also homosexuals, gypsies, the mentally disordered, the mentally handicapped and physically disabled, led to Germany's continued moral reparation, and the establishment of the state of Israel. The 1963 killing of President J. F. Kennedy paved the way for the presidencies of Lyndon Baines Johnson and Richard Milhous Nixon, the B52 blanket-bombing and napalming of rural civilians in Vietnam and Cambodia, the USA's military humiliation with the unceremonious withdrawal of its troops from South East Asia, and the disgrace and removal of its president because of the Watergate scandal. The 2001 terrorist attack on the Twin Towers in New York allowed the neo-conservatives in US politics to advance their programme to a new world order through which pre-emptive military invasions and Western cultural imperialism were legitimised.

It is generally, powerful governments and media, or the victors of an armed struggle that dictate how much excitement is warranted over any killing whether single or mass. There are exceptions, however. When the former Prime Minister of Lebanon Rafik al-Hariri was assassinated in 2005, the public outcry in that country forced Syria, suspected of being connected to the killing, to withdraw its troops who had been there for nearly 30 years. But what are the reverberations on society, if any, from the 'ordinary' murder, the long list of everyday killings where a young man has squared up to another young man, a lover has strangled his partner, a mother has smothered her baby, a drug-gangster has shot a rival, a mugger has knifed his benefactor? These murders are not catastrophic for society or the global village. But nor are they immaterial. Their echo is insidious and toxic.

A minor but vital adjustment in the thermo-balance of the earth's geological belly may be the start of a series of movements in the surrounding crust overlying oceans that gather potency to the point of drowning a city. Momentous murders such as the death of the leader of a superpower or the mass murdering of its citizens by a foreign force are the social equivalents of nature brewing a catastrophe.

Ordinary murder eats away at the fabric of the global society in a similar way to the erosion of natural and human-made obstacles to the sea's constant movement against them. In both cases there is little to notice if observed in the short term, but if calculated over decades or centuries then the rotting of social institutions and poisoning of human probity is akin to the hollowing of cliffs and the salination of low-lying fields. Society atrophies and people are dehumanised, just as the land collapses and the crops perish.

Murder alters the lives of secondary victims, changing their patterns of behaviour, relationships and emotions, as well as potentially leading to physical ill-health. That is, murder destroys life *and* the psychological and physiological integrity of those left behind. But murder also subverts the integrity of global society.

Tertiary victim-hood, however, is not evenly distributed. Hazel May (2001) has argued, society has a moral hierarchy of murder. However, there is also a moral hierarchy of secondary victim-hood. Some murders seem to be more immoral, more disturbing, crueller, and more unjust than other murders, whilst other murders appear to be 'acceptable' or at least not noteworthy. Black-on-black murders in New Orleans and murders between *favelores* (Brazilian slum-dwellers) in Sao Paulo may well be considered to be socially less troublesome in the sense that the perception is of guilt all around (the victims and culprits viewed as blameworthy as each other). Consequently very little sympathy may be socially generated for secondary victims in these circumstances.

Indeed hostility towards low-status communities generally is blamed on endemic violence within these communities. Such murders can be categorised as at the bottom of the moral hierarchy of murder victim-hood, with the parents of murdered (innocent) children at the top.

There is a form of social invisibility in the pain suffered by relatives and friends of those at the bottom of the moral hierarchy of murder. The grieving that these secondary victims undergo because of their personal loss is exacerbated by the unconcerned or negative attitude of the public, media and politicians. Those at the top of the moral hierarchy, however, are socially conspicuous. Their grief is amplified and accommodated in public consciousness.

Hence, tertiary victim-hood becomes skewed towards certain communities in the world. It does so again during times of civil and external warfare. Obviously, the impact of major violent conflicts on the health of individuals can be very great in terms of mortality, morbidity and disability.

By extension, Krug et al. (2002) make the point that social suffering from violence is enormous. In times of armed hostilities, infant mortality generally rises and average life expectancy drops. This is in part due to the increased risk of infectious diseases stemming from:

- decline in the percentage of the population immunised

- population movements and overcrowding in refugee camps

- greater exposure to vectors and environmental hazards, such as polluted water

- reduction in public health campaigns, and lack of access to health care services.

Moreover, public expenditure on health and education systems is likely to be sharply reduced at times of conflict as spending on the military is redoubled. Furthermore, the economy slows: agricultural and industrial production is damaged or destroyed by the enemy; governments have difficulty in collecting taxes; other sources of income (for example, tourism) dry up.

The World Health Organisation, in 2004, published a report specifically about the economic costs of interpersonal violence (Waters et al., 2004). It concluded that it was very expensive. For instance, interpersonal violence costs the USA 3.3% of the gross domestic product. In England and Wales, the total costs from violence (including homicide) have been estimated at US$40.2 billion annually. A single murder in South Africa costs over US$15 000, in Australia US$602 000 and in New Zealand US$829 000. But in the USA, the cost of each murder is over US$2 million. These costs to society are overall and include:

- costs of legal services

- direct medical costs

- costs of policing

- costs of incarceration

- economic benefits to perpetrators

- lost earnings and lost time

- lost human capital and productive value.

However, not all murders add unambiguously to social suffering or maintain their negative effects on individuals. Andrew Murray was 8 years old at the time of the Dunblane massacre and a pupil at that school. When the shooting started, he was herded into the Headmaster's study to escape from the gunman, Thomas Hamilton. He, like other pupils at the school, knew the killer. Although reluctant to talk to the media about the killings of his fellow pupils, he has commented that it has not had a lasting negative effect on him or on the town of Dunblane: 'I was young at the time and didn't really realise how it was a really difficult time for the town, but I think everyone has recovered really well from it and the town has moved on' (BBC News, 2004d). Andrew Murray has become a professional tennis player, winning the junior title at the US Open in 2004 and becoming a member of Britain's Davis Cup tennis squad in the same year. He was to make his first appearance at the Wimbledon Lawn Tennis Championships in 2005. By 2006 he had won a prestigious tennis ATP Tour Title, and became the top ranking British player.

Resolving the devastation of a loved one being murdered was handled in an unusual way by Jo Tuffnell when she formed a relationship with Patrick Magee in which they examined their respective roles as a secondary victim and perpetrator. Magee was one of the IRA bombers who tried to blow up the British Cabinet in the Grand Hotel, Brighton, England in 1984 where the ruling Tory Party was holding its Conference. The bomb was left in a hotel bathroom and it killed two Tory politicians and the wives of three others. Sir Anthony Berry, a Member of Parliament and Jo Tuffnell's father, was one of those killed. Magee was given eight life sentences at the Old Bailey, but was released after 14 years under the terms of the Good Friday agreement. Magee gained a first-class honours degree and a PhD whilst in prison.

A BBC documentary was made (called 'Facing the Enemy') in 2001 about the relationship between Jo Tufnell and her father's killer, and released as a DVD in 2002. It is not uncommon for secondary victims to find an emotional outlet in writing a book about their personal suffering. Holly Wells and Jessica Chapman, both 10 years old, were murdered in 2002 by Ian Huntley. Kevin Wells, Holly's father, wrote a book about his daughter's life and death, and his experiences with the media and the trial (Wells, 2005). The title of the book, *Goodbye dearest Holly*, implies that Kevin Wells was trying to, in the jargon of psychotherapy, 'bring closure' to his harrowing sorrow.

Furthermore, can actual 'good' come out of such devastating 'bad' as a barbaric murder? When Margaret Hassan was killed in Iraq in 2004, the Head of the Catholic Church in England and Wales, Cardinal Cormac Murphy-O'Connor commented that Margaret could be viewed as a martyr, and that her death 'may bear fruit in ultimate goodness' (Murphy-O'Connor, 2004). At the Ecumenical ceremony in the Irish Republic in which tribute was paid to Margaret Hassan, Father Tom Crean commented that her death had 'pierced the very marrow of our beings' and how 'our hearts cry out in pain'. The goodness being referred to here is the acts of sympathy and kindness offered to the secondary victims, and it is the heart of the public that is in pain. What is implied is that there is 'social solidarity' when a high profile murder takes place. A nation is reported as 'in mourning' alongside the relatives.

Personal suffering can be assuaged by specialised support groups. In Britain, the Victims of Crime Trust (VOCT) was established in the 1990s. VOCT has the aim to support those people who have been bereaved by a murder or manslaughter; gain compensation for secondary victims; give legal advice, counselling and respite breaks; and attend trials with secondary victims if necessary. Denise Bulger (now Denise Fergus) is a secondary victim of murder. It was her son, James Bulger, who was murdered by John Venables and Robert Thomson in 1993. She subsequently received support from the VOCT and then became a Patron. Mothers Against Murder and Aggression (MAMAA) gives support to, and campaigns on behalf of, relatives who have lost loved ones from such massacres as that which occurred in Dunblane. Mothers Against Guns (MAG) was set up by Lucy Cope, whose 22-year-old son Damian was shot and killed in 2002 outside a nightclub in London, to campaign against the 'gun-culture' that appears to be gaining a foothold in British cities much as it has done in some North American, South American, Russian and South African cities. This group, as its name implies, lobbies locally and nationally for: the availability of firearms to be rigorously controlled; curbs on the sale of replica guns, some of which can be converted to be used with live ammunition; severe sentences for illegal firearm possession and especially for murder when the weapon was a gun. Again in Britain,

Support After Murder and Manslaughter (SAMM) offers help to families and friends of the primary victim. SAMM also aims to raise public awareness about the effects of murder and manslaughter on secondary victims, and to promote and support research into the effects of murder and manslaughter on society. In the USA, Families of Murder Victims (FMV) was set up to provide support and advocacy, lobby the media and policy makers, and introduce 'anti-violence' education programmes into schools and colleges. Queensland Homicide Victims' Support Group (QHVSG) in Australia was founded in 1995, and aims to provide practical and moral support to the victims of homicide. QHVSG also has a policy of education to draw attention to the impact of homicide on people and communities.

Many of the support groups focus on retribution, campaigning for 'whole life tariffs', or the death penalty. A few, however, campaign against capital punishment arguing instead for reconciliation between secondary victims and perpetrators (for example, the USA's Murder Victims' Families for Reconciliation).

Murder victims' support groups demonstrably supply succour to secondary victims. Devastation can be converted into restoration. However, as 'social enterprises', they also perform the function of mollifying outrage about violence. That is, the efficacy of their lobbying is mainly tokenistic. Gun laws may be tightened, but firearm ownership is not prohibited. Violent videos may be certified 'not for viewing by children', but violence remains a permanent feature of mass entertainments. Public memory of terrible acts of violence is limited to those that excel in atrociousness or peculiarity. Moreover, the comfort gained by secondary victims from instances of socially generalised grief, making documentaries, writing books, pale into insignificance when compared with the sum of personal suffering, and therefore are feeble antidotes to social suffering.

Not exactly an antidote to the personal or social suffering from murder, rather a positive side-effect is the way in which the secondary victims view accomplishments that otherwise would not have been started. Along with such individual achievements is the edifying spectacle of communities pulling together in a collective revulsion and support.

On Saturday, 20 March, 1993 the IRA detonated a bomb in the shopping centre of Warrington, England. Jonathan Ball, aged 3 years was killed instantly and 56 people were injured, including Tim Parry, aged 12 years. Tim died from his injuries five days later.

> . . . those who have not suffered the extra-ordinary and completely unexpected tragedy our families have (his and that of Johnathan Ball], cannot imagine the *devastation* caused . . . [emphasis added]
>
> (Parry & Parry, 1994, p. 157)

On his journey to the hospital where Tim had been taken after the bombing, Colin Parry talks of his anxiety, which accelerated into panic. At the hospital Colin and Wendy Parry were told by the hospital doctor about the severity of Tim's injuries and that he was unlikely to live long. The condition of Tim in hospital produced emotional outpourings (abject grief, blind rage and intense bitterness) amongst the family, a 'shattering' of their lives and 'utter desolation'. Even the hardboiled British press were apparently deeply disturbed emotionally by what had happened to Tim.

As Colin and Wendy Parry remark, news concerning the death of a child is a parent's worse nightmare, especially when unexpected. For the Parrys, the men who deliberately placed a bomb in a busy street to maim and annihilate innocent passers-by were evil, callous, brutal, inhuman creatures. Colin Parry expresses his horror at the realisation that there are people (terrorists) who choose to kill other people, but not only do they kill they don't care who they kill, a means (murder) justifying an end (a political goal).

Colin Parry mentions a host of negative emotions and physical afflictions he has encountered since the death of his son: loneliness; anger; bitterness; frustration; hurt; a 'burden of sadness and emptiness'; 'uncontrolled outpouring of grief'; a 'tidal wave of loss'; and abject pain which permeated 'every nerve-end in an intense assault'. Long after Tim's death he is still experiencing changes in respiratory and circulatory functioning whenever he thinks of his son. Moreover, the sense of failure when a parent loses a child through murder is explained by Colin Parry as a feeling of letting his son down, leaving Tim vulnerable to death.

Along with family and friends, the death of a schoolchild directly affects their fellow pupils, as were Tim's school friends, some of whom were said to have spent days crying. One woman, who helped save the life of a teenager after the bomb detonated, was reported as still suffering from feelings of loss and inadequacy 10 years afterwards. A decade later Wilf Ball, father of Johnathan Ball, was described as still grieving and fighting bitterness (BBC Inside-Out North West, 2003). However, Colin Parry makes the point that these feelings are difficult to explain.

The loss of a young person through murder highlights baldly the ephemeral nature of human existence. It brings into question moral and religious guidance handed out throughout children's lives by parents, teachers and the clergy. In Western countries, the accepted and comforting trajectory of life stages (schools, jobs, marriage, retirement and an increasingly elongated demise) is disrupted by death at an early age. Of course in many developing countries this trajectory is corrupted. Just as in mediaeval Europe, in those countries today, where a considerable proportion of children die through disease, poverty and warfare, there are no realistic reassurances that can be given about the route life and death will take.

It is wrong to assume the death of a child is not also a deeply emotional event for families who have many of their offspring die. Added to the pain of losing a loved-one is the financial deficit for the families. Subsistence farming requires the contribution of young progeny to the division of labour. The wages of young people working in the 'sweat shops' of transnational corporations are vital to their families.

A murdered child provokes impassioned distress from people beyond the usual range of secondary victims. Emergency crews and health care staff deal constantly with the injured, dying, dead and the bereaved. However, their hierarchy of compassion is likely to have innocent children at its peak, and this appeared to be so after the Warrington killings. The Parrys refer to the kindness of police officers, clerics, paramedics, hospital staff, as well as from the football team their son supported.

Moreover, the Parry family received well-wishers' flowers and letters from all over Britain and Ireland. The Parrys mention the kindness and support they received from families and religious leaders across the Protestant–Catholic divide in Northern Ireland, and were greeted with warmth and sympathy from people in the Republic of Ireland. In Dublin, a 20 000 strong demonstration for peace in Northern Ireland was held shortly after Tim and Johnathan's death. There was, according to Colin Parry, a 'collective national awakening' in the Republic of Ireland following the Warrington bombing. Moreover, the death of Tim also gained the attention of members of the British royal family and Prime Minister, the President of the Republic of Ireland, the Archbishop of Liverpool and the President of the USA.

In Hazel May's (2001) moral hierarchy, the murder of innocent children is usually the most morally unacceptable form of killing as measured by media and public reaction. However, there is a moral disjunction made between the unjustified destruction of a child's life by another person and the 'socially-sanctioned' killing by society of children in road accidents. There is rarely if ever anything like the combination of international, national and local interest, that was shown over Tim Parry's death, for young people mowed down by drunken, speeding or careless drivers. Road traffic accidents usually attract only local journalistic comment, and totems of sympathy from the public (for example, flowers from the public placed at the site of the death).

Former President of the Irish Republic, Mary Robinson, wrote a foreword to the Parrys' book. Mary Robinson was President at the time of Tim Parry and Johnathan Ball's murders, and later the United Nations High Commissioner for Human Rights. She refers to the 'Warrington project' as a 'healing initiative' between the people of Tim's town and Ireland. The Warrington Peace Centre (Tim Parry and Johnathan Ball Trust) is an educational charity aiming to help children understand the nature of violent conflict. It encourages children to shape a peaceful and secure world. It was founded by Colin Parry, assisted by his wife. It is not conciliation for the deaths and injuries, observes Robinson, but is an example of the recuperative powers of the human spirit.

But, as Mary Robinson stated in her speech when opening the project, the deaths caused by the Warrington bombing created enormous public interest but this was not the case for most of those killed during 'the Troubles', as the Northern Ireland terrorist war is known. By the mid-1990s, the Troubles had seen 3000 adults and 120 children killed.

The death of Tim Parry went further than media and public interest (as concentrated and extensive as it was), entering the Byzantine arena of Irish politics. Mary Robinson refers in the Parrys' book to the killing of Tim Parry and Johnathan Ball as a dramatic force on her country. Her comments acknowledge, therefore, that the aftermath of (some) murders cuts across national borders. Of course Ireland and the UK are intrinsically connected if only through the terrorism that led to Tim Parry and Johnathan Ball's killings and thousands of other deaths. But the slaying of these children drew a much larger amount of media, public and political attention than usual. Mary Robinson details the large-scale sorrow and disgust in her country over actions carried out on behalf of Irish Republicanism aiming for a united Ireland. She argued that although a united Ireland had been a goal of her people since the Irish Republic was created, this should not be achieved at any price.

It could be that the cumulative effect of innocence, goodness and the years of life lost, produces heightened devastation in secondary victims, which, if publicised widely, becomes owned by tertiary victims. However, there have to be other ingredients beyond these to explain why the death of this boy who, according to his father, mostly enjoyed life and most of the time was well-behaved, gains such interest above another with similar personal credentials: why should Tim Parry's murder become a cause célèbre when millions of children die from hunger, warfare, disease as well as murder?

Part of the answer must be the phenomenon of cultural affinity coming into play. That is, the closer the victim is to the audience in terms of such cultural identities as nationhood, ethnicity and religion then the stronger the reaction. But, there is also a more cynical element at play. It is commercially and/or politically more expedient to 'manage' public responses to violence and threats of violence. Enemies and bogeymen/women are invented, or if they are already available conjured as especially dangerous, to sell news stories and to achieve political ends. Juxtaposed with such demonisation is the management of victim-hood. There can't be one without the other. 'Evil killers' require 'blameless bystanders'.

Colin Parry comments that after Tim's death his son gained 'millions of friends'. This is an aspect of the social solidarity after disaster. It is the media that plays a central role in stimulating and maintaining messages of cohesion within society. Motivated at root by commercial reasons, the media are likely to drop the story when it becomes 'tired'.

Some stories of killings run and run, however, drawing the public's attention to the threat posed to the moral order of society. Moral panics can't happen without a receptive audience, which, through its enthusiastic outrage, incites further media output and eventually political input. A spiral of interest and indignation occurs. Personal grief turns into communal fury and sorrow. Declarations of social change are heralded by the politicians, memorials built, but eventually and inevitably social calm arrives. A story that 'has legs' eventually becomes exhausted.

This is not to suggest that the players in this public drama are not genuinely affected by tragedy. As is acknowledged by Colin Parry, members of the media and (most) public officials displayed honest upset at the death of his son. Many expressed their views with transparent emotional commitment about the injustice of Tim's killing. Moreover, journalists do take up the fight for humanitarian issues at times. However, it would be rare if a moral stand against an injustice could be detrimental to the corporate interests of the journalist's employer. The BBC, as a public-funded media organisation, perhaps is the exception. But not only does the BBC operate as business; its avowal of impartiality means that humanitarian causes may be indulged if the spin-off is higher sales or viewing figures, and if it appears that such support is uncontroversial.

The murder of these children could be considered as a process that affects all levels of victim, but is patently more severe for those close to the murdered person. Colin and Wendy Parry suffered far more than, say, a family in Dublin from whom they received flowers or a journalist who covered their story. Alternatively, rather than the suffering being diluted the further away the original connection to the primary victim, it could be that there are different processes at work.

The distress of the victim's family is not in the same category as that of tertiary victims. Communities, societies and the global village are responding when murder occurs to threaten social stability. The representatives of communities and social institutions may be personally disconcerted by murder but (as with other types of deviance), their function is to protect their organisations, whether this is a government, the United Nations, criminal justice systems, or world free trade. Not all murders, or other forms of social transgression, pose such a threat. Some murders (for example, the serial killing of prostitutes or the killing of a criminal whilst committing a robbery) can actually shore up social values. The death of Tim disrupted the 'natural order' of the lives of the Parry family, recounts Colin Parry. It also, as with other killings near the top of the moral hierarchy of murder, disrupts the 'natural order' of social values.

The Parry family put their efforts in dealing with their loss into working for peace in Northern Ireland. From a psychoanalytic perspective this can be regarded as 'compensation', a mental mechanism that is unconsciously helping protect the 'self' from awful reality of some painful event such as the death of a loved one. Compensation allows for an outlet of feeling otherwise tied to a painful event. In the case of the Parrys, working for peace demands similar emotions to those that were given to Tim. For some, mental mechanisms do not work so positively and a destructive process can occur.

On 11 March, 2004, ten bombs exploded on four trains in Madrid, Spain. As with the Warrington bombs, the bombs in Madrid were indiscriminate killing mechanisms. The trains in Madrid, like the street in Warrington, had ordinary people engaging in everyday activities, shopping and going to or from work. The bombs in Madrid either went off whilst the train was passing through a station or, if they didn't, they were set so to do. Nearly 200 people were killed and over 2000 injured. Bodies were torn apart when metal sheared off the blasted train. Body parts from adults, children and babies were strewn around the tracks and stations. Other people were burned to death in their seats on the trains. An assemblage of petty criminals and radical north-African Muslims, inspired by al-Qaeda internet sites, have been blamed for planting the bombs (Tremlett, 2006a). Twenty-nine people were indicted in April 2006 for mass murder or conspiring to murder (Tremlett, 2006b).

In a BBC interview, the husband of one train commuter describes the 'excruciating discovery' of his wife's death. Whilst watching the post-bombing events on television, he had a 'dreadful feeling' and was 'completely consumed by fear' that his wife was one of the victims (BBC News, 2004e). The shock comes first as fear that something dreadful is going to happen (that is, suspecting that a loved one is dead), and then continues (when discovering that the loved one is dead). At this stage the level of PTSD is likely to increase (worst fears being confirmed), or may subside when the loss is confirmed because the uncertainty of not knowing has been removed. But then the stress will be renewed when informed of the exact way in which death was met if this was painful, and again when identifying the body.

The bombing of Madrid (and Warrington) is an example of rippling victim-hood. First the train commuters become victims, then their relatives, friends and associates, their communities (one neighbourhood, Alcala de Henares, had 40 of its residents killed), the city, followed by the Spanish nation.

The carnage from terrorism is indiscriminate because the specific names, genders, ages and even nationalities of the primary victims cannot be known absolutely. The terrorist may not even care who exactly is killed or what their personal characteristics and social identity are. For the terrorist, the target group is usually the tertiary victims. ETA wants to kill Spanish police offic-ers, state officials, and possibly foreign tourists to draw attention to their campaign for Basque independence and killing that particular officer, offi-cial or tourist is either incidental or a 'bonus'. Northern Irish Loyalist para-militaries killed Catholics and British soldiers during 'the Troubles' because they hated both (Catholics due to history, and soldiers because they repre-sented an unpalatable future) but mainly to stop Ireland becoming united. The al-Qaeda hijackers who flew planes into the Twin Towers in New York would not have known any of those who died in these buildings. They were on a broader mission, to attack the USA and what it represented economi-cally and culturally.

Moreover, the Madrid bombers could not have known that the killing of one Honduran couple on their way to work would leave eight orphans. The couple were the family's wage-earners, and were working hard to provide for their extended family. This family had migrated to Spain from a country with no antagonistic connection to al-Qaeda. Fifty-four of the dead were migrants. It could be argued that the exploitation of migrant labour from developing countries is at the heart of the Western-inspired globalisation that the disparate groups who form al-Qaeda are fighting against. From this viewpoint this family are structurally positioned alongside al-Qaeda rather than being an enemy. Moreover, some of the dead were Muslim.

Advocates of radical and swift social change (terrorists, insurgents, revolu-tionaries and state-backed military interventionists) often justify killing innocent people and deaths from 'friendly fire' (these deaths construed as 'collateral damage') as the unfortunate 'means' to a glorious 'end'.

The mother of the Honduran man killed and his daughter-in-law, were inter-viewed by journalist Peter Popham a year later (Popham, 2005). The mother described how the grief remains almost unbearable, particularly as she lost her only son. As Popham explains, the terrorists' bombs at the macro level had dramatic political ramifications. The Spanish government immediately threw suspicion on the Basque separatists, ETA, rather than wait for the evidence to be prepared. Supportive of the war with Iraq, a position that was unpopular with the Spanish populace, and for what may have been expedient national political reasons jumping too readily to assume it knew who had caused the explosions in Madrid, the government became discreditable. The night before the Spanish people voted in the next general election, held soon after the bombings, a video-taped admission of responsibility for organising the bombings on behalf of al-Qaeda's military commander in Europe, Adu Dujan the Afghan, was televised (Tremlett, 2006). The government was ousted.

The 'Coalition of the Willing', as the countries that sent forces with the USA to invade Iraq were named by President W. Bush, was weakened as the new Spanish government pulled out its troops. Moreover, the Madrid bombs had demonstrated, argues Popham, that it wasn't just the USA that was exposed to terrorist acts of deadly violence. Adu Dujan the Afghan gave the explicit warning that any European city could be attacked (Tremlett, 2006).

At the micro level, human suffering persisted long after the event. Parents had lost their children, children had lost their parents. Wives lost their husbands, husbands lost wives. Friends and colleagues had been lost. This family had its bread-winners taken away who not only supported young and old relatives in Spain but those relatives from their native Honduras. Dreams of a better future with economic security and all that brings (for example, good housing and education) for kin in Spain and Honduras resting on the economic support of the victims, were smashed. The murdered couple had barely managed to maintain these financial responsibilities whilst they worked in low paid employment. Without them, the risk of social and economic failure of their dependants is raised considerably. For some extended family members in the dead couple's country of origin, their survival was endangered because of living so near the poverty line.

As can be seen at times with individuals and families, however, the Madrid bombings had paradoxical consequences. The Spanish nation (and the communities whose residents had been killed in particular) showed signs of being distraught, but also of cohesion and re-affirmation. Devastation, once again, produced kindness. The wounded helped others not as badly wounded as themselves to escape the tangled wreckage, the emergency service personnel braved a scene of carnage they had not previously experienced, long lines of volunteer blood-donors formed at mobile units across the city, political tribalism and campaigning for the up-and-coming general election was put in abeyance, huge demonstrations were held to show amity and compassion for those directly affected by the bombings, and three days of official nationwide mourning was called by the Spanish government. At the first anniversary of their bombings, 192 victims were mourned in Spain in a five-minute silence observed throughout the country. A ceremony involving the King and Queen of Spain and a dozen heads of states took place.

Furthermore, the Madrid bombings had the constructive effect of changing significantly the social status of many of the survivors and that of their families. Many of those travelling on the doomed trains were people from poor suburbs going to work in menial jobs in the centre of the city. Some of these workers were illegal immigrants from such countries as Honduras. The Spanish Government offered the survivors and members of their family Spanish citizenship and financial recompense.

For Giles Tremlett (2006) there is also the possibility that ETA, having killed over 800 people in 30 years of separatist campaigning, may have altered its tactics and moved away from violence. The Madrid bombings caused such widespread disgust amongst the Spanish people, including the Basques, that no one since March 2004 to date has seemingly been killed by ETA.

Sometimes it is the society itself that causes the suffering if that society is chaotic. Murder accentuates social suffering in these situations rather than being the catalyst. Ciudad Juarez is a case in point. Hundreds of women have been murdered in Ciudad Juarez, Mexico. Amnesty International (2003) reported that from 1993 to 2003 about 400 women were murdered there. That figure had risen exponentially, with 2005 having more murders than any other year to date.

Most of the victims were sweatshop or menial service workers, young and poor, although some were children and students. Cultural misogyny is a root problem in the region and set the context in which violence against women is, if not acceptable, then not unusual. Amnesty International (2003) reports on the general climate of violence towards women in Ciudad Juarez and Chihuahua City. Many of the women had been tortured brutally after their abduction, sexually violated and then killed.

Ciudad Juarez has a dense population of about two million. It is a mixture of residential, industrial, commercial and entertainment zones. Alma Guillermoprieto (2003) describes the city as 'a seedy border town'. She observes that everywhere there are junkyards, shanty towns, sprawling suburbs, 'topless' bars and nightclubs, and fast-food outlets. The population is rootless. It is a Mecca for drug cartels, and has one of the highest crime rates in all of the Americas, and an extremely high rate of domestic violence (Vulliamy, 2003a). Chihuahua City, several hundred kilometres south of Ciudad Juarez, has a growing problem of similar murders, as have other cities on the border of Mexico and the USA.

Ciudad Juarez's population is made up of itinerant workers with no support networks, living in shambolic shanty towns in which those employed are adopting the means of succeeding in a capitalist system (that is, working hard) with hardly any possibility of achieving the end (that is, financial security and high social status), whilst others take deviant routes to achieve that end. This city, and other parts of the Chihuahua region, has the classic symptoms of 'social strain' and 'social disorganisation', with amorphous and inequitable residential expansion and income distribution, a soaring crime rate and alleged corrupt officialdom.

Ciudad Juarez is a part of 'Amexico', the geographical segment of Mexico and the USA on the strip of land that forms the porous border separating the two countries. Amexico has a vibrant if 'informal' economy in which tens of millions of US dollars' worth of goods pass through, occupying hundreds of thousands of people. Such a city, with migrant populations moving between Mexico and the USA, engenders vulnerability and predatory behaviour. The shanty towns in particular foment crime and violence, but the state of Chihuahua has a reputation of having a patriarchal culture in which brutality by men towards women is not pursued by the authorities.

Not only women, however, are susceptibly to violence in Ciudad Juarez. The Ciudad Juarez victim support group *Nuestras Hijas de las Casas* (translated as 'May Our Daughters Return Home') has revealed that perhaps 2000 men have been killed, although as with the deaths of women it is very difficult to ascertain accurately how many murders have taken place.

Ciudad Juarez is an economic satellite in the worldwide capitalist market run by transnational corporations. The city developed rapidly due to the setting up of assembly plants (*maquilas*) for global businesses. There are hundreds of *maquilas* in and around Ciudad Juarez. The vast majority of the *maquilas* are owned by USA-based, but transnational, businesses, which make profits of billions of US dollars annually. This thriving economy has a ready supply of (mainly female) cheap labour, but the city's civic planning is haphazard. Women workers in the *maquilas* are second-class citizens by virtue of their gender and are mere cogs in the global corporate market. Workers are dispensable because they can be easily replaced due to the flood of poor women entering the region from other parts of Mexico looking for work. Local managers of the *maquilas* and their corporate bosses do not provide any or adequate protection for their female employees either when going to or coming from work. Their low wages mean that they have to live in run-down and dangerous parts of the city.

According to Amnesty International, both local and national investigators of the murders have gained a reputation of being ineffective in apprehending the killers, and in dealing sympathetically with the families of the victims. Moreover, there have been suggestions that the women have been killed in 'snuff movies' and sadistic pornographic videos, that organs of the victims have been removed to be sold for transplants, and that they fallen prey to satanic rituals, domestic violence, violence associated with drug trafficking and serial killers from the USA crossing over into Mexico. Simon Whitechapel (2002) has theorised about who is responsible for the killings in Ciudad Juarez, suggesting that the city is a 'serial killers' playground', and that the killers are likely to have crossed over from the USA.

In addition, drug dealers, the managers of the global corporations with their businesses in the region, owners of construction and energy industries, landowners, government officials and the police, have all come under suspicion (Vulliamy, 2003b). The corporations operating in Ciudad Juarez are open to the criticism that they are complicit in these murders because they create the bad conditions in which their female employees have to work and live.

Causes of distress to the families of the murder victims, apart from the actual loss of their loved ones, include regular misinformation, and either no arrests or the wrong people arrested. The police have been accused of making invalid identifications of bodies, and of giving inaccurate explanations for how the victim met their death. Guillermoprieto refers to instances of the police returning mutilated bodies to the relatives who later discover that the corpse is not their loved one, thereby causing unnecessary angst. The suffering is then repeated of course when they do have the correct body given to them.

The police are also accused of 'victim-blaming' (that is, insinuating that the women, because of how they were dressed or how late at night they were killed, 'asked for it') and of insulting and ridiculing the families. Families have responded to the accusation that their dead loved one was responsible for her own death by the way she dressed or how late she was out in dangerous parts of the city (for example, leaving a nightclub) by pointing out that some of the murders have been committed during daytime, for example, when going to or from work in the *maquilas*. Such distress has been exacerbated by the suspicion that evidence against those charged with murder is unreliable, perhaps obtained through torture or deliberately falsified (Guillermoprieto, 2003).

The police have bungled many of the investigations. Local non-government organisations (NGOs), the United Nations, Amnesty International and legal officials from the USA have all criticised the Mexican authorities for their handling of these murders, and intimated that the local police are corrupt.

Omar Sharif Latif (also known as Abdel Latif Sharif), an Egyptian chemist who had a criminal record in the USA of violence against women was arrested in 1995 for murder and rape, had his conviction for one murder overturned, his sentence reduced, had another appeal turned down, and (in

2006) remains in gaol serving a sentence reduced from 30 years to 20. Victor Garcia Uribe was convicted of killing eight women in 2004. Ten alleged gang members were convicted in 2005 for the killing of 12 women.

Nuestras Hijas de las Casas attempts to get officials to act efficiently. Its demands are not unreasonable. The group wants officials to find and rescue those abducted, or retrieve their bodies. It wants all of the culprits brought to justice, and for appropriate punishment to be handed out by the courts. Financial reparations should, it argues, also be made to the affected families.

Ciudad Juarez has both 'personal' and 'social' suffering. But there is little social solidarity in Ciudad Juarez because there is an absence of social stability both in the city and throughout that region of Amexico.

SUMMARY

The personal suffering from murder can be described as extraordinary bereavement that affects detrimentally a wide range of people connected with both the primary victim and the perpetrator in a variety of ways. The extraordinariness of this type of bereavement entails not only unique elements of grief, but other facets of psychological as well as physiological distress that have led to its medicalisation as PTSD.

But the 'objective' measurement of personal suffering through the diagnostic construction of PTSD is problematic when what is being relayed is the subjective and idiosyncratic of having a loved one murdered. Furthermore, the medicalisation of personal suffering does not account adequately for the social factors that are either the backdrop to, or main cause of, violence. Nor is PTSD a suitable explanatory model for the social suffering that murder exudes. How could, for example, the suffering exuding from the killing of Tim Parry in twentieth-century England by the IRA and the slaying of Madame Riviere, two of her children, and her unborn child by her other child in nineteenth-century France, be aggregated?

It is common, however, for secondary victims to use the idiom 'devastation' when describing their lives after a murder. 'Devastation' denotes the immense impact on their lives. It is a term that implies many areas of normal functioning have been seriously disrupted. Their customary patterns of eating, sleeping, performance at school or work, interpersonal communication, planning, emotional stability, and physical wellbeing, are interrupted if not damaged irreparably. 'Devastation' also suggests, because they are literally overwhelmed, that it is difficult for them to proffer an exhaustive and exact account of their sensations.

Murder spawns both personal and social suffering. Whilst individual accomplishment and social solidarity can by activated by murder, the negative effects are substantial and are escalating. The totality of suffering from murder is such that it can be described as devastating to humans and to their globalised society. Moral repute, economic development, social planning and political constancy become dislocated, or can never become customary, when so many people in so many parts of the world are exposed to violence.

CHAPTER 5

WHY IS MURDER FASCINATING?

The year 2005 was a good year for Hitler. Or more precisely for his memorabilia, the sale of which continues to thrive 60 years after he committed suicide.

Adolf Hitler (1889–1945), probably the most destructive person in history in terms of human life, was also an artist (and a vegetarian). One of his sketches dating from 1924 sold for £5000 at an auction in England (J. Harris, 2005). The year 2005 also saw the release of the film *Downfall*. The story is of Hitler's final days in his Berlin bunker as the Second World War draws to an end, as told by his last secretary. *Downfall* was a commercial and artistic success.

Moreover, Hitler's picture (along with Heinrich Himmler) fronted the 2005 book *Auschwitz – The Nazis and the Final Solution* (L. Rees, 2005). Other 2005 Hitler books included *Inside Hitler's bunker* (Fest, 2005), *Dictators: Hitler's Germany and Stalin's Russia* (Overy, 2005), *Hitler's British slaves* (Longden, 2005), and *Hitler's canary* (Toksvig, 2005). Hitler's 2005 DVD releases were *Hitler in Colour*, *Hitler in His Own Words* and a re-release of the 1972 Spike Milligan film *Adolf Hitler – My Part In His Downfall*. All of this is despite a massive backlist of artefacts and entertainments already relating to Hitler and the Nazis.

Sir Ian Kershaw, Professor of Modern History at Sheffield University (UK) in his 2005 Open University Lecture observed:

> Never since the war has there been so much about Hitler as recently. It seems at times near-obsessive. And Hitler is a taboo figure like no other . . . Hitler has become the very icon of evil. But that just enhances the *fascination*. [emphasis added]
>
> (Kershaw, 2005)

My search of the internet store Amazon in 2005 found over 3000 books on Hitler, 65 videos, 47 DVDs and 17 CDs. There were nearly 2000 books on Nazis, 13 videos, 156 DVDs and five CDs. The content of one of these CDs (under the nomenclature of 'classic music') is speeches performed by Hitler and Benito Mussolini (1883–1945), the Italian fascist dictator. Yes, someone perhaps at this very minute is relaxing in a hot bath, drinking a glass of soothing wine (Riesling?), whilst listening to the phlegmatic rantings of *Der Fuhrer* and *Il Duce*. Or more likely (given that neither was known for their writing of calming orations – arousing the populace to invade their neighbours requires stirring prose), a would-be tyrant, inspired by these demagogic connoisseurs, would be strutting, saluting and bellowing bellicosity.

But let's not forget that Hitler's regime was responsible for murdering millions.

Murder One also had a very good 2005. Murder One is described by its owners as Europe's leading crime and mystery bookshop, stocking every crime title that be can obtained in the English language (in-print, out of print, newly published, second-hand, reference, anthologies, fiction, non-fiction, hard-backs and soft-backs). It also sells 'romance' books. In 2005, having been retailing its wares for 15 years, the store had expanded into new premises in the centre of London. The blurb on Murder One's internet site (2006) is testament to customer satisfaction both from the business angle and the inherent quality of pleasure gained from its products: 'Please contact us if you have any comments on this site or on the wonderful world of crime fiction. Enjoy! (signed Maxim, Tanya, Jerry, Paulo, Gwen, Maike and Neil)'.

A search of Amazon using the word 'murder' in 2005 listed 13 406 books, 2743 DVDs, 450 CDs, 101 videos, 4 computer games and 30 toys. Investigating the internet in the same year using the search-engine Google revealed over 23 million 'hits' with murder as a focus for their site.

Reviewing Google of course does not produce an exhaustive list of Hitler-Nazi entertainments, nor does it cover what seems to be a limitless number of 'souvenirs' about that epoch in German history). Neither does it provide an accurate picture of 'murder' consumption as a proportion of the internet 'hits' may be duplicates and others not linked directly to the issue of fascination. Furthermore, the increase in 'hits' on Google (to nearly 80 million by 2006) is partly explained by internet search engines becoming more expansive as well as sophisticated in how internet sites are collated and referenced. A similar argument can apply to Amazon (by 2006 its bank of murder commodities had risen to 14 102 books, 3037 DVDs, 578 CDs, 103 videos, 8 computer games and 36 toys). For example, some of the CDs listed as 'classic music' are theme tunes from murder-orientated films or operas. Presumably, one does not necessarily have to be overly engrossed in killing to enjoy Sir Richard Rodney Bennett's composition for the film version of Agatha Christie's 'Murder on the Orient Express', or too committed to religious human sacrifice to appreciate Allessandro Scarlatti's *Cain Overo Il Primo Omicidio*.

That said, the colossal number of internet sites and the vast array of goods sold directly dealing with murder demonstrates its popularity. What is difficult to comprehend, therefore, is the disjunction between the personal and social suffering from murder and the level of intrigue murder affords. It provides millions of people who buy videos, films and books with murder as the central plot, with a peculiar pastime. Murder is a strange hobby because its adherents are using the dreadfulness of murder to gain gratification and glee in the same way as train-spotting, basket weaving, or oriental origami might to others. Take for example the craze for short holidays during which participants pay to play a killer, victim, witness or detective: 'Murder Mystery Weekend . . . Take on a character role in this intriguing murder plot while enjoying excellent home-cooked food, including locally themed dishes . . .' Where was this taking place? Well, it was advertised in the English Youth Hostel Association spring/summer 2006 magazine, to be held in one of its own hostels. To be fair, participants had to be at least 16 years old, and the food probably really was very good.

But let's not forget that murder devastated millions of lives during 2005.

A moral hierarchy of murder, that encompasses perpetrators and victims, points to the high level of repugnance over barbarism from the perpetrator and the innocence of the victim (for example, sadistic killers of children, the Nazi systematic extermination of Jews). A low level of repugnancy is applied to unattributed, understandable and 'acceptable' killings (for example, deaths caused by the activities of corporations, domestic murders, infanticide and euthanasia).

There is another element to a hierarchy of murder, that of the interest shown. Enthralment about morally low-level murder will in the main be relatively low, whereas morally high-level murder usually attracts far more attention.

The interplay between the four dimensions within this hierarchy of murder (perpetrator, victim, repugnancy, fascination) will be mediated by social factors such as 'cultural affinity'. That is, it is far more likely that a country's media will report, the public will take notice and the politicians will act, when a murder victim is from that country (although there will be further divisions of repugnancy and fascination depending on which of that country's ethnic groups that they are from). Multiple and large-scale killings of people belonging to a particular faith group are likely to gain more notice amongst others from that same group than those unassociated with that faith. But in 'failing states' where killings are habitual, then neither repugnancy nor fascination will be elevated unless preposterous or exceptionally symbolic (for example, the death of the leader from one side in the fighting; the uncovering of mass graves by journalists; or the killing of a foreign dignitary).

Naturally, I'm not the only one who is keen to understand why murder is so popular. Elie Godsi comments on the lure of violence generally:

> Violence in all its forms be it murder, manslaughter, rape, child abuse or the many other ways in which we are capable of brutalising each other, fascinates, intrigues and horrifies us at one and the same time. As much as we may be shocked and outraged, we are also very curious. The media focus on the seemingly bizarre; the darker, macabre side of life has reached frenzied proportions.
>
> (Godsi, 2004, p. 33)

Martin Bell (2003) comments on the insatiable desire for all things associated with killing. News services must, to keep their audiences, serve up a diet of warfare, serial shootings and hostage-takings. Television and radio ratings and newspaper sales improve when events turn nasty: allied troops are destroyed through 'friendly fire'; a sniper is loose in the city, killing people at random; a hostage is beheaded. Bell raises the problem of assessing what is the cause and what the effect by asking whether it is the media that prompt blood-thirsty entertainment packaged as news, or are the media responding to a public-led demand?

Peter Conrad admits he is obsessed with the famous British film director, Alfred Hitchcock (1899–1980). In an article titled 'Fatal attraction – our fascination with murder' (2000a) and his book *Hitchcock Murders* (2000b), he writes about Hitchcock's ability to thrill his audience with exemplary finesse. Analysing his obsession with Hitchcock, Conrad reasons that what made Hitchcock a great director was his recognition that murder is a primary human habit. For Conrad, Hitchcock had understood that whilst animals kill to survive, only humans kill because they feel like it, or because they want to know what it feels like. This isn't strictly true as chimpanzees kill other chimpanzees for reasons that are only indirectly to do with self-protection, procreation or food. But as a generalisation humans are the embodiment of intra-species killing. Conrad's proposition is that Hitchcock's films (for example: *Dial M for Murder*, *The Man Who Knew Too Much*, and especially *Psycho*), with their blend of murder and sub-textual eroticism, are the quintessence of human intra-psychic exhilaration.

'Ripper' and 'cannibal' murders are particularly seductive and intoxicating killings, and have become lucrative species of entertainment. They are commonly vicious and gory in their actual implementation and in their media presentation. As with other deeply repugnant murders, the perpetrators are always barbaric. However, the victims are not always innocents. The ripper and cannibal preys on the blameless and blameworthy alike. But what unites ripper and cannibal killings is licentiousness. The ripper and cannibal murder is an erotic drama. The players exude malice and sexual excitement, not sub-textually but candidly. A vividly poignant role is set aside for the occasional sexually naive casualty of a killer with manifest sexual predilections, but the cornerstone of the script usually hinges on the characterisation of the victims as sexually reprehensible or repressed. Within the moral hierarchy of murder, an amalgam of the victim's and killer's enacted or latent carnality outweighs the missing ingredient of virtuousness.

As the audience gorges on the maliciousness and debauchery of the ripper or cannibal, a window is opened on the intricate dynamics of human baseness per se. To enter through this window, I turn to the 'werewolf'. This is not another popular consumers' choice of ghoulish recreation I wish to highlight, as mesmerizing as a murder by a werewolf might be. The werewolf is absent in factual narratives about killings (verifiable examples being as scarce as proof of the Loch Ness Monster), and hence its appearance in fiction is not as intoxicating as the ripper and cannibal. However, the mythical werewolf provides a suitable metaphor for personal and social ambivalence regarding murder. Just as the werewolf metamorphoses drastically from benign normality in the daytime to nighttime savage abnormality, so 'normal' humans and 'ethical' societies on the one hand pledge disgust at and instate penalties for violence, but on the other hand requisition and exhibit malevolence and murder.

RIPPER

As I was preparing to write about Jack the Ripper, I opened my newspaper (the British broadsheet, *The Guardian)* to find a lengthy article on Jack the Ripper. A few days later the same newspaper ran a full-length statement from a contemporary theorist on Jack the Ripper, Patricia Cornwell. Cornwell states that her approach, applying science to the mystery of Jack the Ripper's identity, is intended to hold the (long dead) murderer accountable for the sake of the (also long dead) victims. She also advertises the updated edition of her book *Portrait of a Killer* (originally published in 2003). As I was editing this chapter, up popped Jack the Ripper again. This time it was a BBC survey to ascertain, from a sample of 5000 radio listeners, the 'worst Briton' in the last 1000 years. The list of the top-ten most heinous contained: Oswald Mosley, the leader of a British fascist party before the Second World War; Thomas Becket, the twelfth-century Archbishop of Canterbury; and the thirteenth-century King John. But, gaining more than twice as many votes as the runner-up was, yes you've guessed, Jack the Ripper (*BBC History Magazine*, 2006).

The on-line store Amazon, in 2004, 116 years after the events, recorded 220 books on Jack the Ripper, 14 DVDs, 11 videos and 11 CDs. The internet search engine Google had 506 000 'hits' for Jack the Ripper. The latter referred to articles, games, television programmes, books, movies and theatre musicals. By 2005, the Google hit rate had increased to one million, and Amazon's list was 240 books, 20 DVDs and 14 CDs. In 2006, Google's hit rate had gone up to 1 800 000 and Amazon's 2006 catalogue of Ripper products had enlarged to: 249 books; 21 DVDs; and 1 computer game (but no one had brought out any more Jack the Ripper music).

Hitchcock had directed a silent film, released in 1927 called *The Lodger: A Story of the London Fog*. It was actually a tale based on Jack the Ripper (who in the film was suspected of being a lodger). In this film Hitchcock displays an early skill of linking sex with murder. This was what was to gain him a reputation, as Peter Conrad notes, as a director of note. Hitchcock's cinematic style was to communicate suspense through a collage of visual, musical, verbal and non-verbal messages (including silence). He was the inventor of the 'thriller-killer' genre in films, which now is a winning formula in popular entertainment. Moreover, Hitchcock himself remains popular with *The Lodger* recorded onto DVD in 2004, a boxed-set of his films collated for sale in 2005, and, in 2006, full-page advertisements appeared in *The Guardian* for its give-away DVD of Hitchcock's *The Man Who Knew Too Much*.

Why has Jack the Ripper remained so vivid in the British consciousness and that of people from many other parts of the world, for so long? Why is this unknown killer such an iconic figure? The continued interest in this killer is astounding, commencing in the nineteenth-century and showing no signs of abating. In fact, novel entertainment and criminal investigative technologies mean that yet more ways are available of repeating the story to the masses and drumming-up further academic interest.

Is it just a good tale, having as it does a tantalisingly unsolvable (even with the aid of science) plot and therefore open to sensible and sensational hypotheses whether postulated by the amateur or professional criminologist? Or could it be the mix of ferocious bloodshed and taboo sensuality that is central to this Victorian murder that is so invigorating?

Interest in Jack the Ripper has created bizarre leisure pursuits, none more so than the specialist tours aimed at the lucrative London tourist trade. One of these tours is called 'On the Trail of Jack the Ripper'. Advertised on the internet, there is a picture of a terrified young woman, and a link to a similar-styled video. The sales pitch rests on beckoning tourists to have an 'enjoyable' and 'relaxed' walk along the Ripper's 'murderous route' for two hours. Clearly astute business people, the operators of the tour acknowledge the vagaries of the English climate with a pledge that the tour will go ahead no matter what the weather conditions (presumably pea-soup murkiness would be ideal).

The operators brag in their advertisement that 'On the Trail of Jack the Ripper' is the only 'show' to have contemporaneous photographs of the streets and murder sites, and of the 'poor unfortunate victims'. The audience will, the advertisement claims, be taken along the Ripper's 'bloodstained' and 'bloodcurdling' trail. With so much blood still sloshing around no wonder the tour operators tell their customers that after sifting through the evidence (doubtless using portable DNA-testing kits), they will be able to eliminate the 'fascinating' suspects.

However, not everyone is pleased about Jack the Ripper tours (assuming that the operators of this one are, given that it has been running for nearly 10 years, and a satisfied clientele is proclaimed in their advertisement). Local residents, possibly already mildly irritated at having their habitat described as 'sinister' and 'crumbling' (as it is by those running 'On the Trail of Jack the Ripper'), have expressed anger at the Ripper tourist trade for bringing crowds of people into their streets (BBC, 2001). What they are reported as being especially concerned about is that it is increasing because of the unrelenting interest in Jack the Ripper as entertainment.

A new wave of interest was stirred-up by the 2001 film *From Hell* staring Johnny Depp as the police inspector tracking the killer before another prostitute is killed. Along with the chase between the Ripper and the detective, and the Ripper and victim, a love interest (the inspector has fallen in love with the Ripper's next target), there is a judicious amount of blood spilled (not too much to sicken, but just enough to arouse). These ingredients ensured that the film was a box-office triumph some 113 years after the original murders, and 74 years after Hitchcock's effort.

So, what are the supposed facts surrounding the case of Jack the Ripper? The date is 1888, and the locality is Whitechapel in London's East End. Life is hard in this poor district, industrialisation taking its toll on its workers and worse still on those out of work. To comprehend the awfulness of life in slum areas of nineteenth-century cities, Friedrich Engels' *The condition of the working class in England* is unsurpassed in its rich and disturbing detail. Although Engels (1820–1895) wrote the book in 1845 (and it was published in Germany that year), it wasn't published in English until over 40 years later (and then republished in 1999).

Many improvements in the living and working circumstances of the working classes had occurred during that time, but Engels, in prefaces to later editions and related writings, was to observe that in the East End of London misery, insecurity, degradation and desolation persisted for many (Engels, 1999).

Paul Begg (2004) has written what he describes as the 'definitive history' of Jack the Ripper, but his book also contains background information on

Victorian London. For Begg, the ripper murders became notorious because of the notoriety of that part of London. Reinforcing Engels's observations, Begg argues that the East End was feared amongst the general population in England because the country was in transition, heading towards a fairer distribution of the returns from industrialisation but still with the unsettling sense in the nation's psyche that progress could be reversed. The East End housed a corrupted, uneducated, destitute version of an earlier England. Within that environment prostitution was rife. Prostitution, particularly when it is unregulated, is a dangerous occupation in any city at any time. But in nineteenth-century London, characterised by disorder and anonymity, it was especially perilous. Assaults on prostitutes were unlikely to be reported to the police, and if reported very unlikely to be followed up.

The murder, however, of several prostitutes in a brutal fashion over a few months, their bodies mutilated and frequently with organs excised, could not be ignored. Following Begg's theme, Neil Storey (2004) links the rise of the iconic imagery of Jack the Ripper to the rise of the 'gutter press'. In a country that was the industrial engine of the world, which had the largest Empire in history, the East End was anachronistic. Amidst social mire of crime and privation 'folk devils' were sought by journalists, and Jack the Ripper served that purpose well.

Conventionally, it is the death of five women, from August to November 1988, that has been attributed to Jack the Ripper:

1. Mary Ann Nichols, killed 31 August

2. Annie Chapman, killed 8 September

3. Elizabeth Stride, killed 30 September

4. Catherine Eddowes, also killed 30 September

5. Mary Jane (Marie Jeanette) Kelly, killed 9 November

Jack the Ripper's identity is still not known. Inevitably, there have been contentious suggestions, false lines of inquiry and hoaxes. Hundreds of people at various times have been implicated. However, amongst the regular suspects are:

1. Queen Victoria's grandson, Prince Albert Victor, also known as the Duke of Clarence

2. Sir (Dr) William Gull, royal physician

3. James Maybrick, a cotton merchant from the north of England

4. Aaron Kosminski, a Polish immigrant

5. Michael Ostrog, a convicted thief

6. Montague John Druitt, a barrister and teacher

7. George Chapman, another Polish immigrant

8. Francis Tumblety, a quack doctor from the USA

Crime novelist, Patricia Cornwell (2003) has named the German-born artist Walter Sickert as Jack the Ripper after spending a huge amount of money buying scores of his paintings (and more advertising her theory and book), and submitting them to forensic tests. Sickert allegedly had a penchant for using East End prostitutes as his models.

Surgeons from the era of the Whitechapel murders have persistently been under suspicion because of the level of skill used to kill and dissect the victims. For example, the sexual organs from one body were removed cleanly and the kidney from another extracted expertly with an apparent intention to avoid damaging surrounding tissue. All of this professional butchery occurred for the most part within short time periods, in virtual darkness, and most likely with the knife-wielder more than a little distracted by the possibility of discovery.

Medical practitioners (and royalty) come into the frame again with Sir (Dr) John Williams, a personal friend of Queen Victoria and her former obstetrician being named by great-great nephew, Tony Williams (2005). Sir John, apparently, was obsessed with female anatomy and infertility because his wife couldn't conceive. He also worked at the Whitechapel workhouse infirmary, where he had treated four of the Ripper's victims. Furthermore, Sir John was founder of the National Library of Wales in Aberystwyth.

Trevor Marriot, a retired British murder detective from Bedfordshire, disputes the 'facts' of the Ripper saga. He argues that the tally of victims has been underestimated. However, he is not the first 'Ripper-ologist' to question the number of victims. Philip Sugden (2002), accepting the difficulty in computing an accurate list of fatalities from such a long time ago when investigative methods were crude and bodies not necessarily either found or identified, states that the number was at least four but could have been eight. However, Marriot's version of the killings received a lot of media attention in Britain when his book was published in 2005 because it had a novel slant. Re-examining the medical evidence using modern-day forensic profiling led Marriot to argue that the murders did not stop with Mary Kelly on 9 November, 1888. Jack the Ripper, according to Marriot, went on to multiple killing in Nicaragua, and one in Germany, stopping off on his travels to end the life of one more English prostitute. By infallible police deduction, Marriot concludes that Jack the Ripper's international murder career probably means that he was a merchant seaman. Furthermore, Marriot names the ship carrying its lethal human cargo from murder site to murder site: *The Sylph*.

There are other cases that keep interest in ripper murders alive, most notably that of the 'Yorkshire Ripper'. This killer was labelled a 'ripper' because of the similarities to his forerunner in the previous century, that is the concoction of 'sexual reprehensibility' amongst most of his victims, and the viciousness of the killings (the 'Yorkshire' bit is obvious). But, unlike Jack the Ripper, the killer's identity is not in dispute. Peter Sutcliffe was caught, found guilty and sentenced in May 1981. He was given a minimum gaol sentence of 30 years by the trial judge, but it is probable that he will remain incarcerated for the rest of his natural life. Three years after the trial he was transferred to a high-security psychiatric hospital (where, in 2006, he remains).

'Media panics' are fashioned in the 'gutter press' whenever Sutcliffe is perceived to be enjoying his confinement, allowed anywhere near the public, or a woman is believed to be showing him affection. In 2005, the case hit the headlines again. John Humble, known as 'Wearside Jack' in the media because of his accent, was arrested for sending hoax letters and a tape-recording sent at the time of the murders in which he claimed to be the killer (he was sentenced to eight years imprisonment in 2006). However, when Sutcliffe was still at large, the 'panic' was realistic as his tally was considerable and the police were without a prime suspect (having been sidetracked by the letters and tape-recording). Sutcliffe murdered 13 women between 1973 and 1980, and may have gone on killing.

Sutcliffe was caught serendipitously by two police officers who approached a parked car. In the car was Peter Sutcliffe and a 24-year-old prostitute he had solicited. When questioned, Sutcliffe stated that the prostitute was his girlfriend, but didn't give much credence to the relationship when he couldn't tell them her name. The officers checked his licence plates and found they were false. Sutcliffe and the prostitute were arrested. Intuitively, one of the officers returned to where the arrest had been made. Sutcliffe had been allowed to urinate out of sight of the officers. A knife and hammer were found where he had urinated. Questioned now by a senior police officer, Sutcliffe admitted to being the Yorkshire Ripper. He was later to claim that 'voices from God' told him to rid the streets of prostitutes (Bilton, 2003).

The Yorkshire Ripper's auditory hallucinations did not instruct him, however, to eat his victims. Nor has there been any suggestion that Jack the Ripper digested any of the organs he removed from his victims. That seems to be the pursuit of extraordinary 'ripper' killers.

CANNIBAL

Sometimes Freud can come across as not having a glowing impression of the human psyche:

> It was Freud who expressed . . . in the clearest terms: we are all a bunch of killers. Furthermore, in Anglo-American culture, before the kill we are rapists and sadists, and afterward we become *cannibals*. [emphasis added]
>
> (Duclos, 1998, p. 119)

Freud insinuates that there is nothing essentially extraordinary about 'taboo' human behaviours. Hitchcock realised that there was nothing extraordinary about human fascination with 'taboo' behaviours. His most famous film, *Psycho*, was based on Robert Block's 1959 novel of the same name, which itself was inspired by the 1950s US serial murderer, necrophiliac and cannibal (anthropophagic), Ed Gein. Gein's cannibalism (anthropophagy) was typified by human body parts being made into trophies and ornaments, and, as with Norman Bates in *Psycho*, an unsavoury mother–son relationship.

The legendary sixteenth-century cave-dwelling Scottish cannibal (and possibly an invention of the English), Alexander 'Sawney' Bean, is reputed to have consumed about 1000 people over a period of 25 years. From the 1970s to the 1990 Russian Andrei Chikatilo cannibalised dozens of children and young people. In the same time period, Jeffrey Dahmer, the 'Milwaukee Cannibal', killed 17 people and not only ate some of his victims, but also indulged in necrophilia (Martingale, 1999).

In the case of the German Armin Meiwes, cruelty (sadism and masochism), sex (but not rape as the victim was a willing 'accomplice'), and intra-species cuisine came together. This concoction of degeneracy revolted *and* mesmerised Germans, as well as being of prurient interest to many other parts of the world. Certainly the British press took on the story with relish. Perhaps that was because it was a *German*, and anything that gives credence to the British national game of publicising yet more actions of the 'dastardly Krauts' will get coverage in the popular newspapers.

Meiwes became known as the *Der Metzgermeister* (The Master Butcher). The 'master' appellation is somewhat of an unwarranted aggrandisement given that his butchery, whilst gruesome, had only one carcass. Moreover, it is not usual to find butcher's merchandise enthusiastically donating itself for slicing. Bernd-Juergen Brandes did just that.

Apart from having his slaughterer's skills embellished, Meiwes has also been dubbed 'The Maneater of Rotenburg', as well as the 'German Hannibal Lecter'. The fictional Hannibal Lecter was invented by Thomas Harris.

Harris, largely through his cannibal creation, has become a very successful novelist. The books about Hannibal (*Red dragon* (Harris, 1981); *The silence of the lambs* (Harris, 1988); *Hannibal* (Harris, 1999); *Behind the mask* (Harris, 2006) are best-sellers, and films based on the books box-office hits. The central character in the books and films is an extremely intelligent psychopathic psychiatrist, who gains satisfaction from terrorising his victims, eating bits of them and flirting with crime investigators. He is nicknamed 'The Chesapeake Ripper' in the first book having killed nine people in that area. We know a lot about Hannibal Lecter (the fourth book about him is designated as 'prequel', revealing his life from childhood). We also know quite a bit about Armin Meiwes.

People from Meiwes's home town have provided much detail about him. Added to this are the video-tapes of him prior to him taking up cannibalism (a television documentary about his life showed him on fishing trips with his friends), as well as a later one of him eating fragments of his new lover. In his home town of Rotenburg, this middle-aged computer technician was known to be quiet, polite, friendly and sensitive. He had served in the army. Meiwes grew up with his mother, after his father left the family. His mother, who is reported as being domineering with her son, died in 1999. Since then, Meiwes occupied alone the large farm-house that was the family home, although he did at one time have a live-in girlfriend (who apparently wasn't enamoured by him being not only sexually interested in her but in men, so she left him).

Meiwes had a long-standing sexual pursuit that went further than bi-sexuality. His sexual outlet was fantasising about killing and eating another human (but only if the other person was well disposed to the idea). During the police investigation it became apparent that there are hundreds of like-minded sexual cannibals who contact each other using the internet.

Not many, however, move from fantasy to reality. Meiwes and Brandes did after the latter answered an advert placed on the internet by the former in 2001 (for a healthy man who wanted to be devoured). Brandes went to Meiwes's home, where the two entered a pact – the one to be consumed by the other. Brandes swallowed sleeping tablets and drank schnapps before having his penis cut off by Meiwes. The severed penis was then fried. It was intended that the both of the men eat the now sautéd sexual organ, but Brandes was bleeding profusely and couldn't quite manage this auto-erotic self-cannibalistic feat. So he took a bath instead while Meiwes read a novel. The bath was taken in order to help Brandes die more quickly by increasing the rate of blood loss. It didn't, so the next morning Meiwes stabbed Brandes in the neck, carved up the body, buried the skull in the garden and put the rest in the freezer.

About 20 kg of the cadaver was eaten by Meiwes before he was arrested in 2002 after placing more advertisements on the internet and raising the suspicions of other internet users. But trying to gain a conviction of murder was problematic for the police. Cannibalism is not illegal in Germany. Furthermore, it would be difficult to convict Meiwes of murder as his victim agreed to be killed. Instead, he was convicted of manslaughter in 2004 and sent to prison for eight-and-a-half years. However, there was a retrial in 2006, and Meiwes was then found guilty of murder and sentenced to life in prison.

It is not just the Germans: sexualised cannibalism was committed by Peter Bryant, a British man who was given a 'whole life tariff' in 2005. He had already been found guilty of killing a woman in 1993 (and sent to a secure psychiatric hospital, but set free in 2001), before he killed a man in 2004, eating his brain, which had first been fried. Bryant then killed another man when he was held in a secure psychiatric hospital awaiting trial. However, in 2006, Bryant's gaol sentence was reduced to 15 years by the Court of Appeal. The judge in the 2005 court case was reported as stating that Bryant's violence was extreme, unpredictable, with 'bizarre sexual overtones' (BBC News, 2005d).

Cannibalism has occurred in many different cultures, as a religious ceremony (either an offering to a god, or the ingestion of a deceased relative's spirit), a victory ritual (the defeated enemy become the celebratory meal), or as an exogamous practice (maintaining the genetic purity of the tribe). There is also the issue of 'survival cannibalism', in times of famine, following a ship-wreck, or airplane crash when the only nutrition available happens to be human flesh. But according to Gananath Obeyesekere (2005), cannibalism (other than survivalist) might primarily be a 'mythical representation' of tribal culture as an outcome of misunderstandings between European colonisers and colonised peoples. That is, although cannibalism undoubtedly happens, it is not as extensive as has been traditionally portrayed in anthropology and the media.

What is extensive though, is the fascination about cannibalism. Patricia Walton (2004) argues that the frequency of its appearance in literature, popular journalism, film, television and radio, and how such 'flesh eating' diseases as AIDS and Ebola are depicted, indicates that Western culture is 'saturated' with cannibalism. That may be somewhat overstating the case. However, the internet count in 2006 was 10 800 000 for the search term 'cannibal'. For same year, Amazon listed 164 books, 190 DVDs, 9 videos and 127 CDs under 'cannibal'. Titles of the books included: *Eaten alive! Italian cannibal zombie movies*; *Kathy the cannibal*; and *Teddy bear cannibal massacre*. Film titles included: *Cannibal Holocaust*; *The Mountain of the Cannibal God*; *Please Don't Eat My Mother*; *Cannibal the Musical*; *Cannibal Women in the Avocado*

Jungle of Death; and *Slave Girls from Beyond Infinity*. Available music, apart from the soundtracks of the cannibal films, included: an anthology of songs by Cannibal and the Headhunters; James Chance's album, *White Cannibal*; and all of Fine Young Cannibals' recordings.

What about *Der Metzgermeister*? Well, his notoriety is spreading. His case was reported worldwide, and one or other aspect of the case appears regularly in the German media. Meiwes, however, has attempted to stop the exploitation and 'distortion' of his case through legal action, citing human rights legislation.

The fascination about sex and cannibalism is too powerful not to have outlets. Apart from documentaries, a Hollywood film called in English *Butterfly, A Grimm Love Story* and *Rotenburg* in German, has been made, and a German film called *Dein Herz in Meinem Hirn* ('Your Heart in My Brain'). A book called *Cannibal: the True Story Behind the Maneater of Rotenburg* was published in 2005 by Lois Jones, and many others are likely to follow. Heavy-metal artists have been busy composing tunes about the case: the band Rammstein wrote *Mein Teil* (translated as 'My Part', which is slang for 'my penis'); American band Macabre penned *The Wüstenfeld Man Eater*; and *Eaten* was the title of a song produced by Swedish band Bloodbath.

The video-tape recording Meiwes made of the deathly tryst between him and Brandes has not been made public. Only the judges and lawyers in Meiwes's original trial were shown the video in the first trial. If it did ever leave the control of the courts, it would be interesting to monitor whether or not it became the artefact of specialist subcultures that delve into sexual-cannibalism, or an icon of mass entertainment, Meiwes presented as the authentic challenger to the pretender Hannibal Lecter.

WEREWOLF

Human interest in murder generally, and specifically in rippers and cannibals, is not in doubt. What is going on here? The truth is I'm not certain, but I do have my suspicions. Rather like the scenario at a 'murder mystery weekend' (not that I've attended one), I think I have been presented with enough circumstantial evidence to accuse, but perhaps as yet not convict, the werewolf.

The werewolf offers a theoretical superstructure from which I can hang two propositions that seem to make sense to me at this point in the analogous whodunit vacation. However, it is early in the proceedings. Other clues and complexities will assuredly appear and suspicion fall elsewhere as these progress. However, this book has a deadline, and fresher thoughts will have to await the equivalent in publishing of a 'retrial'.

The first proposition rests on a standard social scientific critique whereby globalisation (whether taken to mean worldwide capitalist expansionism, or a central feature of postmodernist society) drives all areas of human life into the market-place. That is, everything becomes a *commodity*, including murder. Moreover, murder becomes a very saleable product when sexuality is added as (to use the language of advertisers) 'extra value'.

My second submission resurrects Freud's (2006) proposition that violence and sex drive human behaviour. Some of Freud's ideas have been ditched because of their insensitivity towards women and lack of empirical evidence. Freud was not consistent or clear about exactly how in his intra-psychic model violence and sexuality operated. But 150 years after his birth, Professor Eric Kandel (2006), Nobel Prize winner in psychiatry, declared Freud 'a giant', one of the 'great thinkers'. Freud's giant thought was that sensuality (Eros) is bonded with destruction and death (Thanatos).

These two embryonic deliberations are not mutually exclusive. Violence and sex, sold as macabre entertainment packages to a public all too willing to have its primitive impulses titillated, of course, was exploited magnificently by Alfred Hitchcock. What Hitchcock, and all other purveyors of thriller-killer leisure, whether visually, musically, or textually, was engaged in with his audience was a reflexive affiliation. The needs of one (the audience) define the services of the other (the entertainer). This, for Anthony Giddens (1991), is how individuals both construct and are constructed by society. What humans need, want, think and do produces patterns (for example, social class, ethnic identities and consumerism) and institutions (for example, of law, religion, health, education, and Tesco and Wal-Mart) in society. These patterns and institutions then sway what humans value and how they behave. However, this is not a simple cycle of influences and responses one way or the other. The reflexive process is a matrix of complex, inconsistent, flagrant and subtle pressures and reactions. Moreover, humans do not just have their own society badgering them and in turn to badger. The global village (with its overarching patterns and institutions) is in on the game. But it doesn't stop there. Each individual has their own biology and psychology with which to wrestle.

These tussles within humans, between individuals and society, and different forces in society, for Denis Duclos (1998) represent a struggle between barbarism and civilisation. Duclos has described the segments of that struggle concerned with violence as the 'werewolf culture'. Just as the psychiatrist in Hitchcock's *Psycho* considers Norman Bates to have a werewolf personality because his 'self' is disintegrating under the escalating influence of his (dead) mother, so the 'werewolf culture', a symbiosis of pain and plea-sure emanating from violence, is in danger of collapsing into incivility.

However, both individuals and society attempt to deny this 'taboo' source of gratification. A protective shield (for example: moral codes and criminal laws against violent behaviour; certification and warnings about media pre-sentations of violence) has been installed to hide from unpalatable yearnings that reveal the tension between barbarism and civilisation.

> [The werewolf culture] . . . is incapable of acknowledging its urges. It feels obliged to label them as 'bad'. And, if it does not wish to give up these plea-sures, it has to construct an elaborate defense system, an artful procedure by means of which it appears to be disgusted by the things it enjoys and to enjoy doing the things it hates.
>
> (Duclos, 1998, p. 119)

Duclos concentrates on Anglo-American culture, although he does indicate that his thesis can be extended to 'modern society', by which I presume he means the West. No matter, as the USA is the driving force behind a West-ernised mono-culture based on materialist and liberal democratic values, and transmitted (other than by direct military invasion) via high-technology communications and media systems across the globe. As a consequence, vio-lence is an accessible form of entertainment globally.

Commodity

Killing people is big business. Murder is a lucrative commodity. This com-modity, however, appears in various guises and appeals to low-brow and high-brow consumers. On the low-brow side of entertainment is not merely the killer-thriller. Television and radio crime re-enactments of both fictional and non-fictional events are watched by millions of viewers. This mass voyeurism is frequently of violent crime.

Rock Underwood (in Hickey, 2003) calculates that in the USA children are exposed to one million acts of violence as well as 250 000 murders by the age of 18 years. This 'contagion' of violence, argues Underwood is contracted through watching television, reading violent books and comics, and listen-ing to such music as Rap.

One prime example of 'uncultured' gratification is what Godsi (2004) refers to as the media circus surrounding the O. J. Simpson trial. The circus had begun in 1994 after the Los Angeles police discovered the bodies of Simpson's ex-wife, Nicole Brown Simpson, and her friend, Ron Goldman. O. J. Simpson had been spotted driving along a highway in South California, and the ensuing car chase by police and reporters was televised live by camera crews in helicopters flying above what was a slow moving convoy on the ground. Moreover, the 1995 trial of Simpson attracted thousands of national and international reporters, and was televised throughout the world, attracting huge audiences. Media interest has continued, with re-runs of his trial sparked off by, for example, the death in 2005 of Simpson's defence attorney, Johnnie Cochran. Over one hundred books have been published relating to the case according to Amazon.

Duclos observes that although the middle classes may not experience first-hand violence to the same extent as those at the bottom of the social hierarchy, they are not sheltered from the deluge of imagery and literature on the subject. Indeed, Duclos makes the point that the middle classes revel in second-hand violence because for them it is associated with 'outsider groups'. The outsiders form the other side of the werewolf. They are the savages with whom the urbane share a secret natural affinity, drawn together to make whole the werewolf culture.

This mutuality can be seen plainly amongst middle-class academics. The most pertinent example of Janus-faced duplicity I have discovered was an international conference held in 2005 in Budapest, Hungary, titled 'Monsters and the Monstrous: Myths and Metaphors of Enduring Illness'. The aim of the event was to explore the persistent influence of monsters and the monstrous on human culture. Participants were invited from the fields of literature, media studies, cultural studies, history, anthropology, philosophy, psychology, sociology, criminology, health and medicine, theology and youth work. It was the third such conference. I rather assume that there will be a long series of these conferences (the next one was planned for Oxford, UK in 2006). The following are examples of the 2005 themes:

- Children, childhood, stories and monsters; monsters and parents.

- Comedy: funny monsters and/or making fun of monsters.

- Do monsters kill because they are monstrous or are they monstrous because they kill?

- The popularity of modern monsters: the Mummy, Dracula, Frankenstein, vampires.

- The monstrous in popular culture: film, television, theatre, radio, print, internet.

- Religious depictions of the monstrous; the monstrous and the supernatural.

- The monstrous and war, war reportage/propaganda.

The conference organisers also offered to accept papers dealing solely with specific monsters. No suggestions of specific monsters were provided. Special sessions were to be held on eroticism and monsters. Specific examples of 'monstrous sexualities' were provided: bestiality, paedophilia and vampirism.

These examples of papers delivered at the conference give a flavour of how ingeniously the themes were addressed:

- The monster under the bed: adult anxieties of childhood.

- The zombie as barometer of cultural anxiety.

- Ontological anxiety made flesh.

- Monstrous nature: Moby Dick as monster between myth and modernity.

- Feeding frenzy? Media sharks monster *Jaws*.

- Rational, magical, or monstrous spaces: press responses to London's sewer system, 1865–68.

- Monstrous sexualities: sexual ethics in a cold climate.

- Zoocentrically: bestial porno and erotic zoophilia.

- Towards a grotesque phenomenology of the erotic.

- Of monsters, masturbators, and markets: autoerotic desire, sexual exchange, and the cinematic serial killer.

Werewolves appeared in one paper, but only those which were connected to the shoreline of the Baltic Sea, and then only if they were thought to be around during the years 1550–1700.

It's not just lecturers, however. Rome University's faculty of law started to run a course in Mafia Studies in 2004, the first of its kind in Italy. The course was inundated with applicants. Tamsin Smith (2004) reports that the students are captivated as they are told gruesome details of how a Cosa Nostra boss disposed of one unfortunate teenager.

Maria Tatar, in her book *Lustmord* (1997) has written about images of violated female corpses in the decadent German Weimar Republic, which abounded with the sexual mutilation of women in its art. She shows how many of the artists identified with murderers. One of the artists (George Grosz) dressed up as Jack the Ripper and was photographed pretending to stab his future wife. Such 'cultured' gratification from violence is offered by the paintings of Marlene Dumas. Art journalist Adrian Searle admits Dumas's artwork seduces him. What does Dumas paint? Dead perpetrators of atrocities and dead victims of atrocities. Referring to one such painting, Searle (2004) states:

> We don't have to look far – not even to snuff movies – to make a link between sex and death, the petit mort of orgasm and the big sleep . . . From the vicarious intimacy, salaciousness and obscenity of the newspaper photograph, Dumas's paintings return their subjects to a state of something like tenderness, something like life. They are also inescapably erotic.

Searle's frankness about the sexual stimulation that death brings to the observer is unusual, his protective shield lowered for the sake of an honest and public exposé of his feelings towards murderous art, and maybe (we are only privy to Searle's responses not his motives) for the rewards that contentious journalism brings.

However, Thomas de Quincey (1785–1858) had already laid the trail that Searle was to follow when in 1827 he published an essay in *Blackwood's Magazine* with the title 'On Murder as a Fine Art' and later to be replicated in book form (De Quincey, 1925). For De Quincey, murder can, like any artform, be mundane or striking. Whatever moral questions there are concerning a murderous event (and De Quincey accepts murderers need to be punished), this is separate from aesthetical appreciation:

> A sad thing it was [any murder], no doubt, very sad; but *we* can't mend it. Therefore let us make the best of a bad matter; and, as it is impossible to hammer anything out of it for moral purposes, let us treat it aesthetically, and see if it will turn to account in that way.
>
> (De Quincey, 1925, p. 10)

Taking his essay to a degree of controversy that supersedes even that of Searle's (with irony added), De Quincey demands that we dry our tears and make use of the proverb 'it is an ill wind which blows nobody good'. There are, observes De Quincey, fine or poor artistic virtues contained within the 'gallery of murders'. This gallery houses the first murder conducted by Cain onwards. Cain (who in Genesis from the *Bible* killed his brother) is viewed by De Quincey as the 'inventor of murder', and hence, 'father of the art'.

For De Quincey, if an aesthetic response is provoked in the observer of a murder or its reproduction such as awe, abhorrence, or bemusement, then it is logical that the murderer is an artist and the work is one of artistry. The implication of De Quincey's position is that once morality is removed there is no essential difference between examples of conceptual sculpture (such as those constructed by two modern-day merchants of the werewolf culture, Damian Hirst and Tracy Emin) and that of any murder.

De Quincey's tongue-in-cheek essay has given some credence to the propagation of murder as a cinematic product. From Hitchcock to Harris this artform has flourished, and shows no sign of its prevalence in films abating. One wonders if the dead animal (Hirst) and unmade bed (Emin) brand of art will be so enduring, even if there is surrounding such work the scent of death or sex.

The werewolf extends further into cultural crevices than the voyeurism of the mass audience indulging in another 'murder mystery' or news of another atrocity, the art fanatic, the academic specialising in the monstrous, or the student of the Mafia. As uncomfortable as it may be to admit, books written by both murderers *and* by secondary victims are part of making murder into a commodity in a globalised world where everything is susceptible to that process. Writing biographies and appearing in documentaries about murdered loved ones is indisputably worthy both as a catharsis for relatives and friends and a laudable commemoration of lives ended too soon. However, the books, television and radio programmes, and films are 'products' in a media market-place that have value both financially and creatively. The honest intentions of the secondary victims correspond with the public's insatiability for a further meal of death and destruction served up by the media.

Such exposure moves the incidence of murder from a personal event to a social spectacle. The meaning of a particular tragedy is no longer confined to attributes formulated by the secondary victims. It is a different, more diffuse, uncontrollable, and potent phenomenon, reformulated and amorphous, manipulated by contending groups (politicians, journalists, programme-makers and specialised interest groups). It is in the global domain, interpreted and reinterpreted. This is a process of personalisation, de-personalisation, and then re-personalisation. First, the relatives and friends experience the loss as 'theirs'. But, it never remains wholly theirs. The police, lawyers and judges enforce meanings that reflect the concerns of the criminal justice system. Then, the more media and public interest is attracted to the case, the more the killing becomes portrayed in ways that will not coincide with the perception of those nearest to the death because different needs are being serviced. The emotions of the secondary victims become collectivised and marketable. As curiosity and outrage increases and widens it becomes the property of not just the secondary victims but the reader, the listener and the viewer. The zenith of this process is when the story of the murder is made into a book, television and radio programme, or film. Then it is owned by paying customers. The original event has now been consumed.

Creating a commodity of murder applies to earnest films that have been produced about terrible incidents. For example, the 1994 slaughter of 800000 Tutsis and moderate Hutus in Rwanda was made into the film *Hotel Rwanda* (released in 2004). It tells the story of how Paul Rusesabagina, temporary general manager of the Mille Collines Hotel in Rwanda's capital Kigali at the time of the hundred-day long slaughter, saved over 1200 refugees trying to escape the killing. Rusesabagina received numerous human rights awards, and his autobiography, titled *An ordinary Man: the true story behind 'Hotel Rwanda'* (2006) is advertised (on Amazon) as adding to the film's content by examining in detail the role of the United Nations peacekeeping troops and the relevance to the conflict and his actions of his own ethnic background (a Hutu with a Tutsi wife). *Hotel Rwanda* became an American Film Institute prize winner for best feature film, and Oscar prize and Golden Globe Awards nominee in three categories. A DVD, soundtrack and book of the film are available, and Google recorded over six million 'hits' for *Hotel Rwanda* (in 2006). Two other films have been made about Rwanda in 1994. The first, *Sometimes in April* (released in 2005) was made in Rwanda, whereas *Hotel Rwanda* was made in South Africa. It is a fictional account of two Hutu brothers caught up in the slaughter, and an exposé of inaction by the international community to intervene. The second, *Shooting Dogs* (released in 2006), is another fictional account. *Shooting Dogs* is a tale about a British English teacher working in Rwanda when the killing starts, and how he offers his school as a safe haven. This film used actual locations of massacres, employed survivors as part of the crew and cast, and used hand-held cameras. It received critical acclaim, although it courted controversy over the possibility that some of the survivors who participated in the film had a reoccurrence of the PTSD they suffered from the original massacres (O'Keeffe, 2006).

Michael Moore's 2002 film, *Bowling for Columbine* attacks the acceptance of widespread gun ownership in the USA, and in particular the National Rifle Association. The film opens with Moore obtaining a free gun as part of a bank promotion. It was given him on the spot after he opened an account with the bank. It then focuses on the massacre in 1999 of 13 people at Columbine High School in which 15 people, including the killers, died. *Bowling for Columbine* was an Oscar-winning documentary, and one of a very few documentaries to be commercially lucrative.

The Columbine killings had already, however, been consumed live by a large television audience as it unfolded. In Wes Yoder's foreword to the book *Rachel's Tears*, about the killing of Darrell Scott and Beth Nimmo's daughter, he recalls:

> 'Are you watching the breaking news from Columbine High School?' was the first thing I heard when I called a friend who is a news producer at CNN headquarters in Atlanta on that day we will never forget as long as we live. . . . As a nation, we watched the moment-by-moment replay of a tragedy, as the face of evil was unmasked before us. We gasped in horror.
>
> (Scott & Nimmo, 2000, p. xv)

Moreover, as the parents themselves recount, by the time they had written their book the massacre at Columbine had generated a colossal amount of print in newspapers and magazines and coverage on television and radio. What they experienced, as did many people connected with Columbine, was a 'media cyclone'. For them this involved an appearance on the highly popular US television talk-show *Oprah* as well as a meeting with the then President, Bill Clinton, and his wife Hilary.

Proclaiming moral outrage at genocide and gun laws has the intended or unintended outcome of helping to sell a film (or any other product). It is similar to the quality newspapers writing graphic articles, with accompanying explicit pictures, about the abusive nature of pornography. These are fine examples of the werewolf culture.

Eroticism

Schadenfreude is the dominant symbol of the werewolf culture. As the political philosopher Edmund Burke (1729–1797) observed: 'I am convinced that we have a degree of delight, and that no small one, in the real misfortunes and pains of others' (Burke, 1757/1987).

Video-tape footage of the beheading of hostage Ken Bigley in Iraq is available on a number of internet sites, as well as the killing of other hostages. Bigley was killed on 8 October, 2004. Within a few days of the murder of Bigley, one of the internet sites recorded one million downloads of the video (Walker, 2004).

Susan Sontag (2004), in her examination of the joy provided by the pain of others, suggests that it is only since the camera was invented that human calamities have become a spectator-sport. Wars and natural disasters can come into the audiences' homes via electronic media whenever wanted, and the journalist maxim 'if it bleeds, it leads' means that newspapers are soaked in the blood of others. The public was fed the photographs and newsreels in 1945 of the emaciated survivors and the thousands of bodies at the liberated German concentration camps. For Sontag, the hunger for images of people in pain is only rivalled by those of people in the nude. By extension, it could be claimed that images of tortured people have their equivalent in images of people copulating.

It was, points out Sontag, the Vietnam War that offered a daily diet of the misery from cruelty and killing. She refers to two specific horror scenes from that war. These were at the time, and remain, icons of suffering and the witnessing of that suffering: the photograph of a naked 9-year-old Phan Thị Kim Phúc running down a road shrieking with pain from the severe napalm burns on her back (the picture, taken by journalist Huynh Cong Ut, won a

Pulitzer Prize); the photograph of Viet Cong prisoner Nguyen Van Lem being summarily executed by South Vietnamese Police Chief General Nguyen Ngoc Loan (this picture taken by photojournalist Eddie Adams also won a Pulitzer Prize).

Moreover, pictures of killing during war and civil strife have been turned into what Malcolm Foley and John Lennon (2000) label 'dark tourism'. Dark tourism, as with sex tourism, is pandering to an apparently barely controllable lust. The craving of the dark tourist is not for exotic fleshpots, but for exotic graveyards. What the dark tourist seeks is first-hand experience of the scenes of atrocities and their graphic representations. Ostensibly, such historical exhibits are to commemorate the dead, to revile their persecutors, and, in doing so, educate humanity about inhumanity. But they have become part of the accepted sightseer circuit, promulgated by private organisations and governments. Whether it is the killing fields of Choeung Ek, Cambodia, the tunnels of Co Chi and galleries of decimated bodies in Ho Chi Min City, Vietnam, or the D Day landing beaches in Normandy, France, and whether or not it is primarily commemorative or educative, there are emotional payoffs that tend not to be declared.

So, what is the source of *Schadenfreude*? Why do we want to look at and thereby take glee from agony of our fellow humans? Are we projecting the uncomfortable elements of ourselves onto others through media fascination with murder?

Lieutenant Colonel Dave Grossman, Professor of Military Science at Arkansas State University, suggests that fascination of murder is 'pleasure by proxy'. For Grossman, observing atrocity compensates for a lack of opportunity or willingness to carry out the act ourselves. Indeed, Freud's view that aggression/violence was the externalisation of the 'death instinct' could be being taken one step further. Pleasure can still be found without destroying others directly, but indirectly by observing destructiveness.

Freud's psychoanalysis (Freud, 2005) is based on an understanding of the mental distress caused by tensions between different aspects of the self. But Freud was not the first to address the issue of inner torment. In Plato's *The Republic*, Socrates (469–399 BC) describes how human reason may be overwhelmed by unworthy desire, resulting in psychological dissonance between an individual's 'nature', their rational self, and the emotions produced from that conflict. Plato (427–347 BC), through Socrates, relates a story about man encountering a scene of execution:

> It's about Leontion, son of Aglaion, who was on his way up from the Peiraeus [the port of ancient Athens], under the south side of the north wall, when he noticed some corpses lying on the ground with the executioner standing by

them. He wanted to go and look at them, and yet at the same time held himself back in disgust. For a time he struggled with himself and covered his eyes, but at last his desire got the better of him and he ran up to the corpses, opening his eyes wide and saying to them, 'There you are, curse you – a lovely sight! Have a real good look!'

(Plato, 390 BC/1974, pp. 215–216)

So, after an internal struggle and a bit of shouting at his sight organs, Leontion enjoys the bloody sight. This is similar to the 'rubber-necking' phenomenon of motorists slowing down to gaze at a scene of carnage after a road traffic accident, although, as far as I'm aware, few indulge in eye castigation.

The French essayist Georges Bataille (1897–1962) initially wanted to join the priesthood, but he became distracted from that career by Parisian brothels. One assumes it was experiences there that stirred his interest in eroticism. However, another assumption is that even Parisian brothels could not be held liable for his comprehensive erotic curiosity, which encompassed: sadism, human sacrifice, necrophilia, war and fascism (especially the brutal exercise of power by the Nazis). Bataille (1986) acknowledged the contradiction of the werewolf culture, believing that images of pain were intolerable but at the same time tolerated because of their erotic quality. Human sexuality, for Bataille, differs from that of animals because of the potential to indulge willingly in, or be engulfed by, eroticism. Therefore, eroticism is not merely sexual activity, but the anticipation of, not preclusion of, sexual contact and fulfilment. Violence of one sort or another, killing, warfare and especially death, are erotic stimuli. Bataille links death to what he calls the 'little death' that follows sexual climax, the contiguous death in sadomasochistic practices, and death as part of religious ritual and sacrifice.

The flesh of the orgy and the body parts of the corpse (and Bataille's particular penchant was excoriated eyes) were erotically conjoined. Bataille is not alone, however, in revealing 'dark truths' about violently erotic human behaviour.

Michel Foucault, who was influenced by Bataille and the Marquis de Sade, was also fascinated by the link between extreme sexual practices and extreme sado-masochism. Foucault saw liberation from social constraints that dictated parameters to thought, knowledge and behaviour, in what he described as 'suicidal orgies'. For Foucault, ultimate pleasure and freedom is inexorably coupled with death (Miller, 1993). It was the freedom to indulge in unregulated (homosexual) pleasure *because of*, not *despite*, the risks, that led directly to his own demise. For Foucault the ultimate control over living was gained by not being scared of dying. In his biographical analysis of

Foucault, James Miller has recorded Foucault's response, whilst he was lecturing at the University of California in 1983, to an undergraduate student's question about personal autonomy:

> Who could be scared of AIDs? You could be hit by a car tomorrow. Even crossing the street was dangerous! If sex with a boy gives me pleasure – why renounce such pleasure? We have the power . . . we shouldn't give it up.
> (Foucault in Miller, 1993, p. 353)

Foucault died the following year.

Joanna Bourke, Professor of History, University of London, adopts a Freudian approach to determine the erotic nature of killing. In her book *An intimate history of killing* (2000) she examines British, American, and Australian veterans of three wars (First World War, Second World War and Vietnam), and concludes that soldiers enjoy killing. The soldiers are able to dissociate the part of their 'self' that exults in killing from the loving and caring parts of the self, thereby enabling them to return to their families after their war service with minimal disruption to their conscience.

Soldiers infrequently gloat about their killing activities, not because they are ashamed, but because their loved ones and friends may not have understood the intense feelings of pleasure they had undergone. Bourke recalls how soldiers admitted that sometimes these intense feelings resembled sexual climax. Bourke provides the many examples, such as the 'shy and sensitive' First World War soldier who, on bayoneting his first German, found it 'gorgeously satisfying'. From the Vietnam War, a US Marine discloses that he was 'literally turned on' when he saw a Viet Cong soldier die, and in the My Lai massacre (1968), US 'C' Company soldiers had laughed as they sodomised and raped women, ripped vaginas open with knives and scalped corpses.

Moreover, Bourke suggests that, whilst women are offered fewer opportunities to kill, they may indulge in fantasies about what their male lovers, partners, fathers and brothers may be really doing. When female soldiers do kill, they can also feel sexual exhilaration.

Grossman, however, whilst accepting that aggression (and sexuality) is innate, does not believe that it is natural for humans to go as far as killing other humans, let alone go to war against them. In order to get most soldiers to kill, other than the psychopath (who rarely makes a good soldier), they have to be specially conditioned. This conditioning, which is becoming more and more complex, must be aimed at the specific techniques of killing and at dehumanising the enemy. But soldiers still resist this conditioning. Grossman points to the very low percentage of bullets fired in most conflicts actually hitting their targets. Grossman also employs Freud to throw light on why there is this reluctance amongst soldiers to kill despite inborn aggression and sophisticated training:

> In battle we see the id, the ego, the superego, Thanatos, and Eros in turmoil within each soldier. The id wields the Thanatos like a club and screams at the ego to kill. The superego appears to have been neutralized, for authority and society say that now it is good to do what had always been bad. Yet something stops the soldier from killing. What? Could it be that Eros, the life force, is much stronger than ever before understood?
>
> (Grossman, 1996, p. 38)

For Bourke, Thanatos excites Eros. For Grossman, Eros controls Thanatos. However, Grossman accepts that soldiers on killing do have a feeling of elation, but that this is short lived, and replaced by feelings of guilt and revulsion. Whichever way round it is, Eros is in a dance with Thanatos.

Most of the soldiers referred to by Bourke and Grossman are men. What about women soldiers? Women have served in many armies, and today women have an increasingly wide range of jobs, including jet fighter pilots in the Royal Navy, RAF and US Air Force. Female guerrillas, revolutionaries and terrorists have participated in many violent insurrections (for example, Nepal, Cuba, El Salvador, Nicaragua, Guatemala, Colombia, Vietnam, Rhodesia-Zimbabwe and Chechnya). There has also been a significant rise in the numbers of suicide bombers who are female, the so-called 'black-widows' (Foden, 2003).

Moreover, women may be sublimating their murderous eroticism by making connections with men who have committed murder. For example, Scott Peterson was sentenced to death for the murders of his wife and their unborn son in 2005. On death row he became very desirable:

> Prison spokesman Vernell Crittendon said about three dozen women called San Quentin with messages of support for [Scott Peterson] . . . convicted and sentenced to die for the murder of his pregnant wife, Laci. 'Two of them actually indicated to our staff that their purpose for calling was marriage,' Crittendon told CNN. He added that it is not unusual for inmates to get married while on death row.
>
> (CNN, 2005)

Care Longrigg (2005) reports that Peter Sutcliffe, the Yorkshire Ripper, has become engaged to be married to Pam Mills. Mills is 54 years old, divorced and has two grown-up children. She has, apparently, had a long-term relationship with Sutcliffe by letter and then visiting him. But she is not the only woman interested in Sutcliffe. Seemingly he is in constant receipt of intimate letters and requests to visit him.

Sheila Isenberg (1997), in her examination of women who fall in love with men who kill, perhaps going as far as marriage, observes that they frequently become their champions. These women, reports Isenberg, become obsessed with campaigns to prove the innocence of their boyfriend/husband or to gain better conditions for him in prison, and provide financial support and manage his affairs. Although some of the women may be expressing a religious wish to 'save' the murderer, much of the motivation is related to emotional intimacy, including sex. There is, suggests Isenberg, the 'bad boy' appeal.

Female interest in violent and murderous men (as well as violent entertainment) may be a socially-contained and gender-specific outlet. Just as the 1960s' sexual revolution allowed women to express their erotic desires and become more active in the mating game, so women may become more engaged with violence as the behaviour of the genders (in the West) becomes more uniform.

For an evolutionary psychologist, such as David Buss (2005), sexuality is essentially a function of procreation, but also can be associated with violence. Violent men are sought by women as a protective measure in the rearing of offspring. However, I do not accept that women in the twenty-first century hanker after cavemen look-alikes given that males who, in evolutionary terms would have been at the very bottom of the mating pecking order, today get partners and procreate with as much or as little fuss in the sexual playground as hairy weapon-wielding macho men. Furthermore, whilst the violent man is in gaol, conjugal rights may be allowed, but little physical protection for the woman can be offered in her daily life. Still less so if her protective mate has been executed.

SUMMARY

Killing people has been big entertainment since the losers of gladiatorial battles and adherents to Christianity were eaten by lions in the Colosseum of Ancient Rome in front of audiences of tens-of-thousands. The Romans were 'civilised' in many respects. But whilst taking on board what the Romans bequeathed the world, should we not have ditched this primitive absorption with death and destruction by now?

Our lust for gore seems to be unabated. Two thousand years later, murder can still be relished 'by proxy'. Modes for the parading of murder have increased considerably. Murder is now available to enjoy in films, television, books, plays, the internet and on holiday.

The reasons for human insatiability with regard to violence are obscure. I have very tentatively suggested first that it is to do with how everything in the global (capitalist/postmodern) society has been converted into a commodity (including the taboo). This is not social progress. At best it is social stagnation, and at worst social degeneration. Taking a lead from Eric Fromm (1956), the gratuitous mix of violent and sexual mass amusements (along with social and health inequalities, materialism, and pollution) has led society towards an 'insane' state. This insanity is Duclos's werewolf culture.

However, what is it that drives the werewolf culture apart from the commercial incentive to sell violence as a product? As the second cautious proposal, I embarked on an inspection of erotic desire being sated by violence. This is because, as Freud signalled, something very core to the human psyche seems to sponsor the merchandising of murder. Ripping and cannibalising bodies is the epitome of eroticised violence (and the perpetual popularity of Hitler and the Nazis is, as Bataille appreciated, not unrelated to erogenous titillation of the sadomasochistic variety). As Hitchcock might have quipped (had he been a social scientist), the eroticised drive for murderous commodities is the werewolf at the door, breathing heavily in anticipation of tearing apart and eating the body of civil society.

The stories of the IRA murder of Tim Parry and Pierre Riviere killing his mother, sister and brother, whilst both are in the public domain, have not as yet been subjected to extensive expropriation. But this doesn't mean that a would-be Hitchcock or Harris will not at some point extract from, or infuse into, these stories a salacious tinge and thereby make them highly saleable commodities.

CONCLUSION

An ordinary boy was murdered in 1993. Tim Parry, aged 12 years, died because of the deliberately murderous actions of people he didn't know, had never met and had no reason to believe carried a grudge against him personally. Indeed, Tim's killers didn't care who died as long as someone died or was maimed.

Tim's father, Colin, is just one out of the tens-of-millions of people each year who have to deal with the consequences of losing through murder someone close to them. In a few years time, the annual official murder rate will rise to one million. Perhaps it's a friend, neighbour, colleague, son, daughter, wife, husband, mother, or father who has died, and perhaps the anguish never ends completely.

Colin Parry rebuilt his life after the death of his son. In 2004, he was awarded the Order of the British Empire (OBE) in recognition of his campaigning for the victims of murder (specifically terrorism) and for peace and reconciliation in Northern Ireland. What Colin Parry discovered was the therapeutic and moral value of trying to reduce violence and prevent murder. In doing so, he encountered 'social solidarity' amongst family, friends and strangers from many parts of the world.

Indeed, 'the Troubles' in Northern Ireland seem to give birth to both barbarians and heroes. Colin Parry is in the latter group, as are a group of women, the McCartney sisters. Robert McCartney died in January 2005 after having been stabbed following a row in an east Belfast bar. He was 33 years old and a father to two young children. His family have blamed the IRA for the murder, as well as criticising the terrorist organisation for interfering with the subsequent police investigation. The five McCartney sisters instituted a crusade to get the killer(s) handed over by the IRA. Apart from worldwide media attention for their case, they have addressed the members of the European Parliament, met with US politicians, including Senator Edward Kennedy and President George W. Bush, British Prime Minister Tony Blair, and Irish Taoiseach Bertie Ahern. Whilst the McCartney family allege that they have been intimidated by the IRA and have moved homes, the organisation has reportedly expelled three of its members for involvement in the attack – and offered to kill those responsible (BBC News, 2006).

The IRA's alleged assassination proposal leads to the questions asked in the first and second chapters of this book: 'What is murder?' and 'Who commits murder?'. There is not a universal, cross-cultural meaning of murder that can be adhered to in any context and no matter who the victims are and who the killers. Murdering can be sanctioned by the state or by groups with a particular interest in using murder as a tactic to achieve what are considered laudable aims not only by themselves but by other groups or states. Take for example, the Palestinian-Israeli conflict, which has claimed the lives of thousands of civilians from both sides. Palestinian suicide bombers when they blow themselves up in a Haifa or Tel Aviv market or commuter bus are sublime martyrs or evil killers depending on which side of the conflict one's loyalties lie. Israeli pre-emptive or retributive military strikes against specific military targets, but which also incur collateral damage (that is, killing innocent people), are either legitimate self-protection measures or an inexcusable defiance by a Westernised state of international law: in other words 'state terrorism'.

The plot thickens. Those considered vile murderers by one side or another can become heads of state. The militant movement Hamas, which has had a history of violence directed towards Israel civilians and a long-term aim of destroying Israel, won democratically the 2006 Palestinian Parliamentary elections. Hamas's founder, Sheikh Yassin, an old man in a wheelchair leaving a mosque in Gaza City, was killed two years earlier by the Israeli army in a missile attack, which also claimed the lives of seven others and injured scores of others who were in the vicinity (later that year, the new Hamas leader, Abdel Aziz al-Rantissi, was also assassinated along with two of his bodyguards).

Menachem Begin, commander of the Jewish terrorist group 'Etzel', fought against the British over the creation of the state of Israel. This included the bombing of the British administrative and military headquarters (based in the King David Hotel) in Jerusalem. Nearly a hundred people were killed: more Arab and Jewish civilians were killed than British soldiers. Begin became the Prime Minister of Israel in 1977. In 1978, Begin, together with President Sadat of Egypt, was awarded the Nobel Peace Prize.

Defining murder and establishing the murderer, therefore, is dependent on who is doing the defining, and in which historical and cultural context that defining is taking place. This will obviously affect any statistics formulated on murder. But I have very firmly declared my 'realist' hand when stating that Pierre Riviere *did* kill his mother, brother and sister no matter how richly Foucault (1975) has contributed to our understanding of the political and cultural circumstances of nineteenth-century France.

Identifying murder and murderers is swayed by perception. Furthermore, each murder event has specific and unique background factors, performances by those involved and corollaries. I have argued, therefore, that typological inconsistencies can be smoothed out by accepting the distinctiveness of murders, but that in general there are three levels of culpability: people, corporations and governments. For example, would the killer of women, children and old people, some of whom died in the same day whilst the other victims were killed at regular intervals over five years, be a serial killer, mass killer or a child killer? What if the weapons ranged from bombs to knives? Would this mean that the killer was a part-time terrorist? What if the killer was a woman? Would this mass, serial, terrorist, child killer be put in yet another category, that of 'women who kill'? There are certainly obvious patterns to murder, but equally obvious quirks.

The third question of the book has been 'Why commit murder?'. If classifying murder is problematic then so too must be trying to find reasons for murder. Attempting to find a killer's motive, and assessing madness or badness in the killer, are a start perhaps but deeper exploration of causes is necessary. From that exploration I conclude that: there are faults in individuals and faults in society that predispose *some* people to become killers; there can never be a grand theory of predisposition to kill, but there are precipitory factors. These are well known (they include intimidation, indoctrination and desperation). One extremely well known trigger is gun availability:

> 'I just killed a kid', Charles Martin told the emergency services operator. 'I shot him with a goddamn 410 shotgun twice.' He had gunned down Larry Mugrage, his neighbour's 15-year-old son. The teenager's crime: walking across Mr Martin's lawn on his way home. Mr Martin opened fire from his house and then, according to the police, walked up to the wounded boy and pulled the trigger again at close range, killing him.
>
> (Borger, 2006)

As Grossman (1996) reminds us, most humans do not kill no matter what the situation or the means being at hand. Hillyard et al. (2005) provides another reminder: most murders (at least in Britain) have a short premeditation span; they are acts of sudden violence; and out of a huge number of violent acts that occur in a year only a few will end with someone dying.

'Why is murder devastating?,' the fourth question, examined the personal and social suffering inflicted by murder. Murder invokes a particularly virulent form of bereavement. The devastation from murder is frequently medicalised as post-traumatic stress disorder (PTSD). The after-effects of murder on secondary victims are usually long-term. Kathy Celletti has written in the newsletter of Citizens Against Homicide about the murder of her father,

Frank Mezzapelle and the continuing suffering of her family, brought about by his death, that has lasted over two-and-a-half decades:

> Even though this horrific tragedy happened to our family almost 26 years ago, the sadness and the pain still remain. My dad, Frank A. Mezzapelle, was a dedicated and loving husband and father of four children . . . On June 24th [1980], after hiring psychics, private investigators and the help of the police, my father's body was found on a road by a jogger. His body was so badly decomposed that his dental records had to be used to identify him. There was minimal TV coverage. My dad's case still remains unsolved.
>
> (Celletti, 2006)

My claim that murder events are incomparable, must, however, also mean that so is the suffering caused by murder. The medicalisation of suffering results in generalised systems of understanding which do not correspond necessarily to the psychological and physiological impairment of an individual.

Furthermore, the degree of violence across the global village, I have suggested, creates a tertiary victim. Poisonous exudates from the pandemic of murder have made globalised society 'sick'. That sickness is exacerbated by the culture of the 'werewolf'. The werewolf culture is the concept I have applied to the fifth question of the book, 'Why is murder fascinating?'. A human that turns into an animal is, I argue, a suitable symbol for the omnipresent interest in murder. Media outlets for violence are extensive, and expanding. What impels such interest when the suffering caused by murder is so devastatingly obvious? I have tendered two interconnected ideas: murder sells, and sells well when it is eroticised; and murder is appealing because Eros and Thanatos are innate human drives (and some murders – for example, the sadism of the Nazis, ripper and cannibal killings – are more seductive than others because they tap directly into sexual pleasure gained from destruction and death).

Many experts in the field of murder have made recommendations for preventing murder. For Krug et al. (2002) international, national, and local agencies and governments must work together to prevent violence. Nelson Mandela writes with authority on the subject of violence given his personal experiences and political achievements:

> Violence thrives in the absence of democracy, respect for human rights and good governance . . . Many who live with violence day in and day out assume that it is an intrinsic part of the human condition. But this is not so. Violence can be prevented. Violent cultures can be turned around . . . We must address the roots of violence.
>
> (Mandela quoted in Krug et al., 2002, p.12)

Jason Burke (2005) has seven ways to stop terrorism. The most important of the seven involves correcting injustices throughout the world (for example, Chechnya, Kashmir and Palestine) that lead to Islamic militancy. Brookman and Maguire (2003) have the following advice to control violence in the home, on the street, and for people in high-risk employment:

1. More attention paid to domestic violence.

2. More attention paid to the parenting of infants.

3. More manipulation of physical and social environments associated with violence (bars, night-clubs).

4. Reduction in alcohol use.

5. Challenge to masculine bravado.

6. 'Crack-down' on illegal weapons.

7. Safety measures for public workers and prostitutes.

Sandra Bloom (2001) argues that just as we have come to understand, treat and thwart a range of diseases, so the disease of violence must be tackled and prevented. The physical and social circumstances of Western societies changed dramatically, as has the knowledge of the medical profession since the nineteenth century. Better sewage disposal, safer water supplies, improved diets, pharmaceutical discoveries and sophisticated surgical techniques, along with wages to pay for these improvements in living conditions, have undoubtedly improved human civilisation. Because violence is embedded in social institutions and in personal relationships, then all areas of public and private life, argues Bloom, have to be involved in preventative action. Individuals and institutions have to change. She observes that violence has its victims and its perpetrators. However, it also has its bystanders – the rest of humanity that allows the conditions which breed violence to happen and doesn't react at all or act when violence occurs to stop it happening again. This, for Bloom, demonstrates a lack of social responsibility.

Sir Bob Geldof, in his inimitably assertive way, takes up this theme of social irresponsibility with reference to how millions of people are 'murdered' through neglect:

> It's really only the poor that die earliest. They're too weak, mute, unseen and powerless to be noticed. We only properly take a reluctant heed when they begin to die in such numbers it would be impossible to ignore them. There then sets in a sort of tiresome acceptance that the pathetic whimperings and low moans of the soon-to-be-dead should be addressed in some manner.

> We don't generally die of our corruption, or our AIDS or Malaria or other illness, or our trade rules, or starvation, or our political instability, or our debt burdens, or our summer droughts. They do.
>
> (Geldof, 2005)

However, a realistic proposition for murder reduction must do more than make long lists of programmes for a multiplicity of agencies to install or make sweeping statements about the need for radical cultural change. For sure, fixing faulty societies (for example, lessening social and health inequalities) and addressing faulty individuals (for example, improving risk assessment in psychiatry) are highly commendable missions. Anything that confronts 'social atavism' and allows global society to evolve further is to be applauded.

The evolutionary 'stuck-ness' of contemporary human civilisation is steadfast. The litany of fine words against just this one aspect of its profligate and dissolute form are the equivalent of the fiddle-player's calming opus as the capital of ancient civilisation blazed. As with the Romans, humanity today has much about which to be proud. The top of my list of human achievements, having spent much of my childhood from autumn to spring huddled around the one open coal fire in our very draughty family house, is central-heating (and of course that was a Roman invention, abandoned during the middle ages – another atavistic period in human history).

What humiliates humanity, however, is: dross television; petrol-guzzling 4 × 4 motor vehicles; the worshiping of an array of extraterrestrials (that is, the 'gods' of the religions); half the world's population being malnourished whilst the other half is obese; Western women enlarging their breasts and Western men their penis whilst millions die from AIDS/HIV, malaria and tuberculosis; three-quarters of the world either unemployed or under-employed, whilst the other quarter works excessively from youth to old age haunted by the 'spectre of uselessness' whereby global capitalism may dispense with their services (Sennett, 2006); half the world's population live on less than US$2 a day, whilst the super-rich from both developed and developing countries grow in wealth and numbers (World Wealth Report, 2006); superpower military and political hubris causing countless civilian fatalities (Fukuyama, 2006); and the ruination of the very habitat necessary for human survival (Lovelock, 2006). What is required is not an emollient, but an ocean of solvent to unstick the global village from this atavistic state.

A final question: 'Why is humanity stuck with murder?' I call on Freud again. For Freud (2005, 2006) humans are locked in a perpetual battle. The contestants are Eros and Thanatos, antagonistic to each other, but unable to release one another. If the sensual life force (Eros) loses to the force of death and destruction then civilised behaviour retreats. If the combat continues to go the way of Thanatos en masse, then civilised human development does not just stop, it degenerates into barbarism.

Therefore, rather than grand-standing about preventing murder, perhaps all that can be hoped for is when the werewolf calls we are tucked up in as safe a haven as we can find (a part of the world that does not glorify murder), with Eros not Thanatos as our bedfellow (our own life force, and that of those around us, in ascendancy). Whilst Pierre Riviere succumbed to death's compulsion (murdering others and himself), Colin Parry has found the force of life (recovering from the murderousness of others to project human decency and hope for a less violent world).

REFERENCES

Adiga, A. (2003). Prescription for profit. *Time Asia*, 15 September.

AFP (2005). Thai man arrested, freed after confessing to eating corpse. Retrieved 30 March, 2005, from http://www.afp.com

Alton, D. & Tinsley, R. (2004). Sudan Darfur: the genocide continues. Jubilee Campaign. Retrieved 10 November, 2004, from http://www.jubileecampaign.co.uk

American Psychiatric Association (2000). *Diagnostic and Statistical Manual of Mental Disorders (DSM-IV-TR)*. Arlington, VA: American Psychiatric Association.

Amnesty International (2001). Botswana: Amnesty International appalled by secret execution. Retrieved 23 November, 2001, from http:www.amnesty.org.uk

Amnesty International (2003). *Mexico – intolerable killings: ten years of abductions and murders in Ciudad Juarez and Chihuahua*. London: Amnesty International.

Amnesty International (2005a). Report on Colombia 2004. Retrieved 20 December, 2005, from http://web.amnesty.org

Amnesty International (2005b). *China Keitetsi – biography*. London: Amnesty International.

Amnesty International (2005c). *Sudan crisis – background*. London: Amnesty International. Available at http://www.amnesty.org.uk

Amnesty International (2005d). Death sentences and executions in 2004. Retrieved 22 December, 2005, from http://www.amnesty.org.uk

Amnesty International (2006). Death sentences and executions in 2005. Available at http://www.amnesty.org.uk

Andress, D. (2005). *The terror*. London: Little, Brown.

Arendt, H. (1963). *Eichmann in Jerusalem: a report on the banality of evil*. New York: Viking.

Ascione, F. (2005). *Children and animals: exploring the roots of kindness and cruelty*. West Lafayette, IN: Purdue University Press.

Ashcroft, K. (1999). *An experimental investigation to identify neuro-psychological impairment in convicted paedophile offenders*. PhD Thesis. Edinburgh: University of Edinburgh Library.

Asthana, A. (2004). Why my family are fighting for justice – 20 years on. *The Observer*, 28 November.

Bakan, J. (2004). *The corporation: the pathological pursuit of profit and power*. London: Constable.

Bandura, A. (1983). Psychological mechanisms of aggression. In R. Green & E. Donnerstein (Eds), *Aggression: theoretical and empirical reviews* (Vol 1). New York: Haemic Press.

Bataille, G. (1986). *Eroticism: death and sensuality* (trans. M. Dalwood) San Francisco, CA: City Lights.

Baudrillard, J. (1995). *The Gulf War did not take place*. Sydney: Power Publications.

BBC History Magazine (2006). Jack the Ripper is 'worst Briton', 6 (13). Available at http://news.bbc.co.uk

BBC InsideOut-North West (2003). Warrington bombing: ten years on. 17 February, retrieved 17 February, 2003, from http://www.bbc.co.uk

BBC News (2001). Ripper tours spark anger in East End. 27 October, retrieved 10 March, 2006, from http://news.bbc.co.uk

BBC News (2003). Colombia murder rate soars. 24 April, http://news.bbc.co.uk

BBC News (2004a). 'Bullied' teenager killed himself. Retrieved 27 January, 2004, from http://news.bbc.co.uk

BBC News (2004b). Beslan boy recalls hostage horror. Retrieved 9 September, 2004, from http://news.bbc.co.uk

BBC News (2004c). School siege: eyewitness accounts. Retrieved 7 September, 2004, from http://news.bbc.co.uk

BBC News (2004d). Dunblane teenager takes US Open. Retrieved 12 September, 2004, from http://news.bbc.co.uk

BBC News (2004e). The day my wife was snatched away. Retrieved 13 March, 2004, from http://news.bbc.co.uk

BBC News (2005a). Clubs in pact to combat hooligans. Retrieved 2 August, 2005, from http://news.bbc.co.uk

BBC News (2005b). Doctor backs Brown Ale label move. 18 October, retrieved 20 October, 2005, from http://news.bbc.co.uk

BBC News (2005c). Jordan shows 'would-be bomber'. 13 November, retrieved 14 November, 2005, from http://news.bbc.co.uk

BBC News (2005d). Cannibal gets life for killings. 15 March, retrieved 16 March, 2005, from http://news.bbc.co.uk

BBC News (2006). New appeal on murder anniversary. 31 January, retrieved 2 February, 2006, from http://news.bbc.co.uk

BBC Three News (2004). Singer jailed for killing lover. 29 September, retrieved 1 October, 2006, from http://www.bbc.co.uk/bbcthree/news

BBC World Service (2000). When children kill children. 9 November, retrieved 21 March, 2005, from http://www.bbc.co.uk/worldservice

Beck, U. (2005). *Power in the global age: a new global political economy.* Cambridge: Polity.

Begg, P. (2004). *Jack the Ripper: the definitive history.* London: Longman.

Bell, M. (2003). *Through the gates of hell: a journey into world disorder.* London: Weidenfeld and Nicolson.

Bell, M. (2004). Guest appearance on BBC Radio 2 'Good Morning Sunday' programme, 3 October.

Bennetto, J. & Judd, T. (2004). Murder cases under review to identify 'honour killings'. *The Independent*, 23 June.

Berkowitz, L. (1989). Frustration-aggression hypothesis: examination and reformulation. *Psychological Bulletin*, 106, 59–73.

Bilton, N. (2003). *Wicked beyond belief: the hunt for the Yorkshire Ripper.* London: HarperCollins.

Birkbeck, C. & LaFree, G. (1993). The situational analysis of crime and deviance. *Annual Review of Sociology*, 19, 113–137.

Bjorkgvist, K. & Niemela, P. (Eds) (1992). *Of mice and women: aspects of female aggression.* San Diego, CA: Academic Press.

Black's Law Dictionary (1999). Bryan Garner, Editor in Chief. (7th edn) St Paul, MN: West Group.

Blair, J., Mitchell, D. & Blair, K. (2005). *The psychopath: emotion and the brain.* Oxford: Blackwell.

Bloch, R. (1959). *Psycho.* New York: Simon & Schuster.

Blom-Cooper, L. & Morris, T. (2004). *With malice aforethought: a study of the crime and punishment for homicide.* Oxford: Hart.

Bloom, S. (Ed.) (2001). *Violence: a public health menace and a public health approach.* London: Karnac.

Bond, M. (2005). The ordinary bombers. *New Scientist,* 23 July, p. 18.

Borger, J. (1997). In cold blood. *The Guardian Weekly,* 16 November.

Borger, J. (2006). Gunned down: the teenager who dared to walk across his neighbour's prized lawn. *The Guardian,* 22 March.

Bouchet, S. & Vézard, F. (2004). Mort à Vilnius: L`affaire Trintignant-Cantat. Paris: Archipelago.

Bourke, J. (2000). An intimate history of killing: face to face killing in 20th century warfare. New York: Basic Books.

Bouvier, J. (1856). *A law dictionary: adapted to the constitution and laws of the United States of America and of the several States of the American Union* (revised 6th edn). Philadelphia: Childs & Peterson. Available at http://www.constitution.org/bouv/bouvier.htm

Brookman, F. (2005). *Understanding homicide.* London: Sage.

Brookman, F. & Maguire, M. (2003). *Reducing homicide: a review of the possibilities.* London: Home Office.

Browne, K. & Hamilton-Giachritsis, C. (2005). The influence of violent media on children and adolescents: a public health approach. *The Lancet, 365*(9460), 702–710.

Burke, E. (1757/1987). A philosophical enquiry into the origin of our ideas of the sublime and beautiful. In J. T. Boulton (Ed.), *Introduction to 'A philosophical enquiry into the origin of our ideas of the sublime and beautiful'* (2nd edn). London: Basil Blackwell, p. 40.

Burke, J. (2005). Seven ways to stop the terror. *The Observer,* 7 August.

Bush, G. W. (2002). The President's State of the Union Address. The White House, Washington D.C. Available at http://www.whitehouse.gov

Buss, D. (2005). *The murderer next door: why the mind is designed to kill.* New York: Penguin.

Carole, P. (2005). *Harold Shipman: mind set on murder.* London: Sevenoaks.

Cartwright, D. (2002). *Psychoanalysis, violence and rage-type murder: murdering minds.* New York: Brunner-Mazel.

Catalano, R., Bruckner, T., Gould, J., Eskenazi, B. & Anderson, E. (2005). Sex ratios in California following the terrorist attacks of September 11, 2001. *Human Reproduction 20*(5), 1221–1227.

Celletti, K. (2006). Frank A. Mezzapelle. *Citizens Against Homicide Newsletter,* March.

Chomsky, N. (2004). *Hegemony or survival: America's quest for global dominance.* London: Penguin.

Citizens Against Homicide (CAH) (2005). *Newsletter,* February.

Citizens Against Homicide (CAH) (2006). Victims' statements. Retrieved 25 March, 2006, from http://www.murdervictims.com

CNN (2004). Powell calls Sudan killings genocide. 9 September, retrieved 25 September, 2004, from http//www.cnn.com

CNN (2005). Prison: Two women want to marry Peterson. Retrieved 17 March, 2005, from http://www.cnn.com

Coalition to Stop the Use of Child Soldiers (2004). *Child soldiers – global report 2004.* London: Coalition to Stop the Use of Child Soldiers.

Collett, N. (2005). *The butcher of Amritsar: Brigadier-General Reginald Dyer.* London: Hambledon & London.

Conrad, P. (2000a). Fatal attraction – our fascination with murder. *New Statesman,* 129, 20 November. Retrieved 18 May, 2006, from http://www.newstatesman.com/200011200035

Conrad, P. (2000b). *The Hitchcock Murders*. London: Faber & Faber.

Control Arms (2004). Guns or growth? 30 November, retrieved 3 February, 2005, from http://www.controlarms.org

Cope, L. (2004). Quoted in BBC News, 16 August, retrieved 17 August, 2004, from http://news.bbc.co.uk

Cornwell, P. (2003). *Portrait of a killer: Jack the Ripper case closed*. London: Time Warner.

Criminal Justice Legal Foundation (2005). Supreme Court declines further review of California murderer's claims: execution delays may be over for gang founder 'Tookie' Williams. Press release. Retrieved 11 October, 2005, from http://www.cjlf.org

Cromie, W. (2006). *Pill to calm traumatic memories*. Cambridge, MA: Harvard University News Office.

Cross, R., Jones, P. & Card, R. (1988). *Introduction to criminal law* (11th edn). London: Butterworths.

Cummock, V. (1995). The necessity of denial in grieving murder: observations of the victims families following the bombing in Oklahoma City. National Center for PTSD. *Clinical Quarterly*, 5, 2–3.

Daly, M. & Wilson, M. (1988). *Homicide*. New York: Aldine de Gruyter.

Daly, M. & Wilson, M. (1999). An evolutionary psychological perspective on homicide. In M. D. Smith & M. A. Zahn (Eds), *Homicide: a sourcebook of social research*. Thousand Oaks, CA: Sage, pp. 58–71.

De Quincey, T. (1925). *On murder as a Fine Art*. London: Philip Allan.

Dobash, R.P., Dobash, R.E., Cavanagh, K. & Lewis, R. (2002). *Homicide in Britain*. London: Violence Research Programme, University of London.

Dow (2005). The Dow Chemical Company. Retrieved 25 November, 2005, from http://www.dow.com

Duclos, D. (1998). *The werewolf complex: America's fascination with violence* (trans. Amanda Pingree). London: Berg. (Originally published in French as *Le Complexe du loup-garou*. Paris: Éditions La Découverte, 1994.)

Dyer, G. (1985). *War*. London: Guild.

Elliott, C. (2001). *French criminal law*. Cullompton, Devon: Willan.

Engels, F. (1999). *The condition of the working class in England*. Oxford: Oxford Paperbacks.

Faris, R. & Dunham, W. (1965). *Mental disorders in urban areas*. Chicago, IL: University of Chicago.

Fest, J. (2005). *Inside Hitler's bunker*. London: Macmillan.

Fisk, R. (2004). What price innocence in the anarchy of Iraq? *The Independent*, 17 November.

Foden, G. (2003). Death and the maidens. *The Guardian*, 18 July.

Foley, M. & Lennon, J. (2000). *Dark tourism*. London: Continuum.

Food and Agriculture Organisation of the United Nations (2005). *The state of food insecurity in the world 2005*. Rome: United Nations.

Foucault, M. (Ed.) (1975). *I, Pierre Riviere, having slaughtered my mother, my sister and my brother: a case of parricide in the 19th century*. New York: Pantheon.

Foucault, M. (1988). The dangerous individual. In Kritzman, L. (Ed.) Michel Foucault: politics, philosophy, culture. New York: Routledge, pp. 125–151.

Fox, J. (1983). *White mischief*. London: Random House.

Fox, J. (2001). *Chomsky and globalisation (postmodern encounters)*. London: Icon.

Freud, S. (2005). In A. Freud (Ed.), *The essentials of psychoanalysis*. New York: Vintage.

Freud, S. (2006). In A. Philips (Ed.), *The Penguin Freud reader*. London: Penguin.

Friday, N. (1976). *My secret garden: women's secret fantasies*. London: Quartet.

Friday, N. (1993). *Women on top.* London: Arrow.

Friday, N. (2003). *Men in love.* London: Arrow.

Frith, M. (2004). Child abuse review: just one case flawed. *The Independent*, 17 November.

Fromm, E. (1963). *The sane society.* London: Routledge & Kegan Paul.

Fukuyama, F. (2006). *After the neocons: America at the crossroads.* London: Profile Books.

Geldof, B. (2005). Foreword. In M. Wroe & M. Doney (Eds), *The rough guide to a better world.* London: Rough Guides.

Giddens, A. (2003). *Runaway world: how globalisation is reshaping our lives.* London: Routledge.

Gillan, A. (2005). Father and sons found guilty of honour killing. *The Guardian*, 5 November.

Godsi, E. (2004). *Violence and society – making sense of madness and badness.* Ross-on-Wye: PCCS Books.

Goldhagen, D. (1997). *Hitler's willing executioners: ordinary Germans and the Holocaust.* London: Abacus.

Goleman, D. (1996). *Emotional intelligence: why it can matter more than IQ.* London: Bloomsbury.

Gosline, A. (2005). Will DNA profiling fuel prejudice? *New Scientist*, 8 April, p. 12.

Grossman, D. (1996). *On killing: the psychological cost of learning to kill in war and society.* New York: Back Bay Books.

Guillermoprieto, A. (2003). A hundred women: why has decade-long string of murders gone unsolved? *The New Yorker*, 29 September, 82–94.

Haider, Z. (2004). Pakistan Bill proposes death for honour killings. Reuters, 26 October. Retrieved 27 October, 2004, from http://www.reuters.co.uk

Hare, R. (1999). *Without conscience: the disturbing world of the psychopaths around us.* New York: Guilford Press.

Hari, J. (2004). Some people are more equal than others. *The Independent*, 1 July.

Harris, J. (2005). For sale: paintings by the artist formerly known as the Führer. *The Guardian*, 7 November.

Harris, P. (2005). Public enemy: Abu Musab al-Zarqawi. *The Observer*, 29 May 29.

Harris, T. (1981). *Red dragon.* London: Bodley Head.

Harris, T. (1988). *The silence of the lambs.* New York: St Martin's Press.

Harris, T. (1999). *Hannibal.* London: Heinemann.

Harris, T. (2006). *Behind the mask.* London: Heinemann.

Hawk, D. (2003). *The hidden gulag: exposing North Korea's prison camps.* Washington, DC: US Committee for Human Rights in North Korea.

Henley, J. (2004). Murder trial hears clash of opinions on rock star's character. *The Guardian*, 18 March.

Henley, J. (2005). Boy watched Shrek video as he waited to kill his family. *The Guardian*, 25 November.

Hickey, E. (Ed.) (2003). *Encyclopedia of murder & violent crime.* Thousand Oaks, CA: Sage.

Hillyard, P., Pantazis, C., Tombs, S., Gordon, D. & Dorling, D. (2005). *Criminal obsessions: why harm matters more than crime.* London: The Crime and Society Foundation, King's College.

Hitchens, C. (2004). In enemy territory. *The Independent*, 23 September.

Hodgson, J. (2004). *French criminal justice: a comparative account of the investigation and prosecution of crime in France.* Oxford: Hart.

Horowitz, I. L. (2002). (fifth edn, revised) *Taking lives: genocide and state power*. New Brunswick, NJ: Transaction.

Huggler, J. (2004). The bandit king. *The Independent*, 20 October.

Human Rights Watch (2005). Iran: two more executions for homosexual conduct. Retrieved 6 January, 2006, from http://hrw.org

Hyatt-Williams, A. (1998). *Cruelty, violence, and murder: understanding the criminal mind* (Edited and with a Foreword by P. Williams). Northvale, NJ:

International Campaign for Justice in Bhopal (ICJB) (2006). That night 3rd December 1984. Retrieved 18 May, 2006, from http://www.bhopal.net/index1.html

Isenberg, S. (1997). *Women who love men who kill*. Kent Town, South Australia: Wakefield.

Jha, P., Kumar, R., Vasa, P., Dhingra, N., Thiruchelvam, D. & Moineddin, R. (2006). Low male-to-female sex ratio of children born in India: national survey of 1.1 million households. *The Lancet*, 367(9506), 211–218.

Jones, L. (2005). *Cannibal: the true story behind the maneater of Rotenburg*. New York: Berkley Publishing Group.

Kandel, E. (2006). Quoted in interview by C. Kalb, Freud in our midst. *Newsweek*, 27 March, 35–43.

Keitetsi, C. (2004). *Child soldier*. London: Souvenir Press.

Keitetsi, C. (2006). About me. Retrieved 28 March, 2006, from http://xchild.dk

Kershaw, I. (2005). Open University Lecture 2005, broadcast on BBC Radio4. Available at http://www.open2.net/oulecture2005/the_lecture.html

Khouri, N. (2004). *Honor lost: love and death in modern-day Jordan*. New York: Random House.

Klein, M. (1932). *The psychoanalysis of children*. London: Hogarth.

Kohlberg, L. (1969). Stage and sequence: The cognitive-developmental approach to socialization. In D. A. Goslin (Ed.), *Handbook of socialization theory and research* (pp. 347–480). Chicago, IL: Rand McNally.

Krug, E. G., Dahlberg, L. L., Mercy, J. A., Zwi, A. B. & Lozano, R. (Eds) (2002). *World report on violence and health*. Geneva: World Health Organisation.

Lafree, G. (2003). International police and health statistics on homicide: problems, prospects and post-World War II trends. Paper presented to International Conference on Crime, Rome, December.

Lapierre, D. & Moro, J. (2003). *Five past midnight in Bhopal*. New York: Scribner.

Lavrentyeva, T. (2004). The whole town is in a state of psychological disorder. BBC News, 2 October. Retrieved 3 October, 2003, from http://news.bbc.co.uk

Law Commission (2005a). *Law of murder to be reviewed*. Press release, 21 July. London: Law Commission.

Law Commission (2005b). *Bringing the law of murder into the 21st century*. Press release, 20 December. London: Law Commission.

Leggett, T. (2003). Rainbow tenement: crime and policing in inner Johannesburg. Monograph 78, April. Institute for Security Studies. Retrieved 4 August, 2003, from http://www.iss.co.za

Leake, J. (2005). Psychiatrist brings back concept of evil. *Sunday Times*, 13 February.

Legrain, P. (2003). *Open world: the truth about globalisation*. London: Abacus.

Le Monde (2004). Bertrand Cantat will be extradited in France next week. 24 September.

Leovy, J. (2003). The unseen agony of black-on-black homicide. *Los Angeles Times*, 26 January.

Liddle, R. (2005). Reversal of the decline of the English Murder. *The Sunday Times*, 20 March.

Lilly J. (2001). Email in letters section, *New York Metro*. Retrieved 27 March, 2006, from http://www.newyorkmetro.com

Lockwood, R. & Ascione, F. (Eds) (1998). *Cruelty to animals and interpersonal violence.* West Lafayette, IN: Purdue University Press.

Lombroso, C. (1876). *L'Umo Delinquente.* Turin: Fratelli Bocca.

Longden, S. (2005). *Hitler's British slaves: British and Commonwealth PoWs in German industry 1939–1945.* Marsh, Gloucs: Arris.

Longrigg, C. (2005). Women who have killer instincts. *The Independent*, 27 January.

Lovelock, J. (2006). *The revenge of Gaia.* London: Allen Lane.

Maalouf, A. (2001). *The Crusades through Arab eyes.* London: Saqi.

McGreal, C. (2001). Love, loot, lust and loathing. *The Guardian*, 23 January.

McLuhan, M. & Powers, B. (1992). *The global village: transformations in world life and media in the 21st century.* Oxford: Oxford University Press.

Malik, K. (1998). Darwinian fallacy. *Prospect-Magazine*, December. Available at: http://www.prospect-magazine.co.uk/highlights/darwinian_fallacy/index. html, pp. 1–9.

Marriot, T. (2005). *Jack the Ripper: the 21st century investigation.* London: Blake.

Martin, L. (2002). *To die like a dog: the personal face of the euthanasia debate.* New Plymouth, New Zealand: M-Press.

Martingale, M. (1999). Cannibal killers: the history of impossible murders (2nd edn). New York: Carroll & Graf.

May, H. (2000). Murderers' relatives. *Journal of Contemporary Ethnography*, 29(2), 198–221.

May, H. (2001). Social meanings of homicide. Paper delivered at University of Leeds, School of Health Care, Leeds.

Meadow, R. (1999). Unnatural sudden infant death. *Archives of Disease in Childhood*, 80, 7–14.

Medecins Sans Frontieres (2005). Prices of AIDS medicines in developing countries continue to be a concern. Press release, 28 June. Retrieved 28 June, 2005, from http://www.msf.org

Merton, R. K. (1938). Social structure and anomie. *American Sociological Review*, 3, 672–682.

Miethe, T. D. & Regoeczi, W. C. (2004). *Rethinking homicide.* Cambridge: Cambridge University Press.

Milgram, S. (1963). Behavioral study of obedience. *Journal of Abnormal Social Psychology*, 67, 371–378.

Milgram, S. (1974). *Obedience to authority: an experimental view.* New York: Harper and Row.

Miller, J. (1993). *The passion of Michel Foucault.* New York: Simon & Schuster.

Milne, S. & Bodi, F. (2001). Americans are reaping a harvest they themselves sowed. *The Guardian* (Special Issue, 'September 11'), 30 September.

Mitchell, K. & Owens, G. (2004). End of life decision-making by New Zealand general practitioners: a national survey. *The New Zealand Medical Journal*, 117(1196), 934–938.

Mitchell, P. & Schoeffel, J. (2003). *Understanding power: the indispensable Chomsky.* London: Vintage.

Morrall, P. A. (2000). *Murder & madness.* London: Whurr.

Mouzos, J. & Rushforth, C. (2003). *Family homicide in Australia. Trends and Issues*, 225, 1–6.

Murder One (2006). http://www.murderone.co.uk

Murphy, C. (2003). Jordan's dilemma over 'honour killings'. BBC News, 10 September. Retrieved 11 September, 2003, from http://news.bbc.co.uk

Murphy-O'Connor, C. (2004). BBC News, 17 November. Retrieved 18 November, 2004, from http://news.bbc.co.uk

National Commission on Terrorist Attacks upon the United States (NCTAUS) (2004). *The 9/11 Commission (Final) Report*. Washington DC: The National Archives and Records Administration.

Ng, J. (2001). Silent survivors. *AsianWeek*, 22(30). Available at http://www.asianweek.com

Nicol, C., Innes, M., Gee, D. & Fiest, A. (2004). *Reviewing murder investigations: an analysis of progress reviews from six police forces*. London: Home Office.

Obeyesekere, G. (2005). *Cannibal talk: the man-eating myth and human sacrifice in the south seas*. Berkeley, CA: University of California Press.

O'Keeffe, A. (2006). Anger at BBC genocide film. *The Observer*, 19 March.

Oldenburg, V. T. (2002). *Dowry murder: the imperial origins of a cultural crime*. Oxford: Oxford University Press.

Overy, R. (2005). *Dictators: Hitler's Germany and Stalin's Russia*. London: Pengain.

Parry, C. & Parry, W. (1994). *Tim: an ordinary boy*. London: Hodder & Stoughton.

Paul, G. (2005). Cross-national correlations of quantifiable societal health with popular religiosity and secularism in the prosperous democracies. *Journal of Religion and Society*, 7, 1–17.

Peta, B. (2004). Jazz musician shot dead after Pretoria concert. *The Independent*, 6 April.

Pincus, J. (2002). *Basic instincts: what makes killers kill?* New York: Norton & Company.

Plato (390 BC/1974). *The republic* (trans. D. Lee) (2nd edn). Harmondsworth: Penguin.

Popham, P. (2005). One year on: a Madrid family's life after death. *The Independent*, 5 March.

Pro-death Penalty (2005). Retrieved 5 December, 2005, from http://www.prodeathpenalty.com

Prunier, G. (2005). *Darfur: the ambiguous genocide*. London: Hurst & Co.

Redmond, L. (1989). *Surviving: when someone you love was murdered*. Clearwater, FL: Psychological Consultation and Education Services.

Rees, L. (2005). *Auschwitz – The Nazis and the Final Solution*. London: BBC Books.

Rees, M. (2005). The most important developments in the last five years. *The Guardian*, 30 December.

Reid, S. T. (2006). *Crime and criminology* (11th edn). New York: McGraw-Hill.

Reuters News Agency (2004). Killings, abductions fall in Colombia – Police. 30 June, 2004, http://www.alert.net.org

Ribbe, C. (2005). *Le crime de Napoleon*. Paris: Editions Privé.

Robarchek, C. & Robarchek, C. (1998). *Waorani: the contexts of violence and war*. Orlando, FL: Harcourt.

Rock, P. (1998). *After homicide: practical and political responses to bereavement*. Oxford: Clarendon.

Rose, S. (1997). *Lifelines: biology, freedom, determinism*. Harmondsworth: Penguin.

Rugman, A. (2001). *The end of globalization: why global strategy is a myth and how to profit from the realities of regional markets*. New York: AMACOM.

Rusesabagina, P. (2006). *An ordinary man: the true story behind 'Hotel Rwanda'*. London: Bloomsbury.

Rynearson, E. K. (1984). Bereavement after homicide: a descriptive study. *American Journal of Psychiatry*, 11, 1452–1454.

Rynearson, E. K. (1994). Psychotherapy of bereavement after homicide. *Journal of Psychotherapy Practice and Research*, 3(4), 341–347.

Scott, D. & Nimmo, B. with Rabey, S. (2000). *Rachel's tears*. Nashville, TN: Thomas Nelson.

Seale, C. (2006). National survey of end-of-life decisions made by UK medical practitioners. *Journal of Palliative Medicine, 20*, 1–8.

Searle, A. (2004). Fatal attraction. *The Guardian*, 23 November.

Sennett, R. (2006). *The culture of the new capitalism.* New Haven, CT: Yale University Press.

Sereny, G. (1995). *The case of Mary Bell: a portrait of a child who murdered.* London: Pimlico.

Sereny, G. (1999). *Cries unheard: the story of Mary Bell.* London: Macmillan.

Shaikh, T. (2002). London to host Islamic 'celebration' of Sept 11. *Daily Telegraph*, 8 September. Available at http://www.telegraph.co.uk

Sharpe, S. (2005). *Hidden victims: the effects of the death penalty on families of the accused.* Piscataway, NJ: Rutgers University Press.

Shipman Inquiry (2005). The final report (6th). Retrieved 10 January, 2006, from http://www.the-shipman-inquiry.org.uk

Shulman, R. (2006). Health fears for victims of Ground Zero's deadly dust. *The Guardian*, 10 February.

Singer, P. (1975). *Animal liberation.* New York: Ecco Books.

Singer, P. (1979). *Practical ethics.* Cambridge: Cambridge University Press.

Singer, P. (1995). *Rethinking life and death.* New York: St Martin's Griffin.

Singer, P. (1998). Darwin for the left. *Prospect*, June, 26–30.

Smith, M. D. & Zahn, M. A. (Eds) (1999). *Homicide: a sourcebook of social research.* Thousand Oaks, CA: Sage.

Smith, E., Nolen-Hoeksema, E., Fredrickson, B. & Loftus, G. (2003). *Atkinson and Hilgard's introduction to psychology* (14th edn). Belmont, CA: Wadsworth-Thomson.

Smith, T. (2004). Students take on the Mafia. BBC News, 6 November. Retrieved 7 November, 2004, from http://news.bbc.co.uk

Sontag, S. (2004). *Regarding the pain of others.* London: Penguin.

Spungen, D. (1998). *Homicide: The hidden victims – a guide for professionals.* Thousand Oaks, CA: Sage.

Soothill, K. & Wilson, D. (2005). Theorising the puzzle that is Harold Shipman. *Journal of Forensic Psychiatry and Psychology, 16*(4), 685–698.

Starmer-Smith, C. (2004). British tourists urged not to avoid South Africa. *The Telegraph* (Travel Supplement), 3 July.

Stockholm International Peace Research Institute (2004). *Stockholm: SIPRIS yearbook 2004: armaments, disarmament and international security.* Oxford: Oxford University Press.

Storey, N. (2004). *A grim almanac of Jack the Ripper's London 1870–1900.* Stroud: Sutton.

Sugden, P. (2002). *The complete history of Jack the Ripper.* London: Constable and Robinson.

Szasz, T. (1993). Curing, coercing, and claims making: a reply to critics. *British Journal of Psychiatry, 162*, 797–800.

Tatar, M. (1997). *Lustmord: sexual murder in Weimar Germany.* Princeton, NJ: Princeton University Press.

Taylor, P. (2003). *Mental illness and serious harm to others [Expert Paper]. NHS National Programme on Forensic Mental Health Research and Development.* Liverpool: University of Liverpool.

The Australian (2005). Editorial: Against executions. 2 December, 2005. Available at http://www.theaustralian.news.com.au

Toksvig, S. (2005). *Hitler's canary.* London: Doubleday.

Tremlett, G. (2006a). *Ghosts of Spain: travels through a country's hidden past.* London: Faber & Faber.

Tremlett, G. (2006b). Court indicts 29 over Madrid train blasts. *The Guardian*, 12 April.

Union Carbide (2005). Statement of Union Carbide Corporation regarding the Bhopal tragedy. Retrieved 18 December, 2005, from http://www.bhopal.com/ucs.htm

United Nations (2005a). *Human development report.* New York: United Nations Development Programme.

United Nations (2005b). Press statement by Spokesman for the Secretary-General on Darfur, 30 September. Retrieved 13 January, 2006, from http://www.un.org

van Woerden, H. (2000). *A Mouthful of Glass* (transl. from Dutch by D. Jacobson) London: Granta.

Victim Support (2006). *In the aftermath: the support needs of people bereavement – a research report.* London: Victim Support.

Vulliamy, E. (2003a). Murder in Mexico. *The Observer*, 9 March.

Vulliamy, E. (2003b). Murder in Mexico (Part Two). *The Observer*, 9 March.

Walker, D. (2004). Who watches murder videos? Retrieved 12 October. http://news.bbc.co.uk

War On Want (2002). Drug donations: corporate charity or taxpayer subsidy? Press release, 10 June. Retrieved 11 June, 2002, from http://www.waronwant.org

Waters, H., Hyder, A., Rajkotia, Y., Basu, S., Rehwinkel J. A. & Butchart, A. (2004). *The economic dimensions of interpersonal violence.* Geneva: World Health Organisation.

Webster, P. (2004). French rock star to be tried for murder. *The Guardian*, 21 February.

Wells, K. (2005). *Goodbye dearest Holly.* London: Hodder & Stoughton.

Wessely, S. & Jones, E. (2005). *Shell shock to PTSD: military psychiatry from 1900 to the Gulf War* (Maudsley monographs). London: Psychology Press.

Whitechapel, S. (2002). *Crossing to kill: the true story of the serial-killer playground.* London: Virgin.

Whittle, B. & Ritchie, J. (2004). *Harold Shipman: prescription for murder.* London: Time-Warner.

Wilczynski, A. (1977). *Child homicide.* London: Greenwich Medical Media.

Wilkinson, R. G. (2005). *The impact of inequality: how to make sick societies healthier.* London: Routledge.

Williams, (Tookie) S. (1997). The apology. Retrieved 6 April, 2005, from http://www.tookie.com

Williams, (Tookie) S. (2004). *Blue rage, black redemption: a memoir.* Pleasant Hill, CA: Damamli Publishing Company.

Williams, T. (with Price, H.) (2005). *Uncle Jack.* London: Orion.

Winnipeg Police (2005). The Beverley Dyke murder – solved. Retrieved 22 July, 2005, from http://www.winnipeg.ca/police

World Wealth Report (2006). New York: Merrill Lynch and Capgemini.

Yehuda, R., Engel, S., Brand, S., Seckl, J., Marcus, S. & Berkowitz, G. (2005). Transgenerational effects of post-traumatic stress disorder in babies of mothers exposed to the World Trade Center attacks during pregnancy. *Journal of Clinical Endocrinology and Metabolism, 90*(7), 4115–4118.

Zimbardo, P. G. (1971). The power and pathology of imprisonment. Congressional Record (Serial No. 15, October 25, 1971). Hearings before Subcommittee No. 3, of the Committee on the Judiciary, House of Representatives, Ninety-Second Congress. *First Session on Corrections, Part II, Prisons, Prison Reform and Prisoner's Rights: California.* Washington, DC: US Government Printing Office.

Zorn, B., Šučur V., Stare, J. & Meden-Vrtovec, H. (2002). Decline in sex ratio at birth after 10-day war in Slovenia. *Human Reproduction, 17*(12), 3173–3177.

INDEX